Frosted Glass

Sabarna Roy

First published in India 2011 by **Frog Books**
an imprint of **Leadstart Publishing Pvt Ltd**
1 Level, Trade Centre
Bandra Kurla Complex
Bandra (East) Mumbai 400 051 India
Telephone: +91-22-40700804
Fax: +91-22-40700800
Email: info@leadstartcorp.com
www.leadstartcorp.com / www.frogbooks.net

Editorial Office:
Unit: 25-26 / Building A/1
Ground Floor, Near Wadala RTO
Wadala (East) Mumbai 400 037 India
Phone: +91-22-24036548 / 24036930

Sales & Marketing Office:
Unit: 122 / Building B/2
First Floor, Near Wadala RTO
Wadala (East) Mumbai 400 037 India
Phone: +91-22-24046887

US Office:
Axis Corp, 7845 E Oakbrook Circle
Madison, WI 53717 USA

Copyright (c) Sabarna Roy

ISBN 978-93-81115-09-1

Publisher and Managing Editor: Sunil K Poolani
Books Editor: Paromita Ukil
Design Editor: Mishta Roy

Typeset in Book Antiqua
Printed at Repro India Ltd, Mumbai

Price — India: Rs 295; Elsewhere: US $16

in loving memory of Ma

"We even find it painful to be men – real men of flesh and blood, with *our own private bodies;* we're ashamed of it, and we long to turn ourselves into something hypothetical called the average man."
— *Notes from Underground,* **Fyodor Dostoyevsky**

About the Author

Sabarna Roy, 44, is a qualified Civil Engineer from Jadavpur University, Calcutta. He works in a senior management position in a manufacturing and engineering construction company.

An avid reader and a film buff, Roy is widely travelled in India and lives in Calcutta with his family.

He started writing during his university days, mostly English and Bengali poems. He stopped writing after he left university and took up employment. After a gap of 19 years, he started writing once again, mostly to reconnect with himself.

In 2010, he published a book comprising a long story and four long narrative poems titled *Pentacles* with Frog Books.

Roy has a dedicated page on oxfordbookstore.com and can be contacted at storyteller10097@gmail.com

CONTENTS

Fallen Man

1.

Rahul woke up to a foggy autumnal morning in Darjeeling. He generally got out of bed around 5.30. Fifteen minutes later he got engaged in his usual rounds of running and jogging for about ninety minutes around the Observatory Hill and in its by-lanes, followed by fortyfive minutes of stretching exercises. This was his daily routine (for the last ten years), except for a day or two, when he loved to get immersed in the famous Darjeeling mist, lying on his bed. The mist entered his room through the openings in the skylight and after some time made it difficult for him to locate even his arms and legs. Once the fitness routine was over, Rahul would gulp three cups of black tea with his mother by his side, slowly go over the previous day's newspaper in search of some exciting piece of news and then get lost in idle chat with her.

This was one of those mornings when Rahul skipped his outdoor routine. Instead, he fell endlessly into a misty bottomless well, as though blinded from outside life. During these falls, once or twice a year, he saw the image of Mount Godwin Austin appearing in his mind's eye. He had seen the peak from Khardungla in Ladakh long back. The lonely peak, shrouded in a black and white melancholic cloud, had seemed like the blackened eye of a sinister killer hiding behind a spongy veil.

Things happened differently on that day. For a change,

somebody was talking to him in his mind. Normally, he experienced an intense silence during such falls. He was taken by surprise at the sound of the words that he heard. The words were spoken with the softness of rising fog and crooned with the warmth of a mountain tune. There was something philosophical about what he heard. Someone was whispering to him from miles away in a deeply sonorous chant, "A man, who takes himself less seriously than he takes others, has reached personal harmony. A man, who makes fun of himself more than others, has reached personal harmony. A man who attempts to observe events from a distance affected by irony and humour has reached personal harmony. A man who has stopped insulting another's intelligence has reached personal harmony. A man who knows that the past cannot be re-enacted has reached personal harmony. A man, who respects the incongruities of existence, knowing that seeing and not seeing are entwined in the same act of vision, has reached personal harmony."

Who was talking to him? Slowly he fell into a deep slumber. He woke up around noon. His body ached; he felt feverish and his gut was wrenched by nausea. His mother sat by his side. She had taken his head in her lap and was running her fingers through his hair. "You have caught the flu. It's everywhere in town due to the change of season. You should be careful with your health now," she said.

"But I've never been ill for the last ten years, ma. Is the flu more virulent this year?" Rahul asked. "You know, somebody – faceless and formless – was speaking to me in my mind this morning."

His mother looked at her son's face anxiously. "Who was speaking to you in your mind? What did he say? Were you dreaming?" Rahul had heard those dream-like words only once, when he was half asleep, but it was as though he had memorised them, they were etched on his soul. He repeated those lines to his mother amazed at his own performance.

His mother smiled softly. "I was reading those lines from your father's diary this morning sitting by your side when you were asleep. The words got mixed up with the images in your consciousness like a stream of light diffusing through multiple layers of darkness." Rahul felt relieved.

His mother said, "Get up, it's noon already. I want to tell you something. I saw Leila's photograph in the newspaper today. She is an architect of international repute and will be delivering a lecture on 'Environment Friendly Habitation' in the Town Hall in Kolkata, three days from today."

Rahul stared at his mother in astonishment. He seemed to lose control for a fraction of a second, like a hungry cheetah would if it came across a careless deer. It was like a fleeting spark of electricity that subsided and disappeared in no time. Rahul had a strange vision. He seemed to be falling from an icy mountain peak straight into a moonlit ocean.

2.

Rahul lost his father in Calcutta in 1976, when he was barely four years old. He couldn't remember much except the few images he had gathered from the anecdotes his mother recounted. Rahul's father was a wildlife photographer who contributed to international journals on ecology and the environment. His profession took him to far-flung places and he often had to stay away from home. This was one reason Rahul had few memories of his father. His mother, over the years, had arduously compiled all his published and unpublished photographs into beautifully bound collections. She looked at them many times over when she was alone. Rahul could never appreciate any of his father's works and often felt guilty about this.

However, he kept the four photographs that his father had given him, very carefully -- they were a precious memento. He couldn't really remember his father giving him the photographs, but his mother had said so. The photographs spoke to him in a strange language and communicated something which he did not clearly understand. His mother was delighted that he kept these photographs with him always in a cellophane cover to protect them from humidity and dust. There was one photograph of three camels crossing a brightly lit patch of desert. There was another one of a penguin. A third shot showed three white Siberian tigers looking chillingly at the photographer. And finally, there was a top shot of a herd of buffalos crossing the Kalahari Desert to the Okavango basin.

Rahul preferred looking at these photographs in absolute silence, trying to fathom what they stood for, apart from being random moments of life captured by his father a long time ago.

His mother brought up Rahul on her own. Rahul had mentally dissected his relationship with his mother into four phases. Till he turned 14 his mother was a playmate and he would sleep in the shadow of her body. Her scent was warm and deeply intoxicating. She was an epitome of discipline and wisdom and Rahul never disobeyed her. He tried to keep her engaged all the time, especially since the day he saw her crying alone in the library. He felt very sad that day lamenting the fact that he could not make her feel completely happy about life. Occasionally this thought aroused in him a numbing rage.

From the age of 15 to 19, the earlier bond seemed to be slipping away. Rahul slept in a separate room. He had intense sexual dreams. He masturbated at night. But his mother remained the epitome of discipline and wisdom and Rahul never disobeyed her. However, the slave like fidelity of the past was slowly replaced by a silent and glowing attachment. His mother introduced Rahul to two interesting activities around this time. Rahul was good at craft and could make good models. This was a skill he had inherited from his mother who was a senior teacher in the Art College.

Rahul was also very good at climbing trees and negotiating vertical inclines. His mother admitted him to a course in rock climbing and subsequently sent him on mountain treks where he discovered his passion for heights and thin air. It was during these years that he struck a friendship with his classmate Sanjay based on their common passion for making models of mansions, villas and settlements. They copied pictures from art books in the library where his mother wrote serious critiques for her college journal, and proudly displayed these copies among friends and family as original work. Surprisingly, mother never intervened or exposed these lies. Perhaps she realised that his artistic abilities were quite ordinary so she pardoned these pathetic attempts at gaining glory. Rahul had become an occasional smoker by the time he was 18.

Between 20 and 26, he was rarely in touch with his mother. He was madly in love with a classmate, Leila, who was pursuing a degree in architecture;, he often ventured on mountain treks in the upper Himalayas. This was a period best defined by his agony-filled meetings with Leila, falling in love and walking in a world of dreams, losing virginity and feeling good about everything. Then all of a sudden, they broke up because of a joke that turned out to be more far reaching than what it should have been. This pushed him into a bottomless abyss of drugs and cigarettes. In the end it was his mother who stood beside him like a rock. She rehabilitated Rahul with her undying conviction and zeal that she would not lose her son to invisible demons and spirits.

From the age of 27 onwards, mother turned out to be his soulmate and companion. Rahul could not complete a bachelor's degree in architecture, so he took up a diploma course in rock climbing and mountaineering. He went on a few high-altitude mountain climbing expeditions and finally migrated from Calcutta and settled in Darjeeling as a senior trainer at the Himalayan Mountaineering Institute. Although this uneventful life made him feel like a loser, the beauty and silence of the mountain peaks, the chill of the thin clear air and his mother's unconditional support made him feel content and happy about life.

Rahul realised he had not had sex since that fateful night when he separated from Leila. Strangely, he did not feel sad or cheated by this queer turn of fate.

3.

A conversation with Sanjay just after the high school examinations on a grassy patch by the Outram Ghats in Calcutta was deeply engraved on Rahul's mind. It was a cloudy, breezy day that threatened to bring rain. The two had visited the Indian Museum that morning. In the late afternoon they wanted to get drenched by the riverside and proceeded towards the Outram Ghats. When the clouds were dispersed by a strong breeze and it was clear that there was no possibility of rain, they decided to lie down on the adjacent grassy patch and immerse themselves in the scene before them. The river lay between two cities, parts of which were growing rapidly while other parts were crumbling. Two bridges stood on either flank – one under construction for ages and the other, an ageold one.

There were boatmen and pimps, eunuchs and cheap prostitutes, as well as lovers cosying up under trees. Youngsters, who seemed to have bunked school or college, lay about smoking grass. There were beggars and noisy vendors selling food and balloons. Steamers hooted and small boats roved around like flies. Sanjay and Rahul soaked in the environment and looked at the grey sky waiting for night to fall.

"Ma was telling *baba* the other day that your mother, Nilima *mashi*, has sacrificed her life for your sake. Do you realise this, Rahul?" Sanjay asked.

Rahul looked surprised. "Sacrifice? What sacrifice?"

Sanjay tried to pacify him. "I mean, *mashi* never really pursued her career or re-married, making you her first priority."

Rahul was curious, "Did she ever say that?"

"No Rahul, don't be an idiot. Why would she say that? She is not that insensitive. But one can understand this, don't you agree?" Rahul felt foolish. "Yeah, I never thought about Ma in this manner. But she does have a career," he said.

Sanjay was aware of Rahul's mother's calibre. "For a

painter of her potential do you think teaching a few self-styled intellectuals is a good enough career?"

Rahul became defensive, "Not really. But she has been painting on and off. Is she attracted to anybody whom she wants to marry or is she having an affair or something – did you hear anything of that kind?"

Sanjay answered, "No. But she is an attractive woman. Many men may have been attracted to her, I'm sure of that."

Rahul couldn't help asking, "Are you attracted to her?"

Sanjay, though a little taken aback, maintained his calm. "I am. But not in the sexual sense Rahul, otherwise, I wouldn't be discussing this with you. In any case, I don't fall for older women."

Rahul changed the topic. "Ma gifted a painting to your Baren*kaku* titled 'Picnic Portrait' last New Year. Have you seen this painting?"

Sanjay answered excitedly, "Oh my God, It's a masterpiece! I've seen the painting so many times, I know it so well. A family is playing rummy beside a river that flows through a jungle. The members are seated on a fabric mat on the ground, flashing their cards and eating sandwiches. A woman is seen rushing towards this group, making them turn their heads, almost reluctantly, towards her. She is blurting something in horror, anxiety writ large on her face. She is gesticulating towards the jungle. The painting uses a few conflicting moods – the serenity of the river, the deathly silence of the surrounding jungle, the relaxed playfulness of the picnic party, the horror on the woman's face and the greyness of the night that will fall...reminding us of the terror-filled endless night that will follow. I had asked Nilima *mashi*, 'Who is this woman; what is she saying?'

"She had said, 'She is a member of the family. You'll know this if you see the painting.' Her features and clothes mark her out as a family member. Her young son has wandered into the jungle and she goes to find him. She chances upon some evidence that shows that her son is in great danger and runs back to her family enjoying its game."

Rahul said, "I enjoy looking at this painting, too. Is this story so important to understand the painting?"

"I wouldn't say so. It merely illustrates how a person can be lonely in the midst of an indifferent crowd and hostile Nature," Sanjay explained. "But in the absence of a credible story it would have been difficult for the painter to leave such a lasting impression."

Rahul chose to digress, "Do you think we'll get admission to the College of Architecture and Planning?" he asked.

Sanjay was positive. "I think so. I don't think anybody can beat us in the model-making part, which carries seventy per cent weightage in entrance exams."

But Rahul was still besieged by doubts. "Do you seriously want to become an architect?" he asked.

Sanjay answered confidently, "Yes. And you?"

Rahul was in two minds. "I don't know. Actually, I want to work with you. Not by myself. We could open an architect's firm together and do good business and make a lot of money. It feels good to do something together. On my own, I prefer travelling to all the mountains in the world. And yes, I dream of visiting the Great Bath at Mohenjo-daro, some day."

It was now Sanjay's turn to change the topic. "Do you fancy any girl, Rahul?" he asked.

Rahul answered candidly, "If I did, you would be the first to know. Do you fancy anyone?"

Sanjay said in a straightforward manner, "Not really. But if you helped me I would like to rape someone."

Rahul seemed shocked, "Who?"

"Have you seen Gargi in our house?"

"Do you mean Aranida's girlfriend?"

"Yes, of course," Sanjay smiled.

"Boy, I get a hardon thinking of her."

"We could rape her together, man!" Sanjay declared.

Rahul agreed, "That's a great proposal. We could do that. But I might have a complex, flashing my dick in front of Gargi in full view of your sturdier one."

It suddenly began to rain and they got drenched. People were rushing about everywhere and night was falling. Rahul never really understood why this conversation, in such great detail, played out in his mind a million times.

4.

Rahul realised that the College of Architecture and Planning was very different from school on the very first day, at the orientation programme and freshers' welcome party. The environment was independent, intellectually driven and in some sense, implicitly sexual. Students were no longer in uniform. They talked animatedly on a variety of subjects with little relevance to the curriculum. The teachers were dressed casually and didn't try to impose authority. Many of them were attractive women who flaunted their good looks and clothes. Surprisingly, more than fifty per cent of the students were girls from up-market missionary schools, hailing from educated urban elite families. This was Rahul's first impression. During the orientation programme Sanjay and Rahul sat together in the auditorium.

"I'm going to like this buddy, I'm going to like this," Sanjay whispered animatedly.

During the freshers' welcome party they moved apart. Sanjay mingled with many people, most of them senior students. Rahul, meanwhile, eyed a girl in a light green sari, who was clutching a brown manila folder in her left hand and looking at the boisterous crowd curiously. A pair of expensive pens was tucked into her green blouse and Rahul found this style quite attractive. This girl had fine features, fair skin and she wasn't too tall. Her large eyes were dark and deep and well-defined by the beautiful curve of her lashes and brows. Her face, sans make up, seemed crafted by a Venetian master. Rahul stealthily looked at the skin of her abdomen and feet. He felt a tingling sensation and yearned to talk to her, and walk with her by some abandoned lake.

The party began with introductions. Each newcomer was asked to declare his or her name and ambition in front of an energised crowd madly cheering and applauding everything that was said. The ambience was electrifying. Sanjay said, "My ambition is to re-build the Great Bath one day." Rahul knew that Sanjay had cleverly fabricated a credible passion so that he could draw the crowd's attention. Rahul watched the girl from the corner of his eye.

She was looking at Sanjay, impressed by what he had just said. When her turn came she went up to the stage confidently and declared, "My name is Leila, Leila Gupta." (Strangely enough, Rahul was reminded of Sean Connery. 'My name is Bond, James Bond'!). "My only passion is to watch and devour paintings as good as Van Gogh's 'Wheat Field with Crows'. I can't tear my eyes away from the painting.

I first saw a laminated copy in my father's collection four years ago. Van Gogh had said something very interesting while working on this canvas. 'I experience a period of frightening clarity in those moments when Nature is so beautiful. I am no longer sure of myself, and the paintings appear in a dream'." The crowd started clapping.

Rahul didn't clap but Sanjay clapped excitedly. He was sitting in the second row. Rahul did not know anything about this painting. He vaguely remembered his mother speaking about it. There was a pressure building up on Rahul now. He racked his brain and wondered if he had any passion or ambition, at all. Even if he didn't he was sure he could invent something bombastic to draw Leila Gupta's attention. When he went up on stage, he was in a state of delirium and heard himself say, "My name is Sanjay, no, no; I mean that's my best friend's name. My name is Rahul Banerjee. I'm not too sure if I have any passion. But I do love climbing mountains. I'm indebted to my mother for this. I hope, someday, my mother and I will dare to climb a tall peak on our own."

Once Rahul finished, there was a hushed silence in the auditorium. Rahul looked at Leila. She was looking at him too, smiling softly and the smile seemed to spread to her eyes. It was a very private smile, which only Rahul could see. Rahul would remember this smile forever, experiencing torpedo-like explosions within although he looked perfectly calm and unaffected.

After the party was over Sanjay said, "I'm staying back buddy. If you want, you can stay back too." Rahul was not in a mood to stay back. "No, I'm going back home," he said.

It was raining lightly. Rahul lit a cigarette and planned to walk back home when he heard Leila calling him, "I have a car. Can I drop you home?"

Rahul was thrilled and wanted to go with her, but said "No, thank you Leila. I prefer to walk."

5.

By the end of the first semester, Sanjay, Leila and Rahul formed a close-knit group. Sanjay and Leila discussed paintings all the time. Sanjay also showed her printed copies of paintings done by Rahul's mother. Leila was deeply impressed by these paintings and wanted to meet Rahul's mother at once; Sanjay took her over one day when Rahul was away on a mountain trek.

"Won't it be great if the three of us could form an architect's firm some day? What do you say, Leila?" Sanjay asked.

"I've been dreaming about this for some time. But I don't think Rahul would be interested. He seems more driven by mountain climbing." She said.

"Why don't you suggest it to him?"

"You could suggest it too."

"I don't know. He doesn't discuss anything with me, these days" Sanjay replied after a pause.

After the second semester Rahul started bunking classes regularly and the 'gang of three' was reduced to just two highly ambitious students driven by European Renaissance sculpture, Asian mosques and Indus Valley urban planning. Their present was almost clouded by their dreams of a glorious future.

Leila was shocked by a dream she had of Rahul one

night. She called him early next morning and said in a
trembling voice, "When can I see you alone?"

"Alone! Why? Come to my house this afternoon," he
responded.

6.

Rahul and Leila met in Rahul's house that afternoon.
They were alone in the house. Once Leila was sipping tea
and sitting comfortably opposite Rahul, she said, "Where
do you loaf around these days? You have stopped
attending college. I dreamt of you last night. It was a
horrible dream."

"A nightmare? A horrible dream or a bad dream is
often called a nightmare!"

"Don't act smart, Rahul. You've been avoiding Sanjay
and me for a long time now. You are not interested in
attending classes. You don't hang around with us. What's
the matter with you?"

"First tell me about your horrible dream, Leila. Or, is
the fact that I appeared in your dream horrible enough?"
Rahul retorted sarcastically.

Leila was straightforward, "I saw that you had fallen
from a mountain top on a moonlit night and were
screaming for help in a pool of blood. There was nobody
around."

Rahul was curt. "I don't like sentimental situations. I
know you are not sentimental either. What's the matter?
Are you in love?"

Leila looked at him with excitement and hopeless fury
in her gaze. "I don't know. I think I'm in love," she
gasped.

"Oh! We should be celebrating that. Where's the other
lovebird, that moron Sanjay?" Rahul said in a mocking
tone.

At this point Leila slapped Rahul and screamed at him,
"I told you not to act smart, Rahul. Last year, during the
first semester when you came to my house I took you to
my father's library and showed you Van Gogh's 'Wheat

Field with Crows'. I asked you teasingly if you, Sanjay and I could enter the painting together and go for a walk. The moment I mentioned Sanjay's name, you were jealous, I saw it in your face. Deny this, if you can!"

"Okay, I was jealous." Rahul said sheepishly. "I was attracted to you from the very first day. Is it wrong to be attracted to someone and desire companionship? When you don't get the person you want you do feel jealous, as if your soul is burning on a grate of coal. It's true that I should have accepted the truth seeing your growing bond with Sanjay, but then you know it's difficult. I thought I could cure myself if I roamed around in the mountains. Frankly, Leila, I couldn't cure myself. Wherever I went I thought about you. Now, you tell me that you are in love. That's great! Since you'll be the beloved of my very dear friend, it would be sinful even to think about you, as my lover. Maybe the idea of sin works wonders in saving hearts and souls from destroying each other."

"Rahul please get this straight. Sanjay is a friend with whom I love to discuss ideas and to work. I'm attracted to him but in a different way. Let me put it like this. I won't be able to sleep with him or dream of caressing him and protecting him. I won't get anxious about his well being in the middle of the night. But I will drop my guard with someone else because I feel completely safe with him although, it took me a long time to realise this", Leila explained.

Rahul looked amazed. "You mean you don't love Sanjay! You said you are in love. Who are you in love with, Leila? Have you been meeting somebody else of late? Sanjay never told me that."

It was now Leila's turn to hold forth. "I'm in love with a pampered man. A man who thinks it is better to hide his love, has no confidence in his own love and makes no effort to win the person he loves. In a fit of rage and jealousy he takes off to the mountains. He displays an image of detachment and intellectual superiority so that others seem materialistically driven mortals compared to him. But, Rahul Banerjee things don't add up the way we want them to. When you rejected me, I tried to fall in love with Sanjay a million times; I failed. I gave up and tried meditation. Then I saw you last night in my dream, in a pathetic state. Immediately, I wanted to run to you and take you in my arms so that no harm could touch you, ever. I love you, Rahul. I love you." Leila cried and laughed hysterically at the same time.

Rahul took Leila in his arms at once and started kissing her madly, clumsily, and ferociously. Soon they were totally naked, holding each other as they basked in a deep pool of pleasure. They sought to hold back time as they relished the immeasurable warmth of their lovemaking. They looked like a lion and a lioness making love deep inside a cave. It was as though Picasso's painting 'Lovers on the Beach' had been brought to life.

When they were relaxing in each other's arms, Rahul asked "Are you mine?"

"Yes!" Leila said in an instant. "And you?"

"I was always yours. I will always be yours." They wanted to sleep in each other's arms, but Rahul's mother would return home any moment. So they showered, got dressed and thought of going out. Rahul felt like a Sultan.

He said, "Leila don't you think we should call Sanjay and celebrate." Leila replied, "Yeah, I think we should." When they were about to leave, Rahul showed her the four photographs taken by his father.

She wanted to borrow the photographs for a day to observe them in greater detail, but Rahul declined. He couldn't part with them even for a moment, he said. Leila was disappointed. "I would like to see them again," she said. "I would love to show them to you again and again. Tell me whenever you feel like looking at them." Rahul drew Leila close and kissed her eyes. They couldn't control themselves and ended up making love yet again.

7.

Sanjay was overjoyed to know that Rahul and Leila were in love. They were eating in a small Chinese restaurant in Chinatown.

"I hope this will help us set up our own firm quickly" he declared.

"Leila's relationship with me is only a part of the universal picture of our friendship. The firm is a flower on the tree of our friendship." Rahul said.

Leila quipped, "Do you know, Sanjay; Rahul used to believe that I was in love with you!"

"I thought so, too", answered Sanjay innocently. "But that doesn't matter. At least we'll get to see more of Rahul, now. We can plan out the activities of our firm in greater detail and with more confidence. Leila and I have been discussing ideas for a long time. Now it's time Rahul made some contribution."

"Like what?"

"Like, give us some ideas."

Rahul threw up his hands at this. "Ideas! I'm short on ideas, man. I'm an executor. Tell me, what to do and I'll do it. Leila, tell me about your ideas."

"Leila has a few brilliant ideas. Tell us about them." Sanjay added.

Leila explained gushing a little as if her cherished dreams were coming alive, "I dream of doing something in Kumartuli and Ghurni. We can give a proposal to the state government to fund complete rehabilitation of these settlements of artisans bound by ancient traditions; they will of course require sustainable architecture for the artisans to continue to work in the future; modernity has taken a heavy toll on them. Our firm can do the architectural designs that will be in tune with the ethos of the place. You know, I'm also interested in restoration of the Bishnupur terracotta temples and some of the old decaying buildings of North Calcutta. Do these ideas excite you, Rahul?"

"They're exciting, workable and highly marketable keeping in mind the future." Rahul said quietly.

"But you sound sceptical."

Rahul tried to explain his position, "No, it's not that. The ideas and intentions are great. But how do you create a city of artisans; how do you restore decay that arises out of neglect and opportunistic ventures in the name of money and commerce?"

Leila was offended. "What do you mean by that?"

"Our firm will be charging a hefty fee for executing these ideas; right? It seems we're confident that our ideas, if marketed well in the right quarters, will combine the passions of creativity and moneymaking. They will also build a good image for the government and our firm. But the artisans and the people whose cities we restore will hardly be touched or affected. I believe the idea of ethnicity is going to be one of the most sought after ideas in the worlds of art, commerce and politics in the near future. I think it's all right in the cause of money and commerce. I fully endorse and support these ideas and will pursue them with great passion," Rahul declared.

Sanjay intervened at this point. "Are you mocking Leila or are you jealous that you have a lover who can think independently?"

Rahul answered in a lighter vein, "I'm jealous that she has in you, a combatant, I will find difficult to match. After a long time, I felt like giving you guys a thorough lecture."

All three of them broke out in wild laughter and concentrated on devouring their meal.

Leila said, "You are an architect yourself, Rahul. Don't you want to do something independently?"

"I want to, but I don't know what it is. Meanwhile, I don't mind executing whatever both of you feel is good enough. There is still time before we can start calling ourselves architects."

"But didn't you have anything boiling deep inside you when you decided to study architecture?" Leila asked.

"Frankly, no. But nowadays I can sense a wish in my soul. I'd like to plant a tree that will generate a huge shade. I'd like to construct a shelter of mud and clay where people can rest on a sunny day and listen to a sad story by a maverick storyteller. Whenever I see this tree in my mind I visualise the melancholic face of Sarbajaya sitting there, burning with fever waiting for Apu to come back from the city. This image never leaves my mind. Do you remember the scenes from *Apur Sansar*?"

Leila looked at Rahul passionately, quite oblivious of

Sanjay's presence. She was flushed with desire and yearned to offer herself to Rahul. She was so wet between her legs that she felt terribly uncomfortable eating in public view. Once Rahul and Sanjay dropped her home she locked herself up in the bathroom and looked at her face in the mirror seductively like she had never done before. She yearned for Rahul to go deep inside her again and again till she fell asleep from the unbearable lightness of pleasure. She wanted Rahul to appear before her magically every time she thought of him.

8.

The next year, Rahul stopped going to the mountains. He was with Leila most of the time – attending classes, studying, watching movies. They took pleasure in each other's bodies whenever they could. Strangely, Rahul never asked Leila to come to the mountains with him. On the contrary, reaching a mountaintop seemed insignificant when compared to the time he spent with Leila. Time was flowing fast, beyond control. Leila was obsessed with her ideas of an artisan city, restoration of Bishnupur temples and North Calcutta. She made extensive trips to Kumartuli, Ghurni, Bishnupur and North Calcutta. She made elaborate surveys, interviewed locals, sketched and took photographs from various angles and made blue prints of her proposals down to the last pair of nuts and bolts. While she wanted Rahul to be by her side during such preparatory work, the final proposal was always discussed in Sanjay's presence. Sanjay was careful not to invade Rahul and Leila's privacy unnecessarily. He came only when summoned. This implicit sensitivity gave Sanjay enough time to concentrate on his studies and improve his grade card. It turned out that by the turn of the fourth semester Sanjay was ranking second, while Leila came first. Rahul did not get a rank but he got average marks. He concentrated on reading books about mountain expeditions. He smoked a lot and at times, smoked grass as well. Leila didn't know this, or they would end up quarrelling bitterly yet again. Rahul and Leila quarrelled without rhyme or reason. Since Leila was deeply engrossed in her work, Rahul felt neglected at times. He often started a quarrel just to irritate and distract her. While these quarrels began on trifling day to day issues, they eventually led to conflicting opinions on matters pertaining to human history and philosophy, which didn't really concern either of them. Whenever Leila was extremely upset with Rahul she sought refuge in Sanjay, who handled the situation diplomatically without taking any sides. The calculated distance and impartiality Sanjay maintained made Rahul angry, though he preferred to keep silent. Rahul wanted Sanjay to take a stand, even if it was against him.

Rahul did not give up going to the mountains completely. Two months before the third semester examinations, he drew up a plan to visit Gangotri. A day before he was to leave, he met Leila in his house. They were alone and after a furious bout of lovemaking they were locked in each other's arms like lovesick birds in a nest.

"You will leave tomorrow and come back after twelve days. What will I do in this period? I'll feel like killing myself, Rahul! I'll feel terribly lonely and desperate!"

Rahul kissed Leila all over. She moaned in pleasure delighted by his attention. "I asked you to come with me this time. It's not as if I'm leaving you forever. I love going to the mountains, just like you love going to Ghurni and other places."

"That's because of our career, Rahul. Our future. Tell me, do you love mountains more than you love me?"

"I love you and want you more than anything else in this world. You know it."

"Prove it to me then," Leila told him passionately.

Rahul was surprised. "What?"

"Prove it. Prove it, now!"

"But how?"

"Don't go tomorrow," Leila said.

Rahul took a deep breath. "All right. I won't go tomorrow. It's done. Are you happy now?"

Leila kissed Rahul and screamed joyously, "Yes I'm very, very happy."

Leila mounted on Rahul and took him deep inside her. They moved against each other, gasping, like they were rocking in a boat on the billowy waves of a turbulent ocean. They went on till such time they could move no further and fell to the floor breathless, very close to death.

Leila woke up from a pleasant dream and asked, "Rahul, won't you marry me?"

Rahul replied, "Of course, I will. Why, do you have any other plans?"

Leila answered dreamily, "I want to get married to you once our firm is established and we've landed a few contracts. Is that all right with you?"

"Anything is all right with me as long as you're happy," Rahul said taking her in his arms.

"I'm happy with you. But at times, you look blank, as if you are searching for something elsewhere and that is when I feel unhappy and bitterly jealous." Leila declared

Rahul tried to justify this. "That happens to you as well, when you're deeply engrossed in your work or studies or discussing proposals with Sanjay."

Leila defended herself at once. "It's not as if I discuss my proposals with Sanjay alone. You are there as well. But if you don't like my talking to Sanjay…"Rahul didn't allow Leila to complete her sentence and interjected midway, "You are assuming things, Leila. I never said that. Sanjay is my best friend. Even if you sleep with him I won't mind. Get this into your head."

"If that's so I'll sleep with Sanjay. But don't you dare sleep with anybody else! It can't be tit for tat, my dear man." she exclaimed angrily.

Rahul felt maddened and moved towards her again. Leila loved the way Rahul behaved with her.

9.

On a winter night after the seventh semester Sanjay came to Rahul's house. He wanted to stay the night to catch up with his friend. Sanjay complained that Rahul had been avoiding him over the last two and a half years because he was pre-occupied with his beautiful girlfriend. It was high time he realied that one need not do away with old relationships because of new ones. Rahul loved Sanjay's opening move. They had dinner and began to chat. Sanjay had lost some weight and wore spectacles these days. Rahul had failed to notice these changes and felt quite guilty.

"Rahul how is it that you've turned out to be a total veggie?" Sanjay asked.

"What do you mean?"

"You seem to have changed completely after you and Leila started seeing each other. Are you happy now that you are in love?"

Rahul answered, "I'm very happy with Leila. Yeah, I've given up many things but then Leila's presence compensates for everything."

Sanjay asked him openly, "Is it sex which gives you this satisfaction despite the boredom of a constant relationship or are you developing a new philosophy to justify love?"

"We love each other madly, Sanjay. I don't need to justify anything. Yes, sex is good. But it's not as if I only want to sleep with Leila. I want to live my life with her."

Sanjay was trying to lead Rahul in a specific direction. "Rahul, tell me one thing: are there separate types of women that you are attracted to? Those whom you want to sleep with and another type that you can live your life with?"

"It is possible."

"Why do you think so?"

"I don't know, but I think it is quite possible. But that is a matter of individual choice."

"Would you like to sleep with someone if there are no strings attached?"

"But why should she agree?"

Sanjay kept up the pressure. "Think hypothetically, Rahul. Tell me a name. You must have fancied a few movie stars."

"Well in that case I would like to sleep with Zeenat Aman or Bo Derek."

"And who might you like to live with?"

"Jaya Bhaduri or Debra Winger."

Sanjay patted him, "That's perfect buddy. Now tell me, if you can enjoy both the options simultaneously, how will that be?"

"It'll be great but frankly unbelievable."

Sanjay caught him. "You agree, it might be fun. Right?"

"Yes, but is it possible?"

"Well said. Do you remember Gargi? What do you think of her?" Sanjay looked straight into his eyes.

"What do I think her? I don't think of her Sanjay... No... no... no it's not true. Sometimes I do think of her."

"And then you land up with a massive hard-on?"

Rahul accepted that, "Maybe it's true. How is she, Sanjay?"

"Arani*da* has left her. She sings in a bar nowadays and I believe, she is an expensive call girl. She goes out with elite clients."

"Do you meet her quite often?" Rahul asked.

"I do, once in a while. I went to her the day before yesterday. She was talking about you and wanted to meet you."

"Rubbish! I don't believe this crap," said Rahul unbelievingly.

"It's true man. You want to meet her? Tell me. I'll take you to her. Tomorrow, all right. She lives in a rented flat in Tollygunj. She is usually free in the mornings."

"All right. But don't tell Leila about this."

Sanjay exclaimed, "You dirty slave! I won't. My word."

Sanjay confirmed that Gargi had agreed to meet them in her flat the next Sunday around noon. Rahul spent the next four days in anticipation, thinking about Gargi and masturbating.

Meanwhile, he had sex with Leila twice. He felt disturbed and confused with each passing day.

10.

The meeting with Gargi was a turning point in every sense. Rahul had never met a woman like her before. She was extremely raw and physical. She asked Rahul about college life and about his mountaineering expeditions. He told her everything, but he didn't mention Leila. He wondered how Aranida had been comfortable with Gargi. If one looked at her wide eyes, thin moist lips, her fleshy curves and beautifully maintained hands and feet, one was overwhelmed by the urge to enjoy her physicality in the most erotic and carnal manner possible. But most men wouldn't consider her as an ideal lover or wife, Rahul was convinced. Gargi looked like a sex provider in an adult film and yes, she had no soul. Rahul enjoyed sitting so close to her, though he was quite nervous. Erotic images flashed through his mind. He had never experienced this with Leila. He started feeling sick and his head was aching terribly.

Sanjay said suddenly, "I have some urgent work nearby. I'll finish it and join you shortly. Meanwhile, you may carry on and catch up with each other."

When he was leaving, Sanjay winked and Rahul was not sure whether he winked at him or at Gargi. Once Sanjay had gone, he felt a million bubbles bursting in his abdomen. They were bubbles of sexual tension.

Gargi told Rahul about her life in detail – how Aranida was suspicious of her movements, how she got fed up with his obsessive ways, and how she met Robby – an Anglo-Indian percussionist in a band. She told him how she got an offer to sing in a Park Street restaurant and went on to become the lead vocalist in Robby's band. She broke up with Aranida and began to live with Robby. She started smoking grass, and hash to give company to Robby and then fell in love with Robby's younger brother, Delphi.

Rahul wanted to ask Gargi about her parents, and siblings and whether she really entertained elite clients but could not muster the courage to do so.

She offered him homemade pudding, foreign cigarettes and a round of grass. When Rahul felt extremely dry inside and his head reeled under a strange impact of herbal aromas, he suddenly found Gargi's face very close to his. Her tongue flicked animatedly, like a red lizard as she unzipped his pants. Rahul was immobile with fear. He did not respond although he longed for the moist confines of Gargi's body. She whispered into his ears, "I fancied you for a long time. Rahul, I will give you love of a kind you can never even imagine in your lifetime. I'll first take you in my..."

Rahul woke up naked in Gargi's bedroom in the afternoon; hungry, thirsty, and tired. His eyes fell on his limp penis. He could not clearly remember what had happened.

Gargi sat on a stool before a mirror singing an Ann Murray song about lovers meeting on a sand dune. She was casually brushing her shiny black hair, clad in a red negligee.

Rahul asked in a trembling voice, "Did Sanjay come back?"

Gargi said, "No. Are you happy, Rahul?"

"I don't know. I'm feeling tired, hungry and thirsty."

Gargi said coaxingly, "Come baby, I'll clean you with hot water, feed you, make you a drink and find you a taxi to go back home."

"I don't have enough money on me, Gargi. How much are you going to charge me for all this?"

Gargi laughed loudly. "I won't charge you this time. Next time, I will. But you will get a fat discount because of your beautiful eyes."

While returning home, Rahul wondered what he could have done in life to be rewarded with such unfettered pleasure. But, as Leila's face appeared in his mind he was overcome by a powerful feeling of nauseating guilt. In the end, he wanted to rewind his life by a day and skip it if he could. He was all the more surprised by his reaction because he had always felt that such situations and emotions, when shown in movies were untrue and sentimental. He was thoroughly averse to such sentimentality but he was going through a similar feeling of guilt, torment and remorse himself.

At night, he caught fever and could not sleep well. In the morning, when he felt unbearably miserable he decided to rush to Leila and tell her everything and seek her forgiveness. He knew it would be impossible to keep such a secret and carry on in this manner. As he took this decision he started feeling better. The trip to Leila's house that day, seemed as difficult as climbing a steep mountain slope.

11.

As he was about to leave his house, the telephone rang. It was Leila.

Leila spoke in a peculiarly impersonal voice, "What happened to you yesterday, Rahul?"

Rahul was fearful but said calmly, "What?"

"You didn't call or meet me. You didn't even inform me on Saturday about your plans!"

Rahul felt guilty "I will be in your house in ten minutes. Can we talk, then? I need your support today."

Leila suddenly shouted into the phone, "Forget me, Rahul! You bloody grass-smoking, whore-mongering scoundrel! How dare you seek my compassion and support! You are a worthless parasite wanting to feed on my efforts and me. No! After what I saw yesterday in Gargi's flat, I don't want to look at you, ever. Don't come near me in college. Don't come to my house or I'll kill you! I'll complain to the police!" Leila banged the phone down.

Rahul sat down. His world was caving in. He didn't know what to do. He called Leila's home and her mother picked up the phone. When he asked for Leila he was told not to phone again. A thick, black, impenetrable veil descended before his eyes, engulfing him in a pocket of limitless darkness.

12.

In the next seventy-five days, Rahul made innumerable attempts to contact Leila. He telephoned her residence thirty-nine times but was denied access in a curt manner and asked not to call up again. He went to her residence six times but was denied entry. He tried to speak to her in college but Leila remained silent and Rahul was denied any reaction or response.

With every passing day he felt broken and devastated. Each rejection felt like a new fire capable of vanquishing his body and his soul. Overcome by nausea, he stopped eating altogether. His eyes burnt from sleeplessness. Each time he tried to close his eyes he suffered from a recurring dream of being trapped in a long, dark railway tunnel. When he tried to run towards the light he was shattered by the roaring sounds of an approaching train that threatened to mow him down. He locked himself up in his room and rarely ventured out of the house. He had no news of Sanjay. Someone told him that Sanjay had left Calcutta soon after the seventh semester examinations were over, to attend a month long corporate training programme in Bombay.

One night, he landed up in the restaurant where Gargi sang. He wanted her help in procuring hash and marijuana. When Gargi was satisfied that he had enough cash she sent him to someone called Darling*da* on Free School Street.

Rahul met Darling*da* and obtained some of the stuff which he began to consume. It was an experience that changed his life. As the toxic smoke went down his throat his gut seemed on fire. He saw himself running through a sunlit poppy field, like Jessie Owens. He had no memories of the past, no dreams for the future; he didn't feel tired anymore. The air that entered his lungs bore the mixed scents of freshly baked fruit cake, poppy seeds and unknown flowers. Finally he entered a dark cave and was cut off from everything; it was as though he were dead.

When he woke up, all he wanted to do was to return

to that cave. He collected more money and approached Darling*da* again. As this cycle played itself out, Rahul was forced to steal from his mother's purse every day. One day he asked Darling*da* if he could do some work instead of paying for the drugs in cash. "What can you do, Rahul?" Darling*da* asked.

"Anything Darling*da*. I can paint, I can make models. I don't know whether my hands are steady, though."

Darling*da* had replied patronisingly, "That's good, Rahul. I sell ethnic stuff to the foreigners staying in Sudder Street. Like landscapes in watercolours or crayons or charcoal on hand-made paper. Or, paintings of festivals and of old Calcutta drenched in the monsoon. I think I can pay you handsomely for these paintings sell well. Moreover, unsteady hands enrich a painting, my dear. The smoke purifies and amplifies your vision."

Rahul agreed instantly but he did not have the money for paper and colours. It was decided that Darling*da* would provide this material, free of cost. Darling*da* appreciated the stuff Rahul made and kept providing him what he craved for and introduced him to heroin. Rahul stopped going to college and did not appear for the eighth semester examinations. When he realised that the situation was getting worse and his mother would soon find out he decided to leave home. He left a small note for his mother, "Ma, I don't like this life. I'm going away. Please try to forget me, if you can."

13.

Rahul travelled to various places – mountains, beaches, deserts, valleys, plateaus and forests. He travelled on trains, and buses, on the backs of animals and of course, on foot.

He worked as a labourer, a pimp, a travel guide, and as a copy painter and somehow managed to earn a meagre livelihood. His ultimate aim was to return to the hazy smoke-filled world, which had become his home. Wherever he went, he first got in touch with those who could supply adequate quantity of the stuff that kept him afloat. By the end of the year he looked like a scarecrow, his dependence on drugs seemed etched on his emaciated face. He could approach drug dealers without any effort, creating no alarm. This made his life easier and more peaceful. He kept a journal during these travels where he scribbled random thoughts as he moved from one place to another. He believed, these words were not written by him but by another Rahul who followed him like an inseparable shadow.

A few journal entries read like this:

1. *On the waterfront in Benaras I read the words of Jagannath in Ganga Lahari, "Now bind your lovely girdle of battle, and anchor the new moon in your crown with ropes of snakes. Do not take me lightly, thinking me an ordinary sinner, Behold, O River of Heaven!" I walked from Assi Ghat to Munshi Ghat* (Aparajita *and* Joy Baba Felunath *were shot here) seeing the night creeping over the waters of the Ganga. From Munshi Ghat as I travelled into the alleys of light and shadows I was lost in the millions of trades of the old city; temples; ganja and heroin sellers; milk, rabri and malai sellers; lodging houses; travellers; lovers; concubines; countless lingams of* ardhanarishwar; *cows and heaps of cow dung and waste, I was reminded of another walk which I had always wanted to take in the future, to return to the grasslands of my nameless ancestors.*

2. *The storm was rising far away from me. It was dredging with it columns of sand and ash, creating an opaque screen between where I stood and what lay in front of me. I was standing at the feet of the Stoke glacier, on one of the over-hanging verandahs of the Stoke Palace. People talked about the symmetry of Buddhist art. Old thankas hung against the Palace walls. A part of the Palace was converted into a museum displaying various artefacts of the Royal family of Ladakh. The storm raged for a long time and as it weakened gradually it revealed colossal ash mountains across the valley of Ladakh. The Sindhu River flowed through the desert valley, leafless vegetation all around. The River looked like a lonely traveller. As I craned my neck to see the mountain peaks across the valley I sighted a million birds in the sky, violet in colour, flying from one mountain range to the other. Night was falling. The ashen texture of the surroundings*

was slowly dissolving into the impending blackness. The guards in the Palace Museum asked us to leave. I saw a lama kid with a crimson hood on his head, on the road below, looking at my face intently. His eyelashes did not flutter. The eyes were big rounds of black bitumen. As I came out of the Palace and went down the road looking for him, he had vanished. I stayed in a camp by the Sindhu River. It was bitterly cold, dry and windy. As I gulped down multiple puffs, I felt unprecedented warmth spreading through my bones, and I dreamt of the infant lama, the serenity of the Pangyong Lake, the wind, the violet birds and the Sindhu River.

3.   *Last night, I saw the illuminated faces from my past lives shadowed on the sand dunes – the faces of my wives, my concubines, my fathers, my mothers, my teachers, my brothers, my sisters, my husbands and my friends. They were floating around like weightless feathers. I saw them from a distance and they withered one by one.*

Rahul travelled like this for nearly four years. When he was in Haridwar one night, he felt a rocking pain shoot through his entire body, a desert-like dryness tore through his abdomen and a billion lights flashed before his eyes; he lost complete control of his movements. A gentleman caught him on the road, dragged him down to the Har Ki Pauri, made him take five dips in the ice-cold waters of the Ganga and asked him in chaste Hindiwhere he came from. Rahul looked down and was amazed by the sudden revelation of his mother's sad face projected on the flowing surface of the water. The pain building deep inside his body was replaced by a mounting desire to leap on to his mother's lap and sleep in the shadow of her body. Rahul said, "I want to return to my mother."

The gentleman put him on a Howrah-bound train that night, and Rahul returned home emaciated, with soiled unkempt hair and beard, looking like a dried-out leaf without any sap.

When his mother saw Rahul on the doorstep she let out an involuntary cry, as though she had seen a ghost. She took him in her arms and cried inconsolably, like a baby. She could sense the first signs of life once again, "I'm a sinner, Ma, I pray for your deepest compassion and understanding." His mother kissed his tired eyes and assured him, "You'll find all of that here, my darling."

14.

The next four years were like taking a new birth from within the bowels of a grave. Rahul surrendered to the process of detoxification in spite of the pain, the thirst and disorientation that he had to face. He had to withstand the constant interplay of violent shadows in his soul similar to what one experienced in the Dark Ages. Rahul's mother sheltered him by locking him in her own embrace in his moments of fury and pain, standing beside him like a rock. The doctor and the psychiatrist put him on a strict regimen of diet, exercise and medicine. This was the worst storm his mother had faced in her entire life. She had confidence in that beam of light that she could see in her son's eyes, from time to time, and in his unfailing desire to make her happy. Surprisingly, his mother rarely cried during this time, but she suffered extreme exhaustion.

Over a period of time Rahul's health improved and his mother experienced the sweetest moments of her life telling Rahul the stories and fables behind the masterly paintings of the Hindustani, Mughal and European Renaissance Periods. She would read aloud from the writings of Manik Bandopadhyay, Bhibhutibhushan Bandopadhyay and Satyajit Ray. He remained quiet and unresponsive at first but slowly began to open up. Mother and son soon engaged themselves in matters related to aesthetics of art and existence and debated for hours loving the bliss of living a simple life.

They never discussed Sanjay and Leila. Once, Rahul had asked his mother: whether she had ever blamed her destiny for having a son like him. His mother said, "Yes, to have given birth to a man whom I could have easily desired as a lover."

Rahul asked anxiously, "I turned out to be a lousy lover in real life, Ma. Would you have reacted in the same manner as Leila did, had you been my lover?"

Mother replied, "These are meaningless speculations. Events happen at random. An ordeal is an ordeal in the long run."

As Rahul got well enough to move outside the house his mother asked him to look at the photographs presented to him by his father and concentrate on the message hidden in them. His mother said, "Rahul, these photographs are saying something to you. Look at them carefully and you'll know. Will you go back to mountain climbing, my son?"

Rahul replied instantly, "Yes, I will."

Rahul and his mother then moved to Darjeeling.

"Rahul, won't you like to marry and settle down? At times I feel guilty for not doing enough about this. I want you to marry and be happy," his mother said one day.

"Happiness has nothing to do with marriage. I'm happy. I've thought about it. I don't want to marry. I'm sure. I'll hate you if you force me," Rahul replied.

15.

Rahul looked at Leila's photograph in the newspaper a couple of times and read the small news column published beneath it.

FAMOUS ENVIRONMENTALIST ARCHITECT TO ADDRESS THE CITY AT THE TOWN HALL

Ms.Leila Gupta, an architect internationally renowned for her focus on environment friendly architecture, will be in Kolkata on September 27 to deliver a lecture on "Environment Friendly Habitation" at the Town Hall. The programme, organised by an NGO will start at 5:30 pm. Ms. Gupta is reported to have refused to work with the state government citing serious differences of opinion on policy matters pertaining to urban infrastructure and planning. She had clarified her stand at a press conference after her meeting with government officials yesterday. The state government wanted to engage her Sweden-based company as a consultant for an upcoming satellite township on the outskirts of Kolkata. She, together with her architect husband, has worked on a number of projects with the state government in the past, including the setting up of an artisan township in Ghurni.

Rahul read the news item a couple of times. He went out for a walk on the Mall in the late afternoon. The fever and general weakness had subsided by now.

Memories of Leila rushed back to his mind the moment his mother had mentioned her name that morning. By evening, he could look at the past in a detached manner as though these events were part of the plot of a novel he had read long back. While returning home, he had a cup of tea and two pieces of freshly baked fruitcake in a newly built cafetaria on the Mall.

"Ma, I plan to visit Kolkata to hear Leila speak. Will you object to this?"Rahul asked.

"Are you sure you want to do this? Are you sure it won't affect you again? Are you sure of that?" She asked.

"It won't affect me. I'm sure of that."

"Then, go. Re-visit your past one last time and then move on." His mother answered with conviction in her voice.

16.

Rahul reached Kolkata a day before the event. He had returned to the city after a gap of ten years and was aware from newspaper reports that the city was undergoing a massive change. The images of the past that reeked of defeat and chaos were vanishing fast. There was construction going on everywhere. The city's name itself had changed. He went to the Maidan and to other parts of the city and was amazed by the structures of concrete and steel that had sprouted all around. He visited the areas where Sanjay and Leila used to stay; the college where he had studied up to the seventh semester and Darling*da*'s hideout. He looked at Gargi's flat and the restaurant where she performed. He could sense the sadness in his heart. He returned to the guesthouse in Central Kolkata overcome by the heat, humidity and smoke which he was no longer used to. He'd been in danger of being run over by speeding vehicles a couple of times during the day. He fell asleep, exhausted by the day's events and anxious about what might be in store for him the next day.

He reached the Town Hall early the next day, so that he could find a seat from where he could slip away quietly. The programme started an hour late. Rahul had expected that seeing Leila after so many years would have an impact on him. He was curious about her and her activities. And wanted to know about her husband and children. She was dressed formally in a black business suit and her hair was drawn back neatly in a bun. She did not wear any jewellery or make-up. Her eyes sparkled and her skin glowed with health. Her features were as sharp as ever, but she had gained some weight and looked good. She presented a picture of confidence that could never decay something so permanent that it was in direct contrast with his life.

When she was invited to speak she said, "My husband and I left this city eight years ago. During the last two days I have had the opportunity to see the city closely and talk to a few local residents drawn from various social groups. While these people feel that the city is changing for the good, my conviction is that the city is being robbed of its past, of that which forms the essence of all existence. There are memories we do not want to keep, even in our personal lives, but without memories we'll be nowhere. We will be living in an empty space and will feel powerless. Powerful people and organised institutions, including the government, use the trick of selective memory to amass power. This is also happening in this city. The landscape, comprising water, soil, air and various forms of life, both seen as well as unseen, are being destroyed by the instructions of very ruthless people in the name of development to enhance the cause of money and power…"

She spoke in this fashion for about two hours. She unmasked the nexus between the government, the builders, the financial institutions, the mafia and the police. She spoke of how they destroyed the natural habitat and cultural traits of a city, how they flouted the laws of the country and curbed the basic choices that are guaranteed to a private citizen under the Constitution, in the name of development. It was a marvellous speech that combined a deep understanding of complex issues with an in-depth knowledge of history and philosophy. When she was asked about alternatives she said that her company offered various models of eco-friendly habitation, which were in use in various parts of Europe and Australia. A pilot project was under way in Cochin funded through a Swedish grant. "It will cost quite a bit to restore our civilisation. We've trampled it beyond repair in most cases. I think the millionaires and billionaires of this country should shell out some money to atone for the sins they have committed," she said as the audience burst into peals of laughter. "Ladies and gentlemen, this can be good business, too," she added.

"I have told the Chief Minister that the powerless require the deepest compassion and understanding of the powerful."

Rahul listened attentively though he was often distracted by his memories. The closing remark had a strange impact on him.

Rahul watched the rich and powerful leave the auditorium after the programme and waited in a taxi outside. When the Mercedes carrying Leila rolled on to the road, he asked the taxi driver to follow the car. It was a short chase, seven minutes to be precise, from the Town Hall to a five-star hotel. When Rahul was certain that Leila would have walked past the lobby, he went to the reception and asked for the hotel's telephone numbers. He found a public telephone booth just across the road and called the hotel asking to be connected to Ms. Leila Gupta.

After a few seconds Leila came on the line. "Yes, this is Leila. Who is it?"

There was a terrible churning in Rahul's stomach and he felt giddy. He sweated profusely and was dumb-struck. When Leila asked for the identity of the caller yet again, Rahul blurted out "Leila, this is Rahul, Rahul Banerjee."

She did not disconnect the line as she had done in the past, "Leila, I heard you speak at the Town Hall today. It was a nice speech. Coming from you, it sounded nicer. I called to congratulate you and check whether you remembered me at all? I grew melancholic in the evening and ended up calling you."

There was a long pause at the other end.

Finally Leila asked, "Where are you, now?"

"I'm calling from a phone booth opposite your hotel. Actually, I followed you from the Town Hall. I know you won't like this."

There was a long pause again.

"I don't know whether it sounds all right, but I'm free tonight and if it is okay with you please join me at the Chinese restaurant in the hotel. I remember that you like Chinese food. In half an hour. What do you say?" she asked.

Rahul was silent for some time, as though fighting a battle deep within him.

At last, he said, "Okay, I'll come."

17.

Rahul reached early and was ushered to a corner table laid for two.

Leila joined him in five minutes, dressed in a long chocolate skirt and a sleeveless blouse. Her face was glowing and she looked distant and mystical in the soft light. Rahul stood up to meet her. They shook hands. Rahul's hands were cold. Leila's were warm.

She opened the conversation brightly, "So, how is life after so many years?"

"I'm here. It feels good," he said.

Leila asked, "Are you the same cynical person we knew? You know, Sanjay was remembering you the day I took my flight to India."

Rahul couldn't hide the surprise in his voice, "Sanjay!" he exclaimed.

"My husband, Rahul. We opened our own firm just

after college. Once we were established in our work, we got married," Leila explained.

Rahul knew he had to control his emotions. "That's great! I didn't know all this. Oh my God, how is Sanjay, Leila? Is he as bright as he used to be in college?"

"He's a very good husband. Yes, he's very bright. He's full of ideas. He takes care of the marketing and business development aspects. He has made wonderful contacts. We could not have grown without his contacts," Leila said.

"Does he paint these days?"

"Sometimes. But mostly on the computer."

They ordered dinner. Leila asked for a glass of gin and tonic but Rahul preferred to sip cold mineral water.

Leila said animatedly, "You've not aged at all. You're as trim and athletic as ever. Your eyes look deeper and quieter. What do you do, Rahul?"

"I'm a senior trainer at the Himalayan Mountaineering Institute in Darjeeling. I have been living there with my mother for the last ten years."

Leila suddenly asked, "Did you finally graduate, Rahul?"

"No", he replied.

Rahul had expected raging flames of anger to darken his soul because of Leila and Sanjay's betrayal, but he felt no anger at all. He was quiet, deep inside. It was like a bomb that failed to explode because it was damp. He was vexed by his lack of emotion.

As the conversation progressed, he became more objective and realised that another person lurked beneath the beautiful persona Leila exhibited to the world. He noticed wrinkles in her skin, a pale grey texture below her eyes and a slight sag in her back. These were signs of ageing and scars of battles with memories of the past. Rahul was not clear what he wanted out of this meeting.

Leila asked, "Are you married?"

"No," said Rahul and added, "Do you have children?"

Leila said, "No. We are mostly travelling and involved in work. We decided not to have children. I don't think we have the patience to raise children. I had a miscarriage just after our wedding. It was heartbreaking. I didn't want to repeat the experience."

Rahul said, "I hope I've not upset you by asking this."

"No. It's good to talk to you after such a long time."

The food arrived. They started eating.

Leila started the conversation again. "Did you like my speech?"

Rahul said, "Yes. I said so on the phone."

"What do you think? Will my ideas work here?"

Rahul shrugged, "I don't know. I've no knowledge of such things."

"Why is that? Are you cut off from the real world, Rahul?"

Rahul answered philosophically, "I don't know what you mean by the real world, Leila."

"How is it that you landed up at the Town Hall?"

Rahul narrated the sequence of events.

"You wanted to see me. That sounds so good. What did you see in me?" Leila asked.

"There are things Leila, which can't be communicated. I hope you understand that."

Leila fell silent. She was sipping her gin. After some time she looked at Rahul intensely, misty-eyed. "I think you know that you remain, in our minds like an indefatigable ghost. However much we try to expel you, we fail each time." She said almost in a quivering voice.

Rahul asked bluntly, "What do you mean by 'our minds' Leila?"

"I mean, Sanjay's and mine."

Rahul ate the dim-sums quietly. He had finished the soup.

Leila said suddenly, "Have you forgiven us, Rahul?"

"No. I mean, yes. But, I don't want to sit in a position of power."

"You know, you are smart enough to be powerful and not act so. You are a powerhouse, Rahul."

Rahul suspected that she was getting drunk. Tipsy.

Leila shot, "Why did you want to meet me, Rahul?"

Rahul said slowly but firmly, "To see the most

important milestone of my past one last time and move beyond it."

A pall of gloom descended on Leila's face. She looked like an orchard ravaged by a jungle fire. The muscles on her face twitched and she started crying. Rahul said comfortingly "Why are you doing this to yourself? Don't be weighed down by what you did long back. The two of you betrayed me, that's true. I cheated on you and that is true, too. All this seems to have happened in some other life. Who am I to pardon you? I'm no saint. I don't sit on a pedestal, nor do I aspire to do so. You guys destroyed my life. I think this is a valid way to look at what happened. But in reality things happen at random most of the time. Our wishes and interpretations have no meaning. In the end we have to look back at whatever happened with a smile. I would like to leave now. Thanks for the wonderful dinner and for your company, Leila. Goodnight."

Rahul went out without looking back at Leila. He was happy with his performance. Leila wanted to tell Rahul that whenever she crossed the Pacific she requested a window seat so that she could look down at the ocean for, in some strange way, it reminded her of Rahul's eyes.

An Improbable
Love Affair

1.

Rahul felt tired as he came out of the banquet hall. He had spent the whole day arguing environmental issues relentlessly with other specialists at a conference. He walked slowly down the marble staircase, deep in thought, unmindful of his surroundings – people jostling with guarded agendas hanging loosely on their made-up faces, motionless and silent inside elevators yet chirpy in the shops lining the floors of the luxury hotel. As he passed through the grand central corridor, he was struck by a disturbing thought. During the whole day he had lost his temper at least eleven times in the course of these inconsequential yet egoistic debates. The poise and grace he had displayed had slowly slipped at the feigned ignorance and corrupt loyalty of the speakers to the invisible sponsors and beneficiaries of a deep-state. To a point he had argued the merits and logic, but the moment he heard a patronising streak in their voices, something snapped. He felt intense columns of a raging fire lashing at him and consuming him totally.

Water was one of the major topics of discussion – its conservation, recycling along with talks of an imminent third world war being fought between nation states on grounds of scarcity of water were passionately mentioned.

But he rarely found policy-makers talking about specific policies that would encourage rainwater harvesting or the creation of smaller decentralised projects with greater autonomy. Nothing was suggested to discourage the scouring of landscapes and waterscapes by the real estate sharks either. He picked fights with everyone and it was left to the sponsors of the conference to intervene and ensure decorum. In spite of such temperamental behaviour, Rahul was treated with a reasonable degree of awe. Mentally, Rahul made a note of the attention he drew from the crowd, especially the ladies, and was more than reasonably pleased with his performance.

It was not as if Rahul did not believe in what he said. He was convinced that human civilisation was headed towards irreversible destruction given its complete submission to consumption, and the madness only increased as time progressed and technologies evolved. He believed that both Capitalism and Communism (the two contrary philosophies and economies expostulated in the modern world) had been subservient to the human tendencies of endlessly amassing power through the wheeling and dealing of the state machinery, ultimately allowing commercial corporations in cahoots with political and civil institutions to take overall existential control of life, thereby making most of the people feel rootless and alien. In both the systems of state control, a handful of families went on apportioning disproportionate wealth and resulting power through institutional means, thereby creating a permanent disharmony between humans and nature, between men and men, and this had gone to an extent, which (he strongly believed) was beyond repair or reconciliation. He had argued passionately that the state was not ruled by its legitimate politicians but by the leaders of large corporations. His tagline was, "Need less, consume less, produce less. Can we work towards a zero-development society?"

In conversation with an investment banker, a lady friend of his, he repeated this line and drew her into the nitty-gritty of the Free-economy Movement. She was visibly impressed by the show of passion and he was very satisfied with the manner in which a quick impression had been made. They exchanged phone numbers and vowed to keep in touch.

Rahul himself however, did not lead a life where he needed less, consumed less nor produced less. In fact, he was a senior management executive in a large corporation and led a life of privilege and comfort. It was also not as if he did not fight himself to gravitate to the kind of ecological life, which he talked about so often. There was a way, but he just didn't know how to get there, or adjust to the absence of material pleasures in life, nor did he know how to communicate and share in a community. He was very unhappy about this but he did nothing. This was further compounded by the blow Nandana had dealt him. What he said to himself repeatedly was, he would not allow himself to drown in an ocean of grief. He made a mental note of his action plan to emerge from sadness and despair, something which happened frequently these days without provocation or warning.

By this time he had reached the circular hotel lounge with its massive dome decorated by abstract murals in bright colours. Huge cut-glass chandeliers hung from the top mystically reflecting and refracting countless beams of light. He felt insignificant for a moment. Through the glass panels of the revolving door at the entrance, he saw the bespectacled lady climbing into a car with a tall man. He was struck by a strange sadness almost to the point of helplessness. He debated whether to sit for a few minutes on the lounge sofa or to continue walking. But the moment of contemplation was interrupted by the entry of a familiar face. The woman approached the hotel reception; and although she looked familiar Rahul could not identify her instantly. Then, he recalled a film song and zeroed in on the protagonist, the pale but beautiful Vidya Kishori.

It was Vidya, in faded jeans and T-shirt sans make-up. She looked fragile and indifferent and her face evoked strange emotions in Rahul. She was comparatively a new entrant in the film industry. She had revived her family business three years ago by asking her elder brother (a very successful industrial engineer till then) to head production while she herself dealt with the creative aspects. They had worked jointly on three home productions on shoestring budgets. All three films were based on short stories written by practically unknown writers yet contained fresh dramatic elements and were directed by relatively new directors who were willing to explore uncharted territories in mainstream cinema.

Vidya played the female protagonist in all the three films. She had an exquisite face; a strange combination of simmering beauty, intelligence, elegance and character. She was small in frame but had an enduring screen presence. Her eyes had the unique ability to talk and smile radiantly at the same time. But it was the curious mix of melancholy and happiness trapped in them that took one's breath away. Two of her films had been blockbusters but the last one had bombed. However, Rahul had liked her most in the third film. Her character was that of a woman whose husband had left her for another. She played a lonely homemaker who forced by the hardships of life took up work eventually forsaking love for the sake of her adolescent son. She magnificently portrayed rejection and humiliation without recourse to sensational dramatization, the grief so well displayed on her visage that it seemed as if someone had permanently etched it on her face.

There was a scene in the film where her lover asks her, "Don't you need love? Don't you need a relationship to live meaningfully? You are so young. You are so desirable. It shows on your face. Why don't you accept your love for me?" Vidya's character after remaining silent for a long time answers, "I need you. But I also need a good father for my son; I think you'll fail on that count." That scene captured the fierce, invisible conflict in a woman caught between maternal responsibilities and a woman in the throes of passionate love.

Rahul had seen Vidya's films many times over and had silently, without admitting to himself, fallen in love with her. He had deeply yearned to be a part of her production house. He was ready to become a spot boy if required, to achieve this goal. When he shook himself from his reverie

Vidya was no longer in the lounge. With a feeling of love and longing and the proceedings of the conference forgotten for good, Rahul returned home, his heart throbbing hard and fast.

2.

At night he was unable to sleep. A low-grade fever and aching joints made him toss and turn throughout the night. He could not recall when his thoughts of Nandana had replaced those of Vidya. Rahul had been married to Nandana for twelve years. Before marriage they had been involved in an intense, eight-year courtship. Nandana had studied English while he had taken up physics. Both had volatile temperaments yet became college buddies before they felt drawn to each other, it was instantaneous, after that first meeting in the college canteen.

During the years of courtship, their exchanges slowly evolved from engaging discussions on politics, art and philosophy to wild lovemaking at each other's homes at every opportunity. These were punctuated by visits to cinemas and theatre festivals, followed by long-winded intellectual discussions on the aesthetics of art. By the end of the fifth year, when both had completed their masters degree and were to start working, they thought of marrying and starting a family. Like other young lovers of their time, they had rarely discussed marriage and family in the early years of courtship.

Meanwhile, both their families had started knowing each other and were not too comfortable in each others' company because of their innumerable differences. Fundamentally, the differences centred around the fact that Nandana's family considered themselves to be cultural elites whereas Rahul's family considered themselves to be rich and laid great stress on enterprise to achieve material comforts in life. Rahul himself was more comfortable in the relaxed environment of Nandana's family whereas Nandana without confessing to anyone aspired to have a rich husband, plush home, and all the comforts of a lazy life and loads of cash to spend as she willed. She in her heart of hearts hated all restrictions on spending and the moral principles of austerity, which her father emphasised upon during her growing-up years.

Although outwardly she said quite the opposite of what she aspired to, however, in her selection of men, who remained in her close coterie, she allowed only the rich, the brilliant and the successful. Apart from anything else what she genuinely liked about Rahul was his benevolent, soft and unobtrusive nature. While Rahul started working, Nandana enrolled herself in a vocational course, turning down two good offers from reputed publishing houses. Rahul was taken aback by this decision because Nandana gave so much importance to the economic freedom of women. Once Nandana had told flirtingly to Rahul, "Why, you can't take my responsibility, is it? I'm not in the mood to work. I'm still in the learning mode. This course helps me to meet women from different backgrounds. The experience is great. I think this will help me know the specific conditions in which women live and struggle in our country. I can't be pushed to work to a 9 to 5 schedule so early on in my life. In any case, you are earning great guns for both of us. Your family is wealthy. They don't need your money, of course. So, we can have a lot to ourselves; I suppose." Rahul did not respond to this. In fact, later he started encouraging her to get more involved in the course that she was doing. After four months she suddenly stopped studying, citing lack of sufficient intellectual challenge in the course. She concluded; "It's boring talking to pitiful women day in day out." In the process, she wasted ten thousand rupees she had taken from Rahul for the course.

One evening when Rahul said: she should have at least continued with the course for the sake of money that was invested in it, she flared up. She retorted back saying, "What you can only think of is money, money and money! Have you ever tried to imagine what I might want to do with my life? If that money is dearer to you, mark my words, I will return it all to you, with interest, in the next one year. Now stop talking about money Rahul, for god's sake!" Nandana's boyfriends pampered her with undiluted attention. Her style and attitude of a queen bee were carefully accentuated by her charming personality and mouthful of ideas on emancipation of various sections of people in the civil society. Her deft volubility attracted one and all. She mixed unabashedly with men without hiding anything from Rahul. He kept silent; although he was repeatedly pitted and eroded from within by turbulent waves of jealousy. He wanted to revolt against Nandana. But he failed and felt weak in front of her.

One day, when he had muttered something disagreeable she came back sharply at him, "You can't have such a low opinion of my friends. You remain at work most of the day chasing money. That's all right. After all, money is required to start an independent family. I'll be your wife soon. I can't think of marrying anybody else. But I can't accept my suitor being a narrow minded regressive jerk, which I know you are not. You're only torn into pieces by unnecessary jealousy, my baby. I love you. I also love you for your magnanimity. Don't you ever forget that! It's so central to your character." Immediately after this, she drew him to a session of wild lovemaking that seemed to have drowned all of Rahul's fears and anxieties. He knew this relief would sustain him for sometime till the demons flew back inside his soul once again in their cyclical trajectory.

The wedding was marked by magnificent grandeur and done most elaborately although no religious rituals were followed. The warmth of the ceremony lingered with both the families and the couple for a long time. In the first four years of their marriage, Rahul and Nandana lived with Rahul's family. Nandana did not do any housework for two reasons; one, she was not trained by her parents to do such work and she did not have the temperament to do such tedious and menial work. Two, Rahul's house was literally littered with servants and maids and so there was no need for her to work. And so she remained extremely idle for most part of the day. To kill time she started attending seminars, discussions and talk shows on various political, cultural and social issues and in the process, gathered a lot of theoretical knowledge on multifarious facets of life. She also read quite a lot, watched art films and visited the theatre regularly. This exposure converted her into an aggressive critic of life and art. But she refused to do any real work. With time, she became extremely critical of Rahul's family. She also criticised Rahul for getting obsessed with his work and not spending enough time with her.

Nandana was also extremely possessive about Rahul. Gradually, she started suspecting him of cheating on her behind her back and insisted on his not overstaying in office, going on official tours and if he had to go, insisted on taking her along with him. Initially, Rahul relished her bouts of possessiveness. But after some time he started hating them, more so because she would not allow him to reciprocate and be similarly jealous of her. To keep peace in the house and maintain his dignity, he submitted completely to her, nurturing a strained hope that she would eventually begin to understand the underlying principles of equity and fairplay in relationships. Well, that was not to happen.

One thing that Rahul was quite vexed with was: the crueller Nandana turned out to be, the more enamoured, attached and rooted he became to her. To be fair to her, it was not as if she was cruel all the time; sometimes she could be quite loving. But her love seemed to last only as long as she was sure of his complete submission. The second she had any doubts about him, she would grow quarrelsome, and pick fights over the smallest and most inconsequential issues.

One morning, she announced that she had been asked by the editor of a famous national daily to write a weekly column on cultural issues. At first, Rahul was hit by a twang of jealousy. He feared Nandana would soon grow famous and more insolent, pampered and aggressive.

The first subject that she took up was on the decay in traditional art schools in Shantiniketan. Rahul wanted to get involved in her writing, but she clearly turned him down. When she visited Shantiniketan for the research work, he wanted to go with her, but she wanted to make the visits with the editor and not Rahul. Within a month's time Rahul found she was ceaselessly on the phone with the editor on one pretext or the other and meeting him day and night within and outside of office hours. Nandana commissioned two of her classmates from the university to write a series of articles on the assigned subject based on information she had collected during her visits to Shantiniketan. But the information was sketchy and disjointed. She then gave them a few published books on the subject and instructed them to write four articles, which would be published sequentially, and to write them in a manner so devious that would make tracing them back to these books impossible. In a span of one month the articles were written by this team, craftily edited by the editor and published on four consecutive Sundays.

Rahul thought Nandana would now permanently settle in her career as a newspaper columnist, leave him and start living with the editor. But things happened differently. Intriguingly, she became disinterested in her name getting published in articles that were not written by her. She was embarrassed as she was unable to defend her articles when discussions on related topics came up in society circles. Further by this time she was already mentally disengaged from the editor. There was always a lull after the storm was over. Rahul cherished these periods. He wished and prayed that such periods should continue forever because during these times Nandana would be at her weakest best, singing praises of a close knit family life with him and their kids. She would demand impregnation while making love to Rahul. Rahul would always suspect such fantasies, but at the back of his mind he sincerely wanted to believe Nandana was sincere about wanting a family. These periods lasted for a few months, only to be interrupted by another man and another deception in the name of some lofty work. This sinusoidal curve of conjugal existence continued, ranging between periods of extreme fidelity and periods of limitless, unprovoked, indiscreet infidelity for approximately twelve years. In the days of closeness, Rahul sensed waves of infinite bliss cresting on the shores of his flying soul in an illuminated sky. During the nights of separation, Rahul felt stabbed by flying demons and fire spitting evil spirits burning down his eyes and skin brutally with every stroke of raging flame.

Nandana did not conceive after marriage in spite of a few sincere efforts made by her. It could not have been due to any physiological irregularity with either of them because she had conceived once before they were married. She had undergone abortion (against her will) considering the possible problems they could face from their families. Actually, Nandana wanted to keep the child and immediately start a family with Rahul, irrespective of all the odds. She reacted instinctively; she gave a damn about how their families would react or about financial constraints. Rahul had to counsel her to make her understand what was practical and what was not. Rahul did not know that Nandana had conceived with Samar years after their marriage. This time, of course Nandana had walked into an abortion clinic without batting an eyelid. Thereafter, her relationship with Samar had ended abruptly.

In the beginning of this year, when he was basking in another 'spell of sunshine' (as he preferred to call the positive phase) he received a call from Ambarish who was in London. Ambarish was a common friend of Nandana and Rahul. Ambarish had separated from his wife some time back. He was to come to India next month to deliver a few lectures on an invitation to the Jadavpur University. He was planned to stay in the university guesthouse. Out of magnanimity, Rahul invited Ambarish to his house for his entire stay in India, which he accepted without any hesitation. Although Nandana protested at first, Rahul saw a sudden gleam on her face that made him aware of what was to follow. As expected, in a few days time Ambarish and Nandana had become inseparable and were visiting concerts and functions without Rahul. On the twentieth day, Nandana declared that she had decided to move to London with Ambarish, to study in the university where he was teaching. In the next forty

days, Nandana moved out of her home and shifted base
to London; taking a lump sum from Rahul, which she
perceived was her rightful share; along with the ornaments
she had brought from her house and all the rest of her
belongings in three colossal bags. She reached London
on a tourist visa. Rahul cried and howled like a child in
solitude but did not resist the process. He even signed on
the no-objection certificate and faxed it to the UK high
commission required for her visa without any qualms.

A few days after she'd left, Rahul sat in front of the
TV watching cricket. Suddenly, it occurred to him he felt
more relaxed than he had felt in a very long time. He
could not remember the last time he had felt like this. He
knew he would no longer be subjected to the cyclic chain
of gnawing anxiety and expansive relief, which he was so
much used to by then. In spite of being able to break
away, if not by himself but at least out of Nandana's
efforts, and enjoying his new found freedom; he was
shaken by a tide of absolute grief, rejection and humiliation
from a person to whom he had remained devoted and
loyal all this while. He was attracted to a few women (in
two cases the attraction was very intense and mutual)
during his married life but somehow he could not proceed
given his fear of Nandana. However, he had done
everything in his power to make Nandana happy; at least
his conscience was clear. He grew sadder, despite this
overbearing feeling of freedom and detachment from the
rigorous routines of family life; he could not concentrate
while writing and began to feel sexually dysfunctional.

3.

Whatever her faults, Nandana was not a villain or a
wicked person. She was someone who completely
submitted herself to her wild instincts. She was a gambler
with men. However, this alone cannot be held against
her. In a way all of us gamble, quite similarly in mind and
practice. She was untrained in matters related to the civil
world. She was congenitally destined to continually make

errors in judgment. She was continually in need of love, affection and protection, coupled with its explicit demonstration. From an intellectual standpoint she understood the significance of loyalty and the treachery of betrayal, but could not differentiate between both while making a decision for her own life. She did not wish anybody harm. She only wished the best for herself. She shunned the rigours of enterprise and was averse to hard work. She only saw love in somebody else's efforts to make her happy and withstand her erratic personality. When she loved somebody she loved him with so much care that when she was out of love she did not care to rekindle its vigour on her own. She believed love was given by nature and taken away by nature without our knowing.

In her years with Rahul, she had gradually replaced his image and shadow with a father figure instead of a lover and husband who like her, needed attention, love and care. She expected Rahul to be forgiving, as could be expected of a parent under any circumstance instead of the angular emotions of a husband. She wanted to prove that a natural way of living was possible. She wanted to prove that an unproductive person in every sense was the most productive person in seeking one's own happiness and solace. But in her heart of hearts she craved for recognition and acceptance in the conventional sense. This was hardly forthcoming from the motley of people she socialised with who judged people essentially from the outside without knowing the fires burning inside human souls. While judging others they distanced themselves from their own personal fires. Many people were jealous of her ability to pursue pleasure in such a naked manner and to obtain the same at every quarter. Many wanted her to decay and suffer. She was blessed with a strong body and anti-ageing chemicals embedded in her genes. She grew stronger with age. That is why people feared her as if she was nature's most forgiven devil and as such, gods were on her side.

4.

Rahul was an instinctive storyteller. He kept on creating stories of all sorts in his mind. Some were original while the others were his version of already existing stories. He would narrate these stories at length to his colleagues, acquaintances, and friends, on various occasions and social get-togethers. He was widely appreciated for his story telling. In a way, such sessions, helped him to nurture and nourish his ego.

One day Arati, a colleague, friend and an ardent fan of Rahul told him decisively, "Enough of your story telling, Rahul; I won't hear your stories any more. I want you to write them. Don't dissipate your energies by talking and talking."

The conversation kick-started a chain of thoughts. He decided to start writing at least to review the feasibility of the whole process. He started initially with reluctance, stumbling at every word, description, twist and dialogue. Later he gained velocity and a healthy momentum. The speed at which he wrote was reasonably proportional to the speed at which he thought. In one and a half year's time he had finished sixteen stories. Each story ran to an average of twenty pages, which meant he had written over three hundred pages in the intervening period. He took few breaks in between each story since the plots were already conceived in his mind. He also feared that if he stopped he would halt forever.

Having written these sixteen stories he felt he was exhausted with his ideas and would have nothing to write in future. It was also at this time that the Ambarish-Nandana saga had started. For some time he dwelt on each of the stories. He was not able to concentrate diligently while reading them again and again with an objective to prune and edit the text to make them lighter, sharper and less imposing. With every aborted attempt he felt restless and suffered tantalising agony. He didn't know what to do. He even considered making fresh drafts of whatever he had written to date.

He was at a loss as to his next line of action with reference to whatever he had written. He was seriously anxious and somewhat depressed at not being a good enough judge of his own writing. It was then that he started searching for the names of publishing houses and literary agents based in India on the Internet. Having analysed the details, he short-listed three literary agents among many, who according to the declarations made on their respective websites were quite famous and represented established authors. Although, a detailed submission procedure for review of works by new authors was included on these websites; however, he grew a little circumspect about the whole thing. Burying the negative thoughts fermenting in his mind and in his bid to be seen in action he e-mailed six sample stories, to each of these agents with an adequate synopsis and author resume, as per the procedure. This he did without any requisite amount of editing of the stories, barring grammatical and basic consistency checks.

In the following two months he dreamt of various kinds of favourable responses from each of them. He received all the three coincidentally in a gap of two days each in the first week of the third month. All three of them had turned down his request for representation stating that the stories in spite of being original required serious editing. This was a body blow quite different from the response he was used to receiving as a verbose narrator of stories to a live audience. At first, he felt angry at having wasted an enormous amount of time and energy. Later he felt sad and submitted to sustained spells of self-pity. He believed his failure in keeping his wife on his side and wooing publishers with his writings were significant symbols through which nature was communicating a deeper and more meaningful message, something about the times to come. His pitiful thoughts under the circumstances were about what sinful actions he had been party to and how he could have inherited such undiluted humiliation. Did the future hold any happiness for him? Would he be granted a lease of happiness in future? Deep inside his soul he believed he would be. Relaxed by his recent thoughts he waited for something regenerative to happen.

Meanwhile, he read his stories repeatedly, disassociating him from them and found them to be raw and forceful; yet they required definite polishing. He knew the labour involved could be intense and backbreaking compared to writing the first draft itself. He decided to erase the stories forever from his computer and burn the one hard copy that he had retained with him. He did not resort to such destructive strategy finally. Instead, he self-published two hundred copies of his book containing all the sixteen un-edited stories and distributed them to friends, family and colleagues, requesting them to read the stories and let him know of what they thought of them. He did not receive any response over the next six months.

5.

Vidya was uncomplicated yet shrewd in her business approach. Her basic priority was to keep the cost of operations low so that she could maximise her returns on the investment. She worked on stories written by new writers. It also led to fewer complexities in copyright related issues. She worked with a team of new cast, new directors who were passionate about their work and trained technicians.

This had a favourable impact on the cost of making a film. In her approach to finalise a story for a film and her own style of acting she was a realist. She liked stories which were grounded and dealt with the specifics of human relationships, bound within the recognisable realities of our space and time. She avoided highly verbose stuff, surrealism and metaphor laden stories.

Vidya wanted to show her father that filmmaking was not all about chasing stars and presenting their images however incoherently within a badly crafted script. Her father had made good films once upon a time, some of which were critically acclaimed and a few of them immensely successful from a commercial standpoint. A time came when he was infected with the idea of making it big and thought only high-profile stars could help him do so. He did away with all the learning that experience had taught him and almost brought himself and his company to ruin; he did not possess the moral courage to accept his mistakes. Privately struck down by his super inflated ego, he differed vehemently with all the strategies Vidya adopted to run the company. He even yelled at her once, cautioning her that women knew nothing of filmmaking. She had not lost her demeanour in such meaningless family squabbles fully knowing the potency of demons flying within her father's soul. As success trickled in slowly he tempered down and became quieter although he did not appreciate Vidya's efforts or even acknowledge them. Irrespective of the fact that Vidya hated the film industry she became a star herself, both as an actor as well as the invisible backbone of a once-failing production company. Insiders, mostly men, were fiercely jealous of her silent leadership qualities in galvanising a young, committed and talented team of creative professionals. She was feared by some. Nasty rumours flew in all directions about her but she made it a point not to talk to the press except at the press junkets that were essential for her films. She wanted to work with other production houses but no one gave her work. After some time she decided to follow her own path and leave the rest to fate.

An acquaintance in Kolkata had sent Vidya a book of short stories written in English by someone called Rahul Gupta. The acquaintance believed that some of the stories would make good films. Vidya was looking for new material. Her third film had not done too well although the cost had been covered and profit made in the international market.

Vidya finished reading Rahul's book last week. She felt that four stories could be turned into dramatic films. The book disturbed her because it was gloomy and the characters were constantly losing out on life and betraying each other. It was not a smooth read. At places it was too verbose and descriptive to hold the reader's attention. Sometimes the characters engaged in long spells of conversation which were clearly meant to illustrate the writer's point of view and did not contribute to the overall narrative. From an artistic standpoint she felt that these stories required re-writing at places. Yet, there was something in the stories that touched Vidya. All the stories were connected by a common thread consisting of situations, events and characters. In fact there was one story that made her recall a painful event during her stint at the university. But after reading the book she looked at it differently, with pain and with understanding.

In college, Vidya was madly in love with Samaresh. She adored his ruffled hair, moist green eyes, his wiry frame, and the way he smoked and talked about changing the world. They had avoided touching each other as they sat side by side watching Ritwik Ghatak's *Komal Gandhar* in the university auditorium. They came out of the hall and got drenched in the first showers of the season. They walked down a boulevard, holding hands silently, mesmerised by the overwhelming impact of the film. Suddenly, after walking like this for a long while, they declared their unconditional and undying love for each other. Vidya felt that time had frozen, and that she was transported to a world of immortality immersed in harmony and peace. After falling in love with Samaresh, Vidya remained in a constant state of excitement and simmering tension; her health improved and she became a better student and a voracious reader.

Then came the night when she lost her virginity on the terrace of the university administrative building. Vidya and Samaresh had crossed that irreversible limit under the clouds and sparkling stars. She was split between intense pleasure and a monstrous fear of getting caught. She was lost between hazy wakefulness and descending sleep, when she heard disagreeable voices around her. She saw faces, with piercing eyes, encircling her in a human chain preventing her from any possible movement. Samaresh was gone, as if he had vanished into thin air. He had deserted her; Vidya realised. He returned to the university a month later but he didn't approach her, much to her relief. She shuddered with nervous tension every time she thought of coming face to face with Samaresh, again.

Vidya read the sixteen stories again. On a cloudy Sunday morning she picked up the telephone and phoned the acquaintance in Kolkata. "Mookerjeebabu, do you know this Rahul Gupta personally?" she asked.

The reply was, "No. Why?"

"I want to meet him once. I liked a couple of his stories. But I can't decide until I've met him and spoken to him."

The voice at the other end said, "Don't worry madam. I'll get this organised. Do you want this meeting to take place in Mumbai or in Kolkata?"

Vidya replied, "I'm coming to Kolkata next Saturday for a show. I'll leave on Sunday evening or late at night. I can meet him on Sunday morning. Will that be possible? I'll be staying at Kukku's place."

The voice said firmly, "It'll be done madam."

When Vidya kept the phone down she felt a strange sensation creeping up inside.

6.

It was difficult for Rahul to sleep or think reasonably after receiving the invitation to meet Vidya and discuss his stories with her. He wondered if it was a mistake.

He prepared himself for the meeting over the next six days. He tried to anticipate the questions she would ask. Should he ask any questions, himself? He had many questions, but he decided to refrain from asking them. He decided to pose as a man who was far away from the earthly frivolities of life. He would not admit to having seen her films or heard her name. Would that be believable? After much thought, he decided to follow a track that would sound authentic and not shallow or boastful. He wanted to look smart. He looked at himself in the mirror after a long time. A few lines had appeared on his face. His hair was thinning and greying in streaks.

He was getting old. He laughed at himself. What was happening to him? How could he ever hope to attract Vidya?

He told himself that the meeting required no such preparation and he would react truthfully and instinctively as was required at the time. By Sunday morning he had regained his self-confidence. He felt calm. Vidya greeted Rahul in the massive drawing room of her friend's ancestral house. The house stood beside a lake, surrounded by trees. The room where they sat was tastefully decorated and contained antique wooden furniture. The first glimpse of Vidya's face, made him feel weak in the knees. Vidya looked more beautiful in person than she looked on screen. There was a soft glow and a cloud of serenity floating about her face. Her eyes looked deeply compassionate. She showed Rahul to his seat warmly making an intimate gesture of affection. She herself did not sit. She made sure that Rahul was seated comfortably and brought a glass of tender coconut water for him. Rahul was embarrassed.

After some small talk Rahul started feeling comfortable.

Vidya asked, "Didn't you think the stories required further pruning before you published them?"

Rahul said, "Yes. But I was unable to concentrate at that time. My life was in turmoil. I was worried that I might end up burning what I had written if I didn't do anything about them immediately. I was impatient and lazy – both cardinal sins I have to agree."

"You could have hired the services of a professional editor."

"Yes, I could. But at that point in time I was going through a phase of emotional turmoil. I feared I'd lose these stories if I didn't do something with them. In retrospect, I concede I made a mistake."

"Why do you say that?"

"The book is dead. But it satisfies my ego to have a book with my name on it, however insignificant it might be."

"That, I think, is a sentimental way of looking at things.

I've just told you that the book has made a major impression on me. I want to finalise an agreement with you to make two of your stories into films. In fact, I hope we can come to an agreement on this."

"That's so kind of you."

Vidya reacted angrily, "I'm not here to do kind things Mr. Gupta. I'm a film producer and an actor. I know precisely what I need. I've found that in your work. My point is, you have to work harder to convert your stories into world-class literature, which I think is possible, but only if you sit down to chisel and polish your writing. You know that this is the most difficult part of the journey so, I fear, you avoid it and worse still, you try to circumvent it."

There was silence in the room for some time.

Vidya resumed the conversation in an apologetic tone, "Don't misunderstand me. I liked your stories immensely. I also know where they fail. That problem can be addressed. In fact I liked your stories so much that I want them to be widely read and appreciated."

While Rahul was secretly overjoyed he behaved as if he didn't care much.

"I appreciate your point of view. I'll take another look at the stories shortly. I agree they require pruning," he said.

"I hope you'll agree to give me the film rights for two stories."

Rahul was a bit dazed by these developments. "Will you give me some time to think about it and get back to you?" This was not what Rahul had meant to say. He didn't know why he said such a thing.

For a moment there was a shadow of disappointment on Vidya's face. She regained her charm immediately and said, "Okay. Once I get your approval we can work out the details."

"What is it that you liked in my stories?" Rahul asked hesitantly."Well, there are a few nice features. But what I appreciate the most is your clear understanding of loss and betrayal in human relationships."

Rahul suddenly got up, making a move to leave.

"Whom do I talk to after I've decided about the matter? I think I can get back in seven day's time."

Vidya got up, shook hands with Rahul and saw him to the door. "You can talk to me directly. I'll give you my number. Please give me your number too. If I don't hear from you in that time, I'll call you."

Rahul's chest suddenly felt tight. He felt as if he would burst. He felt on top of the world.

7.

Vidya could sense Rahul's veiled attempts to impress her despite his show of nonchalance. She was used to such attempts because she operated in an industry dominated by men. She was, after all, a beautiful, intelligent and enterprising woman. What she disliked was guile. But, with Rahul she sensed a touch of childlike candour. Was Rahul deeply attracted to her? Could he have been in love with her? People fell in love with a beautiful screen persona but that had very little relevance to the actual person. A character in a movie, however charming or disagreeable, could never affect anyone's emotions for a long time because there was no interaction between the image and the audience after the movie ended. So how could Rahul have been in love with her even before they met?

Rahul was a writer deeply involved in his world of characters and events. Writers did not fall in love so easily with actors, she believed; because writers were egocentric and vain. Convinced that they were intellectually superior they considered screen actors to be frivolous, insincere and incapable of understanding the deeper meanings of life. She thought about her own life. Well, she was not merely a screen actor. She was also the backbone of a production company that tried to make films that were different. This, she knew, intimidated a lot of men who looked on her with awe. Her cool, calculated businesslike approach led them to believe that she was a manipulative woman. In spite of achieving success in such a short span of time she was unable to establish her supremacy in this field. It was not as though she had constructed barriers all around her and was not attracted to men. It was just that she didn't have faith in them and found herself unable to trust most men. This was a major impediment in her forming a meaningful relationship with a man to whom she felt attracted. Rahul had left a strong impression on her. Vidya thought about his affectionate gaze and the clean, soft radiance of his skin. Rahul's personality reflected his self-doubt and did not look cultivated for the occasion. She appreciated this trait as she was tired of meeting over-confident, hyperactive men.

Rahul did not call at the end of seven days. Perhaps he had sensed that she would call him anyway. Finally she called him on the ninth day after they had met.

Rahul answered the phone after about thirty seconds. Vidya's heart thumped in her chest but she was not aware that Rahul, too, was leaping with joy.

"This is Vidya Kishori calling. Can I speak to Rahul Gupta?"

"Rahul speaking. Wow! How is life?"

"You were to get back within seven days, remember? Today is the ninth day. Does that mean a clear-cut no to my proposal?"

"No, of course not. It's a yes from my side."

"Why didn't you call me then? Did you want to check whether I was serious?"

"I don't think I can afford to do that with you. Actually I had, misplaced your number."

"Liar!"

"What?"

"Nothing. I only meant to say that you are lying."

"About what?"

"About misplacing my number." Vidya's chest was heaving with tension. She didn't know how she dared to speak to him in such a teasing manner. How would he react? There was a discomforting silence at the other end.

Rahul was quiet for a while. "Yes, I lied to you. Actually, I was not too sure whether you meant what you said."

"Are you convinced now?"

"Yes."

"Thank you. Will you agree to prepare the first draft of the screenplay for both the stories? I will be very happy if you do that."

"I know nothing about screenplays, nothing at all. I don't want to get involved in something that I don't know well."

"There is a team that works on such things in our company. There are people who'll help you on technical matters. All stories rest on the fountainhead of the writers' vision. You'll be the best person to write the screenplays. You'll be paid separately for this work apart from what you'll get for the film rights."

"This has nothing to do with payments and contracts. I just don't want to do it. That's all. I've agreed to give you two of my stories. Do what you want with them. I don't care."

"Well, as you wish. My office will send you a draft copy of the agreement shortly. "

Completely unaware of each other's feelings, they were on the verge of breaking down, in spite of being separated by thousands of miles. Both of them controlled themselves. There was a similar churning deep inside their chests. They hung up without saying any more.

8.

Rahul did not sleep well during the next twenty-four hours. He felt that he had hurt Vidya without any provocation when she was being friendly and reasonable. He had forgotten that Vidya was the only person who had reacted to his stories and that too, with such a fantastic proposal that could make him famous in a short time. And here he was, responding to her proposal in such a boorish manner. He knew he had to talk to her and set things right. He called her that night.

"Vidya, this is Rahul. Can I talk to you now?"

"Yes. What do you want to tell me, now? You don't

want to give me the film rights to your stories? All right. I don't care. I won't send you the draft agreement in that case."

"Vidya, I'm sorry. I understand I've been rude to you, behaved in a most ungentlemanly manner. In fact, I phoned you to apologise and also to suggest something else."

Vidya sounded startled, "What?"

"I'll prepare the initial scripts for both the stories and submit them to your team for approval. They can prepare the shooting script based on that."

"Thank you!" Vidya exclaimed in a voice tinged with relief. "I really wanted you to work on the stories. It makes me more confident to take them up, now."

"I want to explain something."

"Go ahead."

"I had a reason for refusing to work on them, at first. It was essentially personal. These two stories are based on my own life. Working on them again would re-open old wounds and I wanted to avoid that. But now I feel it may be a good way to deal with the loss and move on."

Vidya was at a loss of words. She suddenly wanted to hold Rahul in her arms and caress him like a mother did to an infant. She kept silent for a few moments.

"Vidya are you there?"

Vidya woke up from her reverie, "Of course! I want to tell you something about myself. It may take some time. Do you have the time to talk?"

Then the words came gushing out like a forceful fountain depicting the various facets of her life – sad, happy and melancholy. She forgot that she was talking to Rahul on the phone. She felt that he was sitting by her side listening to her with rapt attention, understanding the crests and troughs of her eventful life. After a long time she stopped. There were tears in her eyes. Rahul, at the end of the line, was desperate to see her and hold her in his strong embrace. He felt aroused.

Rahul and Vidya suddenly realised that their worlds had changed. They were no longer the same people as they were before. Rahul said, "I'm happy you've been so honest. Is this a dream? You've been so benevolent, you've appreciated my work, and now you've become my friend!"

Vidya asked him, "Are you already divorced, Rahul?"

"Not yet. We're separated. We'll submit the divorce papers in court, soon. Nandana has agreed to complete the paperwork without any hassle."

"Can I ask you something?"

"Go ahead."

"Do you still love Nandana? After all, it was such a long relationship."

"I don't love her any more. She lives her life wildly and instinctively. It's complex, but I do not think she is a wicked person. I've always wanted a family, a home with kids that will shelter us from the hostilities of the world. I have nothing to prove. I want to have kids, not to show off my potency, but to enjoy the warmth of plump, sweet-scented babies playing around my feet."

Vidya found a magical echo of her own wishes in Rahul's words. She said, "Will you come to Bombay any time soon?"

"Why do you say Bombay?"

"I love to call my city that way. I love to call your city Calcutta and not by any other name. You didn't answer me."

"I'm coming tomorrow morning."

"It's morning, already."

"Then I'll proceed to the airport right now."

Vidya was indeed so famous that millions of people were envious of what she had achieved in her professional life. However, the simplicity in Rahul's words, made the satisfaction of having crossed professional milestones seem trivial in comparison to the happiness of love. Can love and desire for a person be eternal and undying? Can it withstand the ravages of time? Does it necessarily have to culminate in the domestic confines of rearing a family? A family is about shelter as Rahul said. It is also about chaining individual pursuits as Rahul had written in so many of his stories. These thoughts travelled through Vidya's mind like lightning. She brushed them aside. She knew what she wanted now. She wanted to see Rahul in front of her so that she could touch his eyes and he could touch hers.

"Should I come to your office or to your home when I've reached Bombay?"Rahul asked.

"Home, of course," she replied. "I'll take the day off, tomorrow. I want to introduce you to my family."

"We hardly know each other. Do you really trust me?"

"Can you trust me fully?"

"You are an amazingly attractive woman, Vidya. Half the nation fantasises about you. Young hunks hover around you like flies. I'm an ageing brat. I don't know how I'll fit into your scheme of things."

"You know, I was scared of falling in love with you so suddenly, with such intensity. You are not the type I'm expected to fall in love with. Read the newspapers to know about that in greater detail. But love comes all of a sudden, like a thunderstorm. It comes accidentally, in the most incongruous of circumstances."

"You might soon regret it."

"I might, who knows! You might regret it as well. You can get bored too soon. Your mental image of me could be an illusory concoction of my screen characters and what is written about me."

"No point in speculating about all that. I want to see you now."

"I want to eat you up now, my darling! So hang up and run."

"Hang up and wait."

9.

Events moved swiftly in Rahul and Vidya's lives after this. Rahul's divorce came through and he quit his job in Kolkata and moved to Mumbai. He finished the two screenplays in a couple of months and one of them was already under production. Vidya, for a change, was not acting in this production as she was pregnant. They planned to get married in a month's time. Vidya's brother was making arrangements for a Hindu wedding ceremony on a grand scale. Vidya had bought a new seaside bungalow and Rahul was busy writing a fantasy novel for children and young adults. Vidya and Rahul planned to invite Ambarish and Nandana as well as Samaresh and his wife Kankana to the reception. The leading lights of the film industry would be ignored. Vidya was getting much criticism and being portrayed as an eccentric woman for deciding to marry an outsider like Rahul.

The moral tussle between an ecological life and a consumptive one had died down in Rahul's soul. He was full of happiness and confident of weathering any storm as long as Vidya was beside him. Vidya would gaze into Rahul's eyes wondering whether this man would support her acting career and the responsibilities she had towards her film production unit. She would be very unhappy if Rahul objected to this, but she, on her part, would not do anything to make Rahul jealous or insecure about her in any way. Maybe this could be the key to her happiness.

(This story was presented to a dear friend on her birthday, 11 May 2008.)

Act of Revenge

1.

Rahul checked into a recently inaugurated super-deluxe hotel in Akashpukur, located at the top of a mountain. One afternoon he sat in a corner of the open-air coffee shop sipping lemon tea and sketching on handmade paper made to rest on a large clipboard.

Rahul visited Akashpukur in the second week of December every year to see the first snow fall. He stayed there for a week or so, cut off from the outside world, doing charcoal sketches and drafting a detailed work-plan for the coming year. He finalised the paintings to be done and chalked out a travel programme based on the exhibitions, shows, talks and lectures, which were part of his routine throughout the year.

He spent much of his time walking absentmindedly through the narrow impoverished lanes of Akashpukur. He had deliberately not stayed in his father's cottage, this year. The cottage was built forty years ago when Akashpukur was only visited by a few reckless trekkers, who loved the wild mountain flowers that grew there. Though, his father was a hard-nosed businessman, he had fallen in love with this mountain with its canopy of clouds. Once, on his way to a mountain resort favoured by the British, he happened to come across this place while traversing through the jungles aimlessly on horseback. The scents and colours and the beauty of the misty mountains left a deep impression on him and he decided to build a cottage on the mountain slope.

Rahul looked up from the sketch that he was making and as his eyes swept across the cobalt-blue sky, he spotted a flock of blackbirds flying across the valley. He felt a sudden surge of happiness. The sunshine glowed like melting gold and softly illuminated the universe with golden streaks. The valley was dotted with bushes of fragrant flowers in various colours. There were houses separated by serrated patches of vegetation, with chimneys blowing out grey smoke in an idyllic manner. The air was biting cold, clean and scented by the fragrance of mountain flowers and snow. The mountains looked sombre with patches of green at their base, and a white covering of snow at the top.

Rahul was suddenly aware that a deep silence hung over the entire region, broken only by the sounds his pen made as it flew over the paper and the tinkle of porcelain as he placed his cup on the saucer carelessly. He missed the overpowering darkness, the hidden memories, the timber roof, the wild bushes of red mountain flowers and the dilapidated easel of his father's cottage as he looked at this modern deluxe hotel. It was built like a massive cathedral with its domes, arches and vaults but it had all the facilities that are taken for granted in a modern, deluxe hotel. If he had stayed in his father's cottage his privacy would have been invaded by the retinue of old servants, and local visitors who admired his paintings. These diversions would have come in the way of the process of introspection that he had embarked on. He needed to be in an impersonal environment to connect to the churnings of his soul. So he had registered in this hotel under a different name to avoid recognition.

Rahul looked at the sketch before him. It was the face of an adolescent girl, with aquiline features and enormous eyes. There was in them a hint of pain, mockery, devilish laughter and above all, a burning sense of defiance. The muscles on her face were taut with expectation and anticipation. She had full lips with sensuous curves as if they had been bitten by an army of blood sucking ants while she was lost in a happy reverie. Her nose was sharp and divided the two sides of her face into perfect halves. The eyebrows and eyelashes were untouched and wild, like alpine forests that guarded her eyes. Her hair was uncut. It was deep black and wavy and a part of it fell across the left side of her face. The stark absence of innocence coupled with the air of shrewdness seemed incongruous in that young, exquisitely beautiful face. Rahul shivered, "But that is what Nina is like."

He felt suffocated by a world where, even after years of discipline and training, an artist couldn't look at his own creations without taking recourse to images and symbols.

Rahul didn't want to give final touches to the sketch. He knew his hands had moved involuntarily and mysteriously brought out the image from his subconscious. He wanted to tear it up but he checked himself. He was unable to concentrate any more. In the evening as darkness settled on the landscape and a sudden rush of clouds brought the possibility of snowfall at night, a few thoughts flashed through his mind. There was a time when he'd wanted to do a series of paintings based on Camus' *Plague*. Images of diseased rats, an overwhelming epidemic taking one life after another and Dr. Rieux's hermetic actions sprang to life in his mind just as they were described in the novel. He took out his diary and jotted down some notes.

Outside, the night looked sinister with the snow falling lightly, and the cold seemed to penetrate deep into his soul. He looked at Nina's sketch again, this time in flickering candlelight, and thought of going out for a walk in the darkness and the snow. As he was about to leave his room, his phone rang and he saw an unfamiliar number blink on the LCD screen. He picked up the phone hesitantly after a few seconds. For some time there was silence. As he was about to disconnect an aggressive male voice asked "Is this Rahul Banerjee?"

"Yes, who is it?"

"I'm Nina's lover, Gabbar. Do you remember me?"

"Yes. But why have you called me at this hour?"

"I wanted to tell you something that might interest you."

There was a prolonged silence. Rahul could hear his heart pounding rapidly. "Tell me," he said impatiently.

"I've set your house on fire. It's burning right now. I am standing in front of it. The fire brigade is trying to douse the fire. What can they do; they reached very late. In fact, the walls and the roof are caving in. I'll kill you someday for touching my girl, you bastard! Just wait for me. Wait for me!"

Rahul felt that someone had knocked the breath out of him. When he came out of the hotel, there was a blizzard blowing furiously. Unable to brace himself against the wind and snow, Rahul tripped and fell to the ground.

2.

Rahul was the seventh and the youngest son of an immensely successful businessman. His grandfather was the head priest of a famous temple visited by wealthy seekers of divine intervention. After a long stint in the temple he was dismissed for swindling an enormous amount of money. Rahul, the black sheep of the family, was thirty years old and a gap of twenty years separated him from his eldest brother. His mother had died within hours of his birth, exhausted after birthing every three or four years. Her life had been an endless tunnel of boredom. She had practically nothing to do in the house. Her conjugal life was restricted to gratifying her husband and bearing his children. Her husband pursued commercial goals or set off for distant mountain stations alone. There were innumerable servants and maids who looked after the house. Smart governesses brought up her sons. She spent her time embroidering dramatic battle scenes from the Mahabharata. These were of no use to anyone so nobody took any notice of these marvellous works of art. Her sudden demise created a void for some time, but arrangements were soon made to get someone to breastfeed the infant. Rahul's paternal grandmother took charge of the situation and he was fed under her watchful eyes, by a tribal woman who had enough milk to spare. However, this woman was not allowed to suckle her own child at that time. Rahul's father paid the woman's husband a large sum of money to ensure this.

His six elder bothers turned out to be fine entrepreneurs educated in missionary schools, the best commerce colleges and business management schools in India. But they were different in temperament from their enterprising father, who could grab any opportunity and create success. They built a large-scale steel mill, a construction company, and a trading house that imported FMCG products. The father, rejuvenated by the reinforcement provided by his six sons, consolidated his empire, often breaking the laws, colluding with dirty politicians, corrupting the officers of his clients and competitors alike. He was a megalomaniac and loved displaying his raw business tricks unabashedly. After his first heart attack at the age of seventy, he called his six sons together and distributed the three companies amongst them. Two brothers were given charge of each company. One brother was made accountable for operations and the other for finance, thereby ensuring self-regulation as well as independence in individual functioning. He then withdrew to his cottage in Akashpukur where he died a year later. Rahul's father had understood very early that he was not cut out to be a businessman. This realisation made him lose interest in his youngest son and he turned the boy over to his grandmother. So Rahul was saved the rigorous training and grooming that his brothers had received. With the passage of time a bond developed between Rahul and his grandmother, and it was this bond that insulated them from the chaos in the house. It was his grandmother who showed him the embroidered tapestries made by his mother, one full-moon night. They left a deep impression on him and inspired him to draw and apply colour to whatever he saw around him.

At the age of seven, Rahul drew his first sketch – the ravaged and terribly wrinkled face of his grandmother.

It was not completely life-like. There was something incongruent about the face he etched – the deep set eyes were like those of an aged falcon, the hair that looked like plastic wires, the interplay of light and shadow that captured the timelessness of the face within the confines of time. The sketch astonished her as it revealed the essence of her soul and convinced her that this grandson would live a life quite different from that lived by her son and other grandsons.

Rahul had little interest in studies, but he loved to paint and to read. He drew pictures that illustrated the stories that he read and showed them proudly to his granny, who was full of praise. On his twelfth birthday his grandmother asked him to go and explore every nook and corner of the city – its markets, the riverfront, the poverty-ridden dwellings along the narrow lanes, as well as the opulent localities. Rahul and Kabir, his granny's servant, who was just a little older than him, visited the churches, mosques and cathedrals, the graveyards and the burning ghats, the office buildings in Esplanade and Chowringhee and the various bridges over the next four years. Rahul started painting with watercolors and gradually moved to oil after a few months of training under a retired professor of the Art College.

His granny held a private exhibition on Rahul's seventeenth birthday where six of his oil paintings were exhibited. One showed the Victoria Memorial against the backdrop of menacing rain clouds while another showed the Chowringhee skyline on a sunny day. An imaginary zoo with humans instead of animals, the Park Circus cemetery at night, a gloomy riverside scene and a lonely rhinoceros gazing at the abandoned five-point crossing in Shyambazar made up the other paintings. The exhibition was attended largely by friends and family. The incongruity yet the inherent simplicity of his paintings left a lasting impression on the viewers. Rahul was flooded with appreciation and his grandmother was tremendously happy. At the end of the exhibition she kissed Rahul, brimming with child-like euphoria, and then collapsed, leaving him to fend for himself.

Rahul's father, who had taken very little interest in his son till then, called him soon after to say that he wanted to open a gallery where he could display his works and sell them, too. Rahul kept silent for a while and then declined the offer. His father then said, "If you need anything in future, please let me know." Rahul did not react.

On his eighteenth birthday, Rahul's father gave him a three-storied house by the river with a studio on the first floor. He accepted it reluctantly, enamoured by the panoramic view of the river and the vast space inside. He moved to this house with Kabir the year he started college. He had no interest in studies except that it kept him close to Ritu, with whom he shared a reasonable degree of intimacy from his school days.

In the early years of adolescence, Rahul was disturbed by the changes in his body. He avoided looking at himself in the mirror, immersed himself in work and masturbated frequently. One night he saw Kabir, lying completely naked on his steel cot and masturbating with his eyes half-closed. He was deeply attracted to his face, his hairless chest, and the muscles in his legs. Rahul entered the room hypnotised, and as Kabir opened his eyes moaning pleasurably they yielded to each other like long-lost lovers.

Rahul was disgusted with himself when he started liking Ritu in school. He feared that he was being disloyal to Kabir so he tried to avoid Ritu for some weeks. Ritu loved Rahul's company. She would often come to Rahul's house to taste the pickles made by his grandmother and then stand by Rahul silently observing him at work. Kabir would go in and out of the room keeping a vigilant eye on them both.

One night, when Rahul and Kabir were in each other's arms, Kabir asked, "Are you attracted to Ritu?"

Rahul couldn't look into Kabir's eyes. "Why do you ask? If you don't like her, I won't talk to her," he said.

"She likes you, Rahul."

Rahul pretended to be indifferent, "Maybe."

"Don't you want to sleep with her?"

Rahul said firmly, "No."

"You're lying, Rahul."

"How do you know?"

"I saw you cycling back from school with her on the front bar. You guys were chatting like lovers and your crotch had bulged embarrassingly; it was visible to anybody. You were trying hard to hide your erection, you swine. It was very funny."

Rahul felt trapped. He said, "I always have erections thinking about you, my darling!"

"No, damn it. That one not for me. It was for Ritu. I don't mind you sleeping with Ritu if you allow me to sleep with her, too."

Rahul asked, "Are you attracted to her?"

"Yes."

Rahul was pleased. "Then listen, I'm attracted to her, too."

"Talk to her. Maybe we could sleep with her, together," Kabir suggested.

"She's a decent girl, Kabir. She's not a whore. She won't agree."

"Will you talk to her tomorrow?"

Rahul painted a picture of a solitary cypress beside a range of snow peaked mountains. There was a leopard standing in the shade of the tree. Ritu, dressed in a silver silk gown, was seated on the leopard's back in a relaxed manner. Kabir, dressed like a gladiator sat on a rope swing that hung from one of the tree's stronger branches. Kabir and Ritu gazed deeply into each other's eyes.

When Rahul showed her the painting she was quite baffled.

"A leopard, Rahul! Is it possible to sit on a leopard's back?" She shuddered.

"I don't know."

"And what's this Muslim servant of yours doing on the swing?"

"Devouring your beauty, my empress," Rahul replied.

"But why am I looking at him?"

"You're looking at his face and his body."

Ritu asked perplexed, "Is he attracted to me, Rahul?"

"Yes."

"Are you trying to shock me?"

"Of course, he is attracted to you! He can die for you, Ritu."

Ritu was disgusted. "Does he bathe everyday? Is he clean? And you? Don't you love me, Rahul?"

"Of course, Kabir is clean. And yes, Ritu, I love you too."

"I hope you don't expect me to choose between you and your servant."

"Kabir is my servant. He's my lover too. You could choose both of us together, if you want."

Ritu exploded, "What do you think I am? A whore or what?"

Rahul said calmly, "I think you're a fine attractive girl. A pair of lovers is desperately in love with you. You have to exercise your choice, whatever that is."

At this point, Ritu slapped Rahul and left the house. After a month, Ritu sneaked into Rahul's room without knocking and saw him naked with Kabir. She started sobbing, shocked by the scene. Rahul and Kabir lifted her carefully and laid her on the divan. Slowly, Ritu warmed up to their strokes and was drowned in an unbounded lake of sensations, losing all control.

With a house and a studio at his disposal Rahul began to work very hard. He became very famous and got noticed by art critics, galleries and publishing houses. What he enjoyed doing was teaching the poetics of art to his beautiful niece Sana, the daughter of his eldest brother. She was the only one in his family who remained connected to him. Rahul was twenty-two when he started teaching seven year-old Sana.

3.

Sana was a quick learner. She loved painting with a ferocity that was similar to that of her uncle and was excellent in control of lines and visualisation of colours. Rahul, meanwhile, had built up a grand library of paintings of the European, Japanese, Chinese, Persian and

Bengali masters. He encouraged Sana to study these paintings done in varied styles so that her mind and soul would expand and explore new insights into life.

"Though so much has been painted and sculpted through the annals of Time it is still possible to find your own place in this universe. Look inside your mind, and bring out the images from the darkness on to paper and canvas. A painting may not be an imitation of life, as we know it. But, it must be anchored in our truest sensations. You have to learn that for yourself. By looking repeatedly at the paintings created by the masters you can instinctively understand the process of bringing out images trapped in the darkness of your mind. But it is equally important to see everything around you in an unrestrained fashion, to bring out the essence of things. This will help you form images. I can only help you hone your craft, train you to use line and colour. But only you can decide what you see and what you would like us to see, my darling," he said.

These words created a huge impact on Sana and she craved for the touch of pen, paper, brushes and colours.

Rahul said, "You are the bridge, Sana, between your mind and the screen on which you draw. So, while it is important to activate the process of images leaping helter-skelter, it is equally important to look at these images from a distance, to reproduce their boundaries on canvas."

Sana asked, "Is it like being burnt even when one is away from the fire?" Rahul took her in his arms and brushed his face against her unkempt hair, crooning in delight and ecstasy, "Yes, yes, my darling. Yes." Rahul loved Sana dearly for her face reminded him of his mother.

Rahul taught Sana for eight long years. He made her draw natural objects, animals, the faces of men and women of various ages and in various moods; he taught her colouring techniques used by various masters and lastly, the synthesis of composition. Sana would learn everything like a hungry animal and practice the lessons after school.

When she turned fourteen, Sana, had well-developed breasts and her thin frame had turned voluptuous. Different images blew through her mind like a hurricane. She made a painting that year: it depicted a Prussian blue lake surrounded by mountains with bare, rocky outcrops. A nude girl rose from the bowels of the lake, not like a fairy or a mermaid, but like a real girl of her own age poised between girlhood and womanhood.

Sana had become friendly with a girl called Nina, in school. Nina was dark and voluptuous and about the same age as her. Though good in studies, she desired to break free from the environment that she was in, and to lead a comfortable upper-class life. She complimented Sana on her beauty, on her paintings and begged to be introduced to her mentor, Rahul.

"Take me to Rahul, Sana. I want to learn painting too. If not painting, at least, I can learn to make cartoons," she said.

"Rahul is very busy, Nina," Sana replied. "He doesn't teach students. He paints and delivers talks and lectures sometimes, but he is a fiercely private person."

Nina seemed almost desperate. "You've got to take me to him, Sana, or I'll break into his house and get caught."

Sana asked curtly, "Why are you so interested in him?"

Nina answered, "I went to an exhibition of his paintings with my parents, last winter. I was simply bowled over by what I saw. Raw emotions seem etched in his paintings. Is he like a fierce lion, Sana?"

"He's my master. He's raw. But he's refined. He's a great painter. I'm not saying this because he's appreciated the world over at such a young age but I've seen him from close. He's deeply committed to his work and visualises things in a unique, unattached way and this is what he displays in his paintings."

"Whatever it is, I'm deeply attracted to this man. In 'Self Portrait' he has drawn the figure of a sea-horse. I am curious to know why."

Sana explained, "He's deeply interested in the bodies of animals and has spent years in observing and visualising them. When he draws trees, jungles and mountains, he injects a soul in them and makes them look sensual."

"But he draws men more beautifully than he does women."

"That's only partly true, Nina. Do you really want to learn painting?"

"Yes, Sana. With all my heart."

Somehow, Sana didn't take Nina seriously. Nina frequented discotheques with rich friends, and attended noisy cocaine parties with them. She also had a rough gangster as a boyfriend. One part of Nina demanded constant attention and appreciation. In order to feel less insecure about herself she mixed with people who were more insecure than her. But it was true that she often displayed flashes of creativity and imagination. Sana didn't want to share her teacher Rahul with Nina but one afternoon she broached the subject with Rahul.

Rahul declared that he didn't want a new student, but he agreed to meet Nina, so Sana was happy. She insisted that Rahul tell Nina that, so that there was no misunderstanding between the two friends. Rahul agreed.

On a breezy Sunday evening Sana and Nina came to Rahul's house. They settled into comfortable easy chairs on the terrace.

Nina said excitedly, "Sana calls you by your first name. Would you mind if I call you Rahul too?"

Rahul glanced at Sana naughtily and smiled.

"Rahul, do you know what a great star you are! How does it feel to reach such dizzying heights at the young age of twenty nine?"

Rahul was amused, "Star! You mean a celebrity?"

Nina exclaimed like an excited kid, "Of course! Yes!"

"I would still prefer to be known as a painter, Nina."

"That's humility; I suppose. You are so cerebral. Still you're a smash hit among the masses."

Sana put in, "His paintings are rarely cerebral, Nina."

"Your paintings are raw, violent and at times, terribly incongruous."

Rahul explained, "That's how I see the world in the darkness of my mind."

"But how do you manage to make such crowded compositions in such detail and so sensuously? They haunt a viewer like the theatre of macabre?"

Sana answered this primly, "That's something to do

with craft Nina. Years of practice, observation and visualisation."

Rahul continued, "Yes. I feel all of us think on similar lines. We don't think, do we? Thoughts invade our minds. It's only the sheaths of pretence that make us all look so different."

Nina asked, "Do you pretend too?"

"I do."

"Like, when?"

"Like right now, I want to simply lift you in the air and throw you into the river, but I'm doing no such thing," Rahul said with an awkward laugh.

"Do you really feel that way?"

Sana's voice was cold, "Don't get so serious, darling, Rahul is just joking."

"Were you joking?"

Rahul said, "Yes."

"Has Sana told you why I wanted to meet you so desperately, Rahul?"

"Yes, because you like my paintings."

"That's true. But there's something else."

Rahul looked at Nina and then at Sana. "Something else?"

"Didn't you tell him, Sana?"

"I did tell him, Nina. But don't you think it would be better if you told him yourself?"

"Yes, I suppose so. Rahul, I don't know how to say this, it's embarrassing but I want to be your apprentice, you know. I want you to teach me."

Rahul answered, "I appreciate your feelings, Nina. Kindly understand two things. I do not have the time or the energy to teach. I don't enjoy teaching. Besides, you can't start apprenticeship at the ripe age of fourteen and a half, my dear."

Nina exploded, "You doubt my talent! You think I'm a scatterbrain! You think I've no trapped images in my soul to show!"

Rahul tried to pacify her, "Try and understand, Nina. I don't think any such thing because I've no reason to do so."

But Nina continued thunderously, "Look at my face, Rahul. Look at my body. Don't you think I need to be given another chance? I would sit at your feet. Follow your instructions like a slave. I feel so close to the person that I am when I see your paintings. I can do anything to get you as my teacher. "

Nina was crying at this point of time and Sana had taken her in her arms and was trying to console her. Rahul leant against the parapet and stared out over the river. He looked back at Nina's kohl-smeared face and eyes and thought she was very beautiful. Nina didn't want to be a painter. She wanted to acquire stardom by associating with Rahul. He abhorred the thought and didn't want himself to be violated. "You've rejected me tonight, Rahul. You may want to think about it for some more time. I don't mind. I'll catch up with you some other time."

4.

Rahul was working in his studio late in the night when his phone rang.

"Am I speaking to Rahul Banerjee?" a voice asked.

"Yes. Who is this, please?"

"Don't you remember my voice, Rahul? I'm Nina."

"It's past one in the morning. What are you doing at this hour of the night? Are you in trouble? Can I be of any help?"

"I was just catching up with friends. They were talking about you. So, I called."

"Great. How are you?"

"Not so well", Nina replied. "Did you think about my proposal, Rahul?"

"Yes. Unfortunately, my stand remains unchanged, Nina."

"All right! Can I ask you something? You do conceal a significant part of your life, don't you?"

"Yes. I suppose that's pretty normal."

Nina's voice turned strange. "Why did you refuse to support the cause of alternate sexuality? I understand that a reputed organisation requested you to support their campaign for a change in our archaic laws relating to freedom of sexual choice."

Rahul was stunned, "What do you mean, Nina?"

"I mean, what you just heard, Rahul."

"That's my private life, Nina. It's none of your business!" Rahul's voice boomed angrily.

"I have learnt quite a few things about you, Rahul. First it was out of curiosity. As I delved deeper, I found many untold secrets floating about, just waiting to be woven together. Do so and one can see the dark side of your life!"

Rahul didn't want fear to seep into his voice. He asked, "What do you know, Nina?"

"That you have a past that you want to erase. That you have a present you want to hide."

"Like?"

Nina said teasingly, "Like, Kabir and Ritu. Like, Sana. Like, a couple in Ballygunj whom you visit every weekend for sex. Sana doesn't know about this couple, nor do they know about her. You've already banished Kabir and Ritu from your life. Darling, the world doesn't know any of this. You know that this is not Paris or Milan, London or New York where such a lifestyle could have added to your aura. Do you want all this shit to come out in the papers; do you want to be caught in innumerable controversies?"

"What do you want from me, Nina?" Rahul asked coming straight to the point.

"I want you to teach me, Rahul. Nothing more. Nothing less."

Rahul sighed, "All right. Meet me in the afternoon tomorrow in my studio. But please don't say anything to Sana."

There was a gurgle of laughter and the phone was disconnected. Rahul washed his hands, and fell into bed.

Nina met him the next day. Rahul asked her to sketch an owl, an old woman's face and a landscape. Nina worked with tremendous concentration and Rahul could not believe it was the same girl who had threatened him with blackmail the previous night. She wore a knee-length green skirt and a sleeveless orange top. She was unkempt, disorderly, and dark. She was manipulative and this put Rahul on his guard. But Nina had a sparkling independent mind.

Rahul had experienced so much adulation, fame and money that he treated the men and women around him with disdain. He liked Sana because she was a devotee, her devotion bordering on paranoia. She had taken Rahul's member in her mouth when she was twelve years old, convinced that this piece of flesh was a brush too and if she caressed it with her moist, red tongue over and over again she would see the whiteness of god burst forth like a fountain. Sana obeyed Rahul with a pounding heart, in awe and submission.

He liked the couple in Ballygunj, Shyamalan and his wife Nayana, because they were devotees too. Rahul was their only hope. They were lost in a world of temples and infertility clinics when Rahul arrived on the scene and vowed to impregnate the woman with his seed if the man agreed to sleep with him occasionally. At first, Shyamalan was aghast, but then he succumbed to Rahul's demands. Rahul delayed the conception till he finally got bored with the couple.

Rahul criticised and found fault with whatever Nina drew but she made the corrections painstakingly and was slowly evolving a style of composition and colouring, which was based on an imitation of Rahul's early paintings. One day, Rahul asked, "Why do you copy my paintings?" Nina shot back, "You copy, too." Nina came to Rahul's studio at odd hours to avoid being caught by Sana and Rahul was faced with the task of hiding the canvasses and drawings she made.

One evening Nina asked Rahul, "Why don't you use me as your model? This will give me ample time to look into your eyes and dive inside those pools of madness, those fiery caves and furnaces of imagination."

Rahul said, "You must know Nina, I don't use models for my paintings."

"You can always start. It'll be a new experience. Painters

are not complete if they don't do nude study, are they?"
Nina asked.

"Who filled such trash in your head? This is another
trick to seduce me. Do you love me, Nina?"

"No. I'm in love with someone else."

"Who's that?"

Nina laughed. "Curious?"

"Somewhat."

"His name is Gabbar. He's a college dropout. He's a
drug peddler but doesn't push it himself except for a few
tablets of Ecstasy on weekends. Well, he sniffs cocaine at
times and drinks quite a lot. He kidnaps guys for fun.
And for money. He nearly killed a group of boys for
roughing up his ex-girlfriend. He makes me scream and
laugh in bed. He's got a great body and carries arms 24x7!
Guys in power use him and are shit-scared of him. What
more?"

"I'm zapped by your taste in guys. Can I get to meet
him once? Well, you can model for me together, if you
like."

"Do you want your head beaten to pulp?" Nina
exclaimed. "If you mention the idea of undressing me in
his presence, he'll blow your head off, Rahul. He's not
going to roll down his underpants for you. Moreover, he
doesn't know that I come here. I can introduce you to
him on some pretext. I'll call him when Sana is here.
Okay?"

"All right."

A few days later, Sana told Rahul, "It seems Nina has
got over her lust for you. She is in love with a gangster.
Can you believe it? She wants to come over to your place
with this guy named Gabbar, show him around the place,
the river front and have a cup of tea here, with your
permission, of course. What should I tell her?"

"You decide."

"I don't think, we should refuse her", Sana said.
"Besides, we'll get to see a real gangster from up close."

"As you wish, Sana. Next Sunday, in the afternoon, if
that's all right with you."

They met on Rahul's sprawling terrace with bottles of

wine, cigarettes, ashtrays and plates of snacks close at hand. They chatted and drank and smoked effortlessly. The breeze from the river in the early winter afternoon made things appear lighter than they were.

"You know Gabbar, Rahul is a famous artist. He's an icon. I showed you his 'Self Portrait' in that book of paintings I bought at the Oxford bookstore. You laughed at it. Rahul, when we were coming here this afternoon, Gabbar asked me if we'd have to dive into the Bay of Bengal to meet you, the sea-horse!"

Gabbar was quick to apologise, "Sir, I hope you'll excuse me for such remarks. Actually I'm not artistically inclined at all. But I respect people like you who do such great things and make our country proud."

"Art doesn't make anybody great. Real life does. In fact, I'm truly awed by your magnetic presence. You seem to represent daring as no artistic symbol can. When I look at the curves of your muscles, your brown eyes, the shape of your hair, beard and moustache and the revolver bulging in your pocket I'm reminded of Renaissance sculptures. You could be the ideal material for an artist, Gabbar. You don't understand art you say, but you're the fountain of art my man," said Rahul.

Gabbar seemed quite perplexed and said, "I don't understand you, sir."

"Don't bother, darling" Nina interjected hastily. "How do you like the river from here?"

"Sir, how much does this property cost today? Must be running into billions, no?"

"My studio is priceless. Without the studio, is this property worth anything? I can't say!"

"I'm told your paintings sell for millions of dollars. Is it true?"

"Yes, they do." Sana declared.

"What I don't understand is, how are paintings priced?"

Sana seemed intent on provoking Gabbar. "How do you estimate the ransom when you kidnap somebody, Gabbar?"

"It's simple. By estimating what the man can pay

quickly without borrowing too much and informing the police. But how is it done in the case of art, which you either like or dislike?"

Rahul said, "I don't know, Gabbar. Is it so important for you to understand this?"

"Yes, just in case I plan to steal some of yours! Besides, my babe is an artist too. If I know the worth of her works, I can put a price on her head."

"I like you, Gabbar. I want to paint you and Nina someday. Will you pose for me?" Rahul asked.

Sana told them, "This will be a great deviation from Rahul's body of work. He has not done portraits or individual body studies before. He must be really impressed with you, Gabbar to make such an offer."

Gabbar was new to all this. "But what's the offer?"

Sana spoke on Rahul's behalf, "I think Rahul wants you both to pose together for a painting. A painting that will be a revelation of your souls, your essence."

"Will you agree to be a model, Gabbar? And you, Nina?"

"I don't know. Ask him," Nina replied.

"Model! I mean, what do we have to sell?"

Rahul explained, "You don't have to sell anything, damn it! I'll make a painting of your bodies against a beautiful background. This will be different from anything I've ever attempted in the past."

"Our bodies! Your painting will sell, of course. But what sort of an arrangement is this? Will you give us a major cut or what?"

Sana said sarcastically, "You should feel obliged, Gabbar that Rahul sees something in you that's worth capturing for posterity."

Gabbar asked, "What?"

"You're an icon of daring, Gabbar."

"And, what about Nina?"

"She's an icon of daring, too. But a different sort."

"What do we need to do for all this?"

Nina told him, "Be naked in his studio as long as he wants us to!"

Gabbar was flabbergast, "You too, Nina, that too in

front of him in my presence! You bloody shameless bitch! You're acting like, it's okay with you! I'll smash your face! And you, mister and you, Sana! Don't ever make such wild proposals again. Let's get out of here, Nina baby."

Sana said in a mocking tone, "You don't understand, Gabbar. You're revolting against the idea of public nudity. But no art is possible without the purity of relationship between the model and the artist. The essence of the human soul is etched in the divine and sublime curves of our bodies, which only an artist can see, and make us see. As Rahul said, both of you will be frozen in the frame of his painting for future generations to admire, and wonder about the eternal chemistry that fuels hearts in a human act of valour."

Gabbar was enraged, "I don't like you, Sana. You're on his side. You're brainwashed to the core. I don't like paintings. I don't like hocus-pocus. I like cinema posters of action films in bold colours. Come on, Nina. Let's move. Fast."

After Gabbar and Nina stormed out of the house, Rahul and Sana sat in silence for a long time. They were immersed in the hazy darkness of the late evening. A wind was blowing from north. They suddenly burst into peals of laughter and fell into each other's arms.

Sana bit Rahul's ears sharply, "Do you want Nina to throw off her clothes and model for you?"

Rahul was surprised, "No, Sana. It was a bloody joke. On this ox of a man named Gabbar."

5.

Nina did not come to Rahul's studio for a month. It was already the end of November and Rahul would leave for Akashpukur soon. Suddenly one evening, Nina turned up in his studio. "Thank god, Sana is not here", Rahul thought. Nina looked withdrawn. She came over to Rahul, put her hands on his shoulder and looked into his eyes with piercing sharpness as if she was trying to read his mind. Rahul's face was motionless and betrayed no emotion.

At last, Nina spoke, still looking into his eyes, "Did you and Sana have a good laugh after we left?"

Rahul didn't reply. She repeated her question furiously. Rahul said, "No."

"Liar," Nina snapped. "You think he's a clown. Do you pity me for being involved with someone like that?"

Rahul drew Nina close. "Do you see that divan, Nina, with the embroidered bedspread? Look at it closely. It's a battle scene from the Mahabharata. See the face of Yudhishtira mouthing a lie for the first time in his life. See the shades of cunning and integrity intertwined on his face. Can you see the look of bewilderment on Dronacharya's face? My mother painted this long back. I've preserved this to use it in a painting when the right image springs to mind. I've got it today. Throw off your clothes and lie on the bedspread with your eyes gazing far away while I draw you, diving into the artesian wells of my memory."

Nina threw off her clothes without any resistance, and took position as she was told. Rahul looked at her intently. He could not disconnect himself from his subject. He was trained to exist in a state of absolute control at an unfathomable distance from the subject and the images playing in his mind while making a painting. He saw this earthy girl prostrate before him desperately trying to conceal her soul under an aggressive sheath. Rahul was suddenly aroused by Nina's greyness, the way he was once aroused years ago by the carnal colours of a peacock's wings. He put the palette and brush aside and moved away from the easel where a new canvas was mounted. He felt delirious with desire to violate this pale nymph waiting to be immortalised in his painting.

Rahul stared at Nina's face, her armpits with tufts of freshly grown hair, the black erect nipples on her small breasts, her navel, the patch of curly hair between her legs and the fragile swell of muscles on her body from close. He was taken aback by the scent of her flesh, uncorrupted by soap, or perfume. This was a scent, which was damp and sour and reminded him of wood, buried in soil. This was a scent that aroused him. This was the scent, which he had smelt on Sana and Kabir and lost his way. Rahul said, "Nina I want to make love to you. It's not possible for me to draw you without getting rid of my fever."

Nina replied, "But I'm your model, now."

"You're my apprentice first," Rahul said, defending him.

"What about the purity of relationship between the model and the artist, the apprentice and the master?" Nina asked.

"You are a woman and I am a man, Nina."

"You're a man, Rahul. I'm still a girl."

"A girl who screams and takes delight in bed with a gangster", Rahul said trying to mock her, "But your body looks absolutely unsoiled and untouched. You lied to me."

Nina explained, "The day I first sat on Gabbar's lap kissing him passionately, I could feel him swell with lust. I was scared. Suddenly, he clasped me tight, brushed his face against my cheeks and whispered 'Not now, Nina. We have enough time for this when you've grown into a complete woman, in mind and body.' I felt horribly rejected. I felt sorry for him because he had to curb his desire for my sake. That made me do something terrible. He cried. I don't know, why. I wanted him to be decent with me. But I wanted him to be wild too, the way he was with others. "

"Would you like me to touch you with lust?" Rahul asked almost breathless with desire.

Nina gasped, "Will you rape me, Rahul?"

There were footsteps on the stairway. Rahul dismissed it as a figment of his imagination.

Rahul's voice was hoarse, "Will I have to rape you, Nina?"

Nina closed her eyes. There was a shadow of fear on her face. But it was soon replaced by a deluge of waves of submission.

Nina whispered, "Do whatever makes you happy."

Rahul plundered her virginity like a rabid horse, unleashing a storm in her, but she bore the pain in silence. Suddenly Rahul heard Nina say, "How will Sana feel if she sees this wild scene? Will she be inspired to paint 'A black mermaid raped by a horse'?"

There were sounds of footsteps on the stairway and Rahul felt like a trapped animal, a convict barricaded on all sides by militiamen.

6.

As Sana rushed out of the house there was a typhoon raging in her soul. She had surrendered to Rahul's excesses for years because she would do anything to please her master. She was indebted to him for the craft and composition she had learnt at his feet. But she was not willing to compromise her rights over him, gathered through years of toil. She worshiped him like a true devotee. She had disbelieved Nina when she told her what Rahul had done to Ritu and Kabir, how he had banished them from his life to reconstruct a past so that he could control his future; how he used people's weaknesses to fulfil his sexual needs. Sana had slapped Nina when she said that Rahul was soulless, merciless and in essence, a devil re-incarnate, and that he had made Sana a collaborator in all his deeds without her knowledge. She wished she were dead when Nina further told her that Rahul had already accepted her as his apprentice and they were meeting for months in his studio, behind her back.

Nina had challenged Sana to come to Rahul's studio on a specific day, if she wanted proof. Sana wished she hadn't gone to see the sight that seemed to annihilate her soul. Her whole persona rocked with seething anger rising from the ashes of humiliation and a desire for revenge. She knew where to go to seek revenge. She decided to meet Gabbar and tell him what Rahul had done to his girl.

7.

As Rahul got submerged under tonnes of snow on an abandoned street of Akashpukur he saw images of his father, his grandmother, and a black woman with wiry strands of hair breastfeeding an infant. Pictures of Kabir, Ritu, Sana, Nina, Gabbar, Shyamalan and his wife Nayana rushed through his mind. He saw his house, his studio and unfinished canvasses on fire. He had painted pictures day after day in search of a force that was pure like coral, unfettered and capable of driving his soul. Slowly, a blanket of darkness and silence enveloped him and drew him into a bottomless abyss.

Midnight Conversation

1.

Rahul had been to this spot by the river on two earlier occasions. These were in connection with office get-togethers at Arijit's house. Arijit was a colleague in office, who was quite close to him. His house was nearby, just a short walk from the riverbank. Rahul did not drive down today, nor did he go to Arijit's house. He took a taxi to the B.T. Road junction and then a rickshaw brought him to the riverbank.

It was a neatly paved ghat that Rahul visited on the riverbank. People washed and cleaned and bathed there in the mornings and late afternoons. The ghat had a red cement platform along its perimeter where people could sit. It had probably been constructed a century ago, but it still displayed rare craftsmanship despite the numerous cracks that had developed. There were two ancient banyan trees just beyond and people who sat on the ghat to enjoy the beauty of the landscape were thankful for their cool and comforting shade. There was an adjoining ghat, with proper gangways and adequate anchoring facilities that was used by people who wanted to cross the river. A few fishermen preferred to use this ghat, so two boats were always tied to a tree on the bank. There were a few mansions – old and dilapidated – in the background; but the bustling, commercial area was a short distance away. The ghat was rarely visited by lovers or drug addicts because it was infested with snakes.

Rahul loved this ghat for some strange reason. On the last two occasions that he had come here, he had experienced an unknown calm welling up inside his soul. He had sat in the shade of the banyan trees enjoying the wide expanse of the turbulent river in high tide and viewing large passenger boats with open sails driven by the wind. He had seen a few industries on the other side with their chimneys spewing black smoke into the air and their pipes leaking dark effluents into the river. He'd been thrilled to see a large grove of dark bamboo trees. As darkness fell in the evening he'd felt a chill in his bones as he thought of the stories that the dilapidated mansions around the ghat could tell.

But, on this visit, Rahul merely sat there for hours. It was a cloudy day with a strong breeze and an occasional drizzle that soaked him completely but he continued sitting there quite oblivious of his physical state. There was no one on the ghat, or on the road beyond. The sky looked menacingly dark. He feared the river might overflow with the rainwater and the incoming tide washing away its banks, the ghat and the surrounding mansions with brute force.

Rahul was thinking about his life – his wife and daughter. He was devastated by Reena's declaration that morning and didn't know how to share it with their daughter Reema, who was barely seven years old. Reena had asked him to work out the modalities for a quick divorce. She wanted to move out at once and there was no room for further deliberations or negotiations. Sanjay's face flashed across his mind. Rahul couldn't believe that their affair had been going on for such a long time. He felt so violated and torn apart that he longed for a tall wave to rise from the river and crush him with all its might.

It was then that he suddenly passed out as thirst, hunger and nausea finally took their toll. He had not consumed a drop of water or eaten a morsel of food since Reena had announced her decision that morning. He refused water because he wanted to hurt himself physically, to convert his mental agony into physical hardship, to multiply his suffering to a level beyond the limit of endurance. This was the only way he could counter the humiliation. He had gulped down three pegs of neat whiskey within a span of half an hour before leaving the house.

Lightning flashed in the sky and on the verge of passing out he remembered the name of this place – It was Nayantara Ghat.

2.

Nayantara was sitting on the second floor verandah of her ancestral house knitting a yellow pullover on a modern knitting machine, enjoying the scenic beauty of the river on a cloudy, rainy day. She loved the monsoons more than any other season. The river then looked like a strong man, full of vigour, in the process of making ferocious love. She imagined the seductiveness of the river, with its dangerous playful movements, to be directed solely at her. Nobody watched the river with so much longing and desire as Nayantara did. She loved the dark grove of bamboo trees on the opposite bank, which, on such a day appeared farther away than it really was, as if it had retreated by a few miles. She thought of wild animals running about inside the grove, at such times.

She remembered how she and her brothers were told that they would be banished to this bamboo grove (where the darkest, wildest, and the most ferocious animals lived on the flesh and blood of errant children) if they disobeyed their elders. The images of terror that the bamboo grove aroused in her mind in childhood and adolescence didn't leave her completely. On such overcast days tinged with grey, these images of wild, enticing dangers escaped from the darkest recesses of her mind and played themselves out before her eyes.

She wondered how long she would be able to stay in this mansion. She was in touch with a few people interested in buying this seventy-five year old decaying structure. She also wondered where she would go, and whether she would be able to survive without this view of the river. At times, when she thought of her uncertain future, she felt a slight tremor in her heart. She had always treated the river as her sole companion since her parents died nearly two decades ago. Once her brothers moved to Delhi and Hyderabad no one was interested in this mansion any longer.

Nayantara was the sole resident of this dilapidated mansion that had crumbled for lack of maintenance. This majestic mansion, with fifteen rooms on three floors, once housed twenty-four members of her family, including the servants. A hundred and fifty people could dine together in its garden and terrace. But that was long ago. The garden was now wild with bushes and creepers where evil spirits took shelter. Nayantara's grandfather had left her some jewellery and a sum of money that she invested in a post office monthly-income plan. Seven years ago, she dropped out of college and bought a knitting machine. She soon became proficient in knitting pullovers and woollen garments. These were sold to a wholesaler in Chowringhee. Her pullovers, with their stylised abstract designs, and excellent quality sold quite well. The money from these transactions, coupled with the monthly interest from the post office, ensured that she could live comfortably enough. However, she was in a position to maintain only two of the fifteen rooms, a bathroom, a kitchen, and the verandah on the second floor overlooking the river. All the other rooms in the mansion were closed, collapsing under the burden of neglect and decay.

Nayantara had two close friends – Kartik*da*, a sixty-six year old retired post office clerk and Shyamal, a young school drop-out who sold onions in the local market. Kartik*da* had been visiting their household since grandfather's time. He had become a part of the family and would often sit on the verandah discussing local issues with her grandfather. Nayantara grew up before his eyes so he had a special affection for her. Even after grandfather and other older members of the family passed away Kartik*da* remained loyal to the household and helped Nayantara in whatever way he could. Shyamal was the son of Kunjabihari, the vegetable vendor, who came to the mansion to sell vegetables. Grandmother would sit on the verandah while Shyamal's father sat on the steps and the two would talk about everything under the sun apart from negotiating the prices of vegetables that grandmother had chosen for the day. Shyamal would often accompany his father on these trips. Nayantara's mother had continued this tradition and when Kunjabihari died; his son also became an integral part of 'Bishnupriya House'.

The three gossiped for hours and discussed weather forecasts, commodity prices, local crimes and serious moral issues at times. Strangely enough, Nayantara and Kartik*da* were liberal in their views while Shyamal was a staunch conservative. Kartik*da* and Shyamal read the newspaper with interest but Nayantara had not touched a newspaper in the last twelve years and since there was no television in her house, these two were her only windows to the outside world.

On Mondays, Kartik*da* and Shyamal had dinner at Nayantara's house. Kartikda would buy seasonal fish and Shyamal would buy vegetables, mustard oil and basmati rice for the feast. The men would arrive at Nayantara's house in the afternoon, play cards and enjoy some flaked rice with pickle oil and fried vegetable in the evening.

One Monday afternoon after a game of cards, Nayantara said, "Kartik*da*, why are you looking so sad today?"

"My son has got a job in Mumbai. The salary is three times of what he gets here, so I can't refuse permission, but I don't want him to go. He's a simpleton. People will manipulate him and he'll be in trouble. What will become of him I worry my dear Nayana! And then this money will not be of use to anyone."

Shyamal said encouragingly, "Don't worry Kartik*da*, nothing will happen to him. Mumbai is a city where people go to earn a living. Migrants understand the isolation and problems faced by other migrants. There's a magical bond. They say that's the charm of Mumbai. But please ask him to stay away from the touts of the film industry."

"I'll tell him that. But I don't know what he'll eat, how he'll run his house and wash his clothes there! He knows nothing of the practical aspects of life."

"The standard remedy in such cases is to get him married." Nayantara suggested.

Kartik*da* seemed remorseful. "We thought about that Nayana, but he is not willing to get married now."

Nayantara tried to cheer him up, "All right then, let him be. It's good that he wants to learn things in his own way, on his terms. This will improve his personality."

Shyamal rationalised, "You know, one tends to become irrational about everything concerning one's own children. It happens."

"How can you say that?" Nayantara asked.

"I'm telling you what I've seen."

Kartik*da* spoke up, "What have you seen?"

"Do you know that Bimal*babu*'s son was accused of eloping with Radharani-*kakima*'s daughter? She went to the local police station and forced the OC to meet Bimal*babu* in his house and threaten him with dire consequences if his son didn't return with the girl in twenty-four hours. The fact is that Bimal*babu* has no control over his son. But when he found that the boy's character was being maligned in public, he called that girl a whore. Bimal*babu* and Radharani kakima had a big fight that day. Two days later the couple returned. They'd got married at the Kalighat temple and had spent two nights at a hotel in Uttarpara. They sought the blessings of both the families." Shyamal said.

Kartik*da* suddenly changed the subject. "Nayana, would you mind if I wrote to your brothers requesting them not to sell your ancestral home?"

"I don't want you to do that. This house will have to be sold."

Shyamal was a bit concerned. "Have you decided where you will go after that?" he asked.

Kartik*da* too voiced the same sentiment, "You've never lived anywhere else, except for those two years when you were married. I worry about you," he said.

Nayantara said firmly, "Don't worry. If I need help

I'll ask for it. Let's not spoil this evening with all these worries."

A streak of lightning tore across, illuminating the sky. Nayantara's eyes fell on a human being sprawled on the ground at the ghat. He seemed unconscious, abandoned. She lost sight of the man once the flash of lightning was gone. "Kartik*da*, Shyamal there's a man, lying on the ghat. He may be dead or bitten by a snake. I feel he needs help. Take these umbrellas. Go and help him," she cried.

Kartik*da* and Shyamal lifted Rahul on to a makeshift stretcher with the help of two street beggars. They laid him down on the floor of the living room in Nayantara's house. As she sprinkled water on his face he opened his eyes slowly and looked around, deeply embarrassed.

Nayantara smiled warmly, "You are in my house. Please feel comfortable here."

3.

They took care of Rahul and tried to ensure that he regained his strength and composure as soon as possible. At first, when he drank a glass of water there was a sudden churning in his gut and he threw up; this repeated a number of times. He felt pain when he urinated, but the pain subsided after a while. Nayantara gave him a pair of clean pyjamas, a vest and an embroidered cotton shawl that had belonged to her father. He ate a light meal of rice and tangra fish curry, and fell into a deep dreamless sleep. Once he was asleep, Nayantara told her friends, "I don't think he can get back home tonight. It is raining heavily, too. He can go back, tomorrow. Please have your dinner. It's already quite late. Shyamal, can you stay here tonight? I don't want to be alone with a stranger in my house." Shyamal agreed at once.

They ate their dinner silently, speculating on the various aspects of the drama in their own minds and soon Kartik*da* left for home. Rahul was asleep in Nayantara's bedroom adjacent to the verandah and Shyamal slept on the divan in the same room. Nayantara lay down on a couch and thought about the stranger who seemed sad, and vulnerable like a soul returning from a city of ruins. Unrelated images shuffled through her mind. She saw the dark, angelic face of her father, the haunting black eyes of her mother and the fleshy lined face of her grandfather. Caught up in the tremulous conflict of these images were the sound of rain and the noise of the river outside. When she woke up suddenly around midnight, she heard Shyamal snoring loudly but there was a light in her bedroom. She peeped in and saw the stranger staring closely at the three framed photographs hanging on the wall.

One was a photograph of the family taken in the garden on a sunny winter afternoon. Her grandfather was seated on a red leather-bound chair. His wife, her grandmother, was seated at his feet. Her mother, a voluptuous woman, was standing behind her grandfather's chair with her youngest brother in her arms, while Nayantara was seated on her grandfather's lap. Her father was standing in a corner looking elsewhere, tentatively resting his right hand on his younger brother's shoulder like a blind man. Her grandfather was the centre of attention here. The second photograph showed her grandfather and her mother strolling by the river. The third photograph showed her grandfather, her mother and Nayantara in the shade of a large tree. They were playing with a huge ball.

Once Rahul had studied the photographs he went on to the verandah looking thoughtful. He was quite oblivious of Nayantara who was watching him. They were now standing on the verandah in the darkness of the universe, looking at the ferocious river; one was weighed down by a sense of melancholy and lamentation while the other experienced a simmering sensation of longing and desire.

4.

Nayantara and Rahul conversed like long-lost friends that night, though they had never met before.

"Are you feeling all right now?"She asked.

Rahul was quite overwhelmed with gratitude. "Quite all right. I don't know how to thank you people. I've put all of you in an embarrassing situation. I'm genuinely sorry for all this."

"Don't mind my saying so but you gave us some dramatic relief in our otherwise boring lives," Nayantara joked, "But I'm curious about something. Did you attempt suicide tonight?"

"No. I didn't make any such attempt. But it's true, I did want to die."

"You don't look like you belong to this place."

"True," Rahul acknowledged, "Actually, I like this place. I have a colleague who lives nearby. He brought me to this ghat two years ago, and I took a liking to this place almost at once. More so, because of its name – Nayantara."

"I was named after this ghat."

Rahul was surprised, "Is your name Nayantara too? All right, now I remember the older gentleman was calling you Nayana."

"Yes. There is a story behind my name. Would you like to hear it?"

Rahul was interested, "Tell me," he said.

"My mother told me this. She'd go for a stroll in the evening with my grandfather during her pregnancy. They would sit on the ghat and he would tell her stories about ghosts entrapped in the bamboo grove on the opposite bank. My mother would feel very scared as evening approached and urge him to hurry back home. One day they saw a green snake on the floor of the ghat. My grandfather said 'Rani, if you give birth to a son we'll name him Nayan and in case the child is a girl we'll name her Nayantara.'"

"Do you live alone in this house?"

"Yes. Why?"

"Don't you feel scared in this vast empty space full of decay and smelling of death, and this ferocious river…?" Rahul couldn't complete his sentence as Nayantara butted in at once, "I love the river. I can't live without it. But very soon, I'll have to learn to do so."

"Why? This is your house. You needn't leave it if you don't want to; you have such wonderful friends here. Was this house built by your father?"

"My grandfather built it. He got this piece of land as dowry. He traded in wood, made a fortune and spent most of his time and energy in building and designing this house. He studied foreign journals to imitate western styles of architecture. You'll find that all the other mansions on the riverbank are mere copies of our house because they were all built later. He named it 'Bishnupriya House' after his wife. It is inscribed on a moss-eaten marble tablet by the iron-gate. I remember my grandfather on his deathbed, a huge man made small by fate, innumerable diseases and sorrow."

"Did he suffer from melancholia?"

"His only son, my father, did nothing in life. He only wrote poetry, which my grandfather didn't like," Nayantara told him. "They had terrible fights over this",

"Have you read your father's poems?"

"Yes, I've read quite a few."

"Did you like them?" he asked, yet again.

Nayantara gave a candid answer, "Some of them were good. But most were the rantings of a terrible dark mind. He was obsessed with a fear of wild animals. At one point there were hundreds of foxes in these parts. He would lock himself up for days together in fear of foxes entering our house. My grandfather would yell at him for being such a sissy. He didn't change. One day he fell from the roof and spent the last nine years of his life paralysed. Ma and I would nurse him. He cried a lot."

"Are you an only child?"

"No, I have two brothers. They are happily settled in Delhi and Hyderabad," she told Rahul.

"Don't they come here to visit you sometimes?"

Nayantara didn't seem to like this question. "No, not often," she said.

"Do you feel lonely?"

Nayantara knew it was time to change the subject. "Are you interviewing me? Don't you feel ashamed shooting so many questions at a lady?"

Rahul was apologetic, "I'm sorry Nayantara*debi*. I'm extremely sorry. I got carried away by the atmosphere here. I apologise, once again."

"You don't need to be sorry at all. I was only pulling your leg. By the way, you seem to have recovered quite well."

"I must thank you once again for taking such good care of me," Rahul was truly grateful.

"Were you depressed and disturbed today when you came to this lonely ghat?" Nayantara asked.

Rahul was quiet for a while. "I was. In fact, I still am," he said.

"Why?"

"You won't understand," Rahul tried to evade the question.

Nayantara seemed hurt. "All right."

"I didn't mean to hurt you. Have you ever been married?"

Nayantara said, "Yes, briefly, for a period of two years. I ran away with someone when I was twenty-two. He was nice and sweet. He wouldn't let me do any work outside the house, but he couldn't hold on to a job for long. Then, one day while returning from work a speeding truck hit him and he died on the spot. My in-laws asked me to return to my parents' home. I came back. I've been here since."

"Didn't you feel like getting married again?"

"Yes, once or twice but by then the focus had shifted to my brothers. Is something wrong with your marriage?" Nayantara asked.

"Yes. It's breaking up. My wife wants to divorce me and marry her childhood friend Sanjay."

"Was your marriage an arranged one, or did you marry for love?"

"It was an arranged marriage, nine years ago. We have a daughter who is seven. Actually, Sanjay had become an integral part of our family. I saw nothing wrong in him or his attitude or even in Reena's attitude towards him. I always felt he was like a brother. We bonded well. We stood by each other in times of need," Rahul said.

"Does that make the weight of betrayal heavier?"

There was hurt and anger in Rahul's eyes as he said, "Yes, of course! They betrayed my trust. I don't understand how Reena could lead a double life for so long. After all, it can be extremely stressful and agonising to hide things continuously."

"Don't we all do that?"

Rahul sounded cynical, "That's a cliché. Yes we all do that. But being involved with another man even as one lives in a family with a husband and child, for so many years! I think that's quite different. I don't understand, why didn't she marry Sanjay in the first place?"

"Did you ask her that?"

"I did. She said it's only recently that she felt like marrying him. She also hinted at my not being an exciting lover and at her not being able to carry on with this physical torment for her entire life," Rahul was surprised that he could discuss all this with a complete stranger.

Nayantara continued, "She must have been sleeping with Sanjay in any case."

Rahul was almost hysterical, "I've started doubting whether Reema is my own daughter!"

Nayantara tried to calm him, "It doesn't matter. Does it?"

"I don't know. I'm not sure."

"Will you be selling off this house soon?"

"Yes, my brothers want to dispose of this property at once. They call this house 'a property', and once sold, the money will be divided amongst us equally. A fair deal, no?"

Rahul asked, "Will you move to some other place, then?"

"Yes."

"Where?"

Nayantara answered thoughtfully, "I've not thought about it yet. But I shall go so far away that I don't see this building being broken down and converted into a riverside motel."

Rahul hesitated a bit before continuing, "You know Nayantara, I wanted to ask you something."

"About what?"

Rahul said "The family photographs in your bedroom."

"What about them?"

"Don't you have any other photographs of your parents? Or of your parents with you and your brothers – I mean the usual family photographs that hang on people's walls?"

Nayantara was caught off-guard and said curtly, "What's that got to do with you? But tell me how could you identify my relatives in those photographs?"

Rahul told her, "I'm a specialist in reading and analysing photographs. Years of experience really! Actually, it's nothing but common sense. Somehow, the photographs seem odd. It's as if the person who selected them had a motive: he wanted to erase the memories of your father. Am I wrong?"

"This was my grandfather's room. The photographs were selected by him, not me. But my father can be seen in the group photograph. Didn't you notice him?"

Rahul agreed, "He does. But, even in that photograph he is standing in a corner far removed from everyone else. I feel that's odd and want to ask why?"

Once again Nayantara tried to fend him off, "What's that to you, and what are you looking for, anyway?"

"I don't know. But, it does look a bit disturbing as I said, it makes one sad."

Nayantara fell silent. She looked at the river as though in a trance. It was not clear what emotions were aroused in her by these questions. After a while she whispered as though resigned to fate, "My father was impotent. My grandfather stopped sleeping with my grandmother after my father was born. He was disgusted with her for giving birth to a mentally retarded child. In the later years he slept with my mother, so we were fathered by our grandfather. Maybe this has something to do with his selection of photographs."

5.

They didn't speak after this. It had stopped raining and soon the sky cleared and the sun emerged. Rahul got into his soggy, soiled clothes and set off on his journey to a different world. He had decided that he would not contest the divorce proceedings, but he didn't know what he could do about Reema.

Nayantara looked at the three photographs, dusted them and put them away. She finished her morning chores and settled down with the knitting machine. Thoughts about the future were brewing in her mind. Nayantara decided to settle down in an ashram in Benaras once the house was sold off and she had received her share.

An Incident in the Past

1.

Rahul remembered the smouldering blue flames and the spools of fire splintering like massive fireflies in the chemistry laboratory. The air was heavy with the sharp odours of unknown chemicals. The beakers, pipettes, cylinders, the tiled slabs and glazed walls were suddenly aflame as though hit by a powerful streak of lightning. Rahul was in a state of panic as he saw the arrows of fire hurling towards him but he remained rooted to the spot. Minutes later, hot speckles of orange, red, yellow and blue chemicals had plunged into his eyes. He felt a searing pain in the core of his skull and his face was drenched in blood.

Rahul would often sneak into the school laboratory after everybody had left and the campus was deserted. He would tear himself away from the concerns of the world and experiment with the chemicals and apparatus hoping to find answers to the innumerable questions that plagued his mind, night and day.

That was the last time he had seen light. Thereafter, an impenetrable darkness had been embossed on his consciousness and he was continually haunted by memories of light and shadows and the residual images of what he had seen in the past. As time passed, these memories faded. As a blind man, Rahul gradually trained himself to make sense of the physical world through smell and touch.

He met with this accident at the age of fifteen. By this time, he was involved amorously with Mita, who was three years senior to him in school. Mita was the elder sister of his best friend Sandipan. They called her Parveen Babi in school, for she had a voluptuous body and looked older than her age. Rahul would recreate, fuse and destroy, the images of Mita and Parveen Babi every night before going to sleep since that fateful afternoon. It was like a game to reconnect to a time when he could see. There was another face that was deeply enshrined in his soul. It was the face of one of the most beautiful and elegant women he had ever come across – his mother, Kabita. His eyes yearned to see her.

2.

It took six or seven years for Rahul to accept that he was a blind man and that he would have to acquire the necessary skills to cope with the change. In the initial years he shuttled between ophthalmologists and hospitals in various parts of the world nursing the faint hope that someone would restore his vision.

But the optical nerves were so badly damaged, that even a transplant would not guarantee sight. Since his father had died long ago, his mother accompanied him everywhere, but this attachment was on the verge of breaking down when he was on the threshold of adolescence.

Rahul's mother was always by his side, encouraging him almost a hundred times more than when he was an infant. The situation was further complicated by Rahul's reluctance to accept his state. Getting an adult son to bathe, clothe himself, eat and sleep day after day resulted in a great churning of emotions and tormented her soul. She underwent this conflict without rancour and after a period of time acted more like an automaton. However, when her eyes fell upon the cadaverous cavities that had replaced his large black eyes, a strong wave of nausea threatened to overpower her that was beyond her control.

A violent storm seemed to be running her down. She cried bitterly, but she knew that she had to banish thoughts of death for the sake of her son.

"You have to accept Rahul that life does not end, just because you've become blind. There are so many skills and opportunities available today. You just refuse to acquire them! What a good student you were once. I'm coaxing you, for your own sake. What will happen to you after I'm gone, have you ever thought about that?"

Rahul paid no heed to his mother. He just kept silent and refused to answer or to please her in any way. Sandipan and Mita dropped in at Rahul's house quite often. As Rahul withdrew into himself he lost contact with his friends. His mother was an excellent singer of kirtans and bhajans. Sandipan played the guitar, the banjo and the mouth organ. Mita was a singer of considerable repute. She sang Tagore songs as well as sentimental country hits. Whenever Mita and Sandipan dropped in, their music – filled up a great void in his life; this provided an element of gaiety to an otherwise sombre atmosphere. Though he pretended to be untouched by their efforts, music and melody excited him and gave rise to new desires and hopes.

Two things irritated him – Sandipan and Mita always made additional efforts to make him happy. They also made a great effort to inform him about current affairs. Rahul found this irritating for he found no reason to stay connected to the world. Mita made no effort to come close to Rahul. In fact, she ensured that they were never alone and painstakingly avoided all personal interaction and physical contact. At times he felt that Mita and Sandipan were vessels of hope cleverly employed by his mother. Their main agenda was to entertain him, and to keep him abreast of the outside world; to incite and challenge him to move beyond his disability. He hated these efforts to make him move beyond his tragic circumstances. But he appreciated the music that they created for it stirred in him an unnamed urge that resonated in his soul.

Seven years passed in this manner, and then there was a sudden upheaval in his life within the space of a month.

His mother died of a cerebral attack and Sandipan announced that he was going to Germany on work. Mita invited him to her wedding with a young and famous poet. Rahul felt like he was hurtling to his death even as images of the past flashed before his eyes.

3.

Rahul recovered quickly this time because his very survival was at stake. He had to react to the changed circumstances so he turned pragmatic and invited his grandmother to stay with him as his guardian and housekeeper. He enrolled himself in a blind school. He acquainted himself with details of his considerable inheritance with the help of the bankers with whom his mother kept all her savings. He made intelligent investments out of a portion of this inheritance so that regular expenses were taken care of till such time as he would have a steady source of income.

He lived an austere life, resigned to his fate. At times he was overwhelmed by a sense of agitation and later by an ocean of grief. The people he knew and loved – his mother, Sandipan and Mita – had left him, one by one. He aggravated his loneliness by avoiding new relationships and refusing to make new friends. He spoke very little in school. He went on in this way till he suddenly realised that he was being sentimental and foolish, and that his refusal to accept his blindness was the cause of all his misery.

Rahul wondered whether he should kill himself or make an attempt to live differently. He didn't want to die, but he didn't know how to live differently. It occurred to him that blindness had endowed him with different sensibilities. The images and sensations that played in his mind from a time when he could see, and the ones that had gradually formed over the years when he was drowned in an unending tunnel of darkness were critically different. It was not as if he was cut off from the universe. In fact, when he turned blind he became the universe. He realised he had become less aware of the contours of his own body, and felt more connected to the plasma of existence outside himself, to the ether beyond his skin. He felt his blood and nerves had become more porous to the air outside and could catch hitherto unknown sounds, tastes and smells from close and far away worlds.

Rahul was also acutely aware of physiological changes occurring inside his body. These amplified the sensations imprinted on his consciousness by the outside world, to which he felt exceedingly connected. At times he felt like a receptor of hidden and dangerous signals from the outside world. Could he convert all these into something that would cease to make his life look like a lame excuse, a sad pantomime? It struck him one night that he might achieve this objective by surrendering to music, a feat that also aroused him sexually.

4.

The very next day Rahul set out on this quest. The music teacher in school was versatile and could play a variety of instruments. He was also highly dedicated, accomplished, and had shaped a number of gifted students into fine musicians – both vocalists and instrumentalists. Rahul spent the next three years learning to play the flute, the violin and the Spanish guitar. He listened to Indian and Western classical music as well as folk, rock, reggae and jazz. He immersed himself in Mozart and Chopin, but also drew inspiration from the songs sung by the bards and fakirs of Bengal. The music teacher, after years of exploration, had found in him a passionate friend. This cemented their bond. Rahul realised at last that he had to discover his calling. His teacher advised him to concentrate and listen to his inner voice.

For days together he disconnected himself from all music and dived within. At first, he didn't hear anything. It took eleven days for that faint tune to reach his ears. It sounded like the stirrings of a distant tornado played out on strings and percussion instruments, like a series of waves followed by the loud chants of a strange woman's voice bursting with intense pain and ecstasy. He sensed it was an orchestra playing inside him. He could convert the sensations he felt into simple notations of music. He heaved a sigh of relief. Rahul rushed back to his teacher and declared that he had found his calling. He would form a team of musicians and create original music. The teacher was overjoyed. Rahul formed his orchestra over the next four months with a number of instrumentalists and three singers. They called the orchestra The Darkness Band. The name was highly criticised. But they didn't care.

"We'll create music that is snatched from the throes of darkness and bring it to light. The world glorifies light and equates darkness with the land of the evil. But light and darkness represent nothing by themselves. They are only two inseparable states of existence. We live in permanent darkness. We are not enemies of light. We know light like nobody else in the whole world knows it," Rahul said.

Over the next year Rahul wrote, composed and directed four original scores each running to twenty or twenty-five minutes. He named them 'Light', 'Fall', 'Darkness' and 'Only Darkness'. When the music was played in the auditorium before the students, the teachers and guests on the school's foundation day, there was a hushed silence at the end of the programme, finally broken by rapturous applause.

Rahul, the musician, was born. The principal decided to hold a special concert on Republic Day when the governor, a connoisseur of western classical music and a distinguished violinist himself, was to be the special guest at the school. The governor was rendered speechless and embraced Rahul and his fellow musicians and invited them to his residence in the Raj Bhavan for a special programme on Poila Boishakh.

Over the next ten years The Darkness Band became famous and Rahul became an icon for millions of people. He became rich and many considered him a sex symbol, too. However, he was extremely lonely, confined as he was within the walls created by his sycophants and the endless routine of paid sex and cocaine. He feared relationships because he was haunted by people slipping away. He had grown paranoid about keeping his musicians faithful to his band. All of them had grown into independent worthy musicians, by now, yet they didn't forsake him or the band, for the greener pastures of the film and music industry.

At times, Rahul felt like running away, of putting an end to this life of success, which over the years had made him unhappy and distanced him from the real world of people and ideas. But success had brought acceptance of his talent along with the comforts of life. He, who had yearned for name and fame, now craved anonymity. How would he have felt if his mother was by his side, if Mita and Sandipan were there to talk and argue about life? Could he have become an equally successful scientist had he not lost his sight? He was known to be a champion of the disabled, but he felt more disabled as he tried to conquer his own disability.

He stopped composing original scores and his band members became restless playing old compositions. He lost his mentor during this period and stopped listening to any new music for quite some time.

5.

It was a summer afternoon when Rahul was brooding over his past in his quiet studio in the suburbs. His domestic help informed him that there was a lady, accompanied by a young child, at the gate, who wanted to meet him. There were innumerable requests of this sort everyday; the guards and the helps who worked for him were trained to fend off such incursions. This time, it seemed, the lady was determined not to budge without meeting Rahul, so he finally agreed.

"All right, call her in. Make them sit in the outer lobby. I'll join them in a minute," he said. He wondered who this desperate and stubborn lady could be. What was her motive in meeting him at this hour of the day? He didn't know too many women except those who were connected to him professionally and the select list of whores whom he patronised. But none of them was likely to disturb him without a prior appointment. He felt perplexed and apprehensive as he proceeded towards the lobby.

Suddenly a faint whiff of perfume tickled his nerves and he felt himself break out in goose bumps. He stopped, supporting himself by holding on to the doorframe with his outstretched hand. With his free hand he pushed his dark glasses close to his eyes so that the mangled flesh was not visible through any careless gap. He gained control over himself in a moment and walked into the room, "Is that you, Mita? I can't believe this! It's been ages. Is that your son?" he asked.

There was no immediate reply. He sat down expectantly and only then did the voice – gravelly, almost hoarse and unfeminine, a voice that reminded him of Shubha Mudgal, said, "Yes, it's me, Rahul and yes, this is my son. I've come here for a purpose."

Rahul reacted cautiously holding his breath, "Purpose? What purpose?"

Mita replied dispassionately, "I fear we might end up saying a few things which may not be appropriate for a child's ears. I hope you'll appreciate that. Can someone take my son to a place where he'll be comfortable?"

Rahul felt completely overpowered. At a different level, he was also amused that someone who had deserted him and whom he could never get over, had to return to him after so many years. Did she need him for something? He could sense a sweet cloud of revenge looming large in his chest. He asked a help to take the boy into the studio, play some music and get him some toys. He also asked for tea or coffee to be served to his guest. Mita declared that the child loved music and would remain entertained, he didn't need toys. She also spelled out her preference for black, sugarless coffee.

Mita said unexpectedly, "You think I left you, betrayed you. Isn't that so?"

Rahul replied carefully, considering and weighing

every word, "What's the point in discussing all this today? I'm not interested, really. Tell me, what brings you here now?"

"I know you won't believe me. But the fact is I've wanted to meet you for the last seven years. I couldn't gather enough courage earlier."

Rahul looked startled, "You don't seem lacking in courage."

"Don't slight me, Rahul. I agree it was mean of me to have left you the way I did. But it was difficult to think of my future chained to a self-loathing blind man at that point in time. Please try to understand. We're not as virtuous as we want others to be. That's a fact of life. Besides I became terribly attracted to Kaushik then. He was a poet, a magician with words, ideas and images; revered and adored by one and all. I was blinded by an idea of conquering him and having him as mine, my own."

Rahul didn't speak "Don't you want to know what happened to me after that? I'm not a celebrity like you, so my life doesn't get splashed in newspapers, magazines and on TV. People don't gossip about me in street corners," she continued.

"Tell me, Mita," Rahul said.

"I betrayed you certainly, that too at your weakest hour, at your time of need. I think I was cursed forever because of that. My relationship with Kaushik soured. He turned out to be a womaniser and incidentally, he was a bad poet too. I lost control of my life. Then I became pregnant. Pipal was born. He was born blind. When the doctors informed me I thought of you at once, like one remembers a bad dream. I knew I was being punished for betraying you and would have to carry the cross till my last breath."

"For the first two years I felt like disowning Pipal and running away to a carefree world. I even tried killing myself. It was then that I read about your band in the newspaper and bought a few CDs of your music. It was like being hit by a thunderstorm. It was powerful and vibrant, gay yet sad, something that came from your soul. I found that your music pacified Pipal when he cried. He used to cry so much when he was a baby. In fact, he reacted to your music like one does to hypnosis. Pipal, in many ways, changed my life. Kaushik left me. I became an outsider in my in-laws' house. My parents had died. Sandipan didn't keep in touch. One day I was looking at Pipal intently. He was listening to one of your CDs and smiling in his vacuous manner. It suddenly occurred to me that he was fragile and frail and would need me by his side, forever. My fury vanished. I drew him close and he surrendered himself to me instantly. I developed a unique and comforting bond with Pipal as time progressed. My self-esteem was restored. I started working, bought a house and divorced Kaushik."

"Although Pipal took up a lot of my energy and time, he gave me hope. His blindness and his love for your music made me think of you, so here I am, Rahul. Frankly I feel relieved, almost weightless, talking to you."

"You said you'd come with a purpose. What's that?"

"I can go down on my knees to beg you; I can do anything for this. Will you coach my son, Rahul? Will you be his music teacher and mentor? My son is good. He needs somebody like you to train him."

"But I don't teach, Mita. It's not something that I've ever done in my life."

Mita tried to persuade him, "You can always start. Maybe that could rejuvenate your life, and also the lives of so many people lost in darkness without hope. You can actually touch people's lives more radically by teaching these children of darkness. I've noticed one thing, Rahul. You've been stagnating over the past few years. You have created nothing new, as though you're lacking in inspiration and ideas. Maybe you need to teach at this stage of your life."

"It amazes me to think of the lengths you travel to get your desires fulfilled!" Rahul exclaimed.

"I'm a lonely woman with a blind son. I must know the art of persuasion, Rahul. If I fail I will be nowhere, blown off like a speck of dust. "

Rahul asked, "Does your son sing or play any instrument?"

"He has a sonorous voice, and can whistle very well. I want you to teach him some stringed instrument or the piano and also train his voice."

"I'll think about it and get back to you. Is he very naughty?"

"Yes. He's a rascal. But he becomes very co-operative in a musical environment."

There was a spell of tense silence punctuated by intermittent sounds associated with the drinking of tea and coffee and the munching of cookies.

Rahul could not believe that he was sharing this with Mita. He heard himself say, "At times, I doubt whether I'm treated at par with the musicians who can see. There's a political correctness in society to champion the cause of underdogs and minorities. For the last few months, I've had a feeling that I'm overrated as a musician. Maybe that's why I can't create anything that's new. My pool of fecundity has dried up."

Mita said compassionately, "It happens to the greatest of the great. You can't judge yourself solely on that parameter. But you must understand that sighted people are overwhelmed by your ability to surmount physical odds, to create such fantastic music. It's true that a bit of sympathy does play a part and that may not go down too well with critical judgment. But we're compassionate animals, Rahul. We react instinctively and with passion. I don't think it's possible to do otherwise."

"My point is that at times blindness could be an asset instead of a handicap. It could refine your musical sensibilities more than if you could see. People have to look at things in a detached manner without the politics of judgment. I'm not, for a moment, glorifying blindness for god's sake. But things have to be seen in perspective. I feel let down when I'm introduced in hush-hush tones as a blind musician, as if I belong to a rare species in need of careful preservation. They say I have overcome blindness, and I'm described as a champion of the disabled. Well, I'm not. I don't think I would have been a musician had I not gone blind. I can't explain this but I've experienced many sensations, which I don't remember having when I could see. It was this that helped me to become a musician. There are a great number of fans who are overwhelmed by the fact that I can't see, and yet, I can conduct an orchestra and create seemingly complex music. They've already declared me 'great' before they've listened to my music critically and with the attention that it deserves. They don't have the balls to call a blind man's work inferior in any way. An appeasing audience kills one's artistry, my dear. I'm sorry, I think I'm boring you with gory talk," Rahul said realising that he had been talking for a long time.

Mita asked, "Are you happy with your blindness?"

"That's not the point, Mita. You're not happy, though you can see. But if you ask me today whether I'd like to get back my vision, I'll say I don't know. I've made peace with my world of darkness. But I do have the curiosity and desire to see, like I did long ago."

"Does that happen with Pipal too?"

Rahul said, "I don't think so. Because he has never experienced light, whereas I know light."

"Does that alter his comprehension of the world?"

"Of course, it does."

Mita felt that a burden had fallen off her shoulders. "I can't explain, Rahul, how wonderful and liberating it is, talking to you! I had feared you might not want to talk to me, or might even throw me out of your house. But I also believed you would be kind and forgiving," she said.

"Mita, please don't shower me with such praise. Well, I also have a purpose in prolonging this conversation."

She asked, "What?"

"You know I've gone back a billion times to that fateful day and the cataclysmic event that robbed me of my sight. Sometimes, I feel it was not an accident. Somebody tried to hurt me grievously beyond repair. And I suspect it was linked to my relationship with you."

Mita was not prepared for this. "Why should you think like that? Why at all? You would regularly sneak into the school chemistry lab to do your experiments with chemicals. Were you trained enough? No. Did you seek any professional guidance? No. Something must have gone wrong in the process and resulted in an explosion. Why are you unnecessarily getting depressed with such thoughts of malice when it was only an unfortunate accident?"

"How sure can you be of that, Mita?"

"I'm not an investigator, Rahul. But I've no reason to doubt what is obvious."

"Mita, do you remember Samiran?"

"Well, I do. He was the star sportsman in school. He was in my batch."

"Right. He was also the boy with the best toned body in school, remember?"

"Yes, but how is that relevant?"

All these years Rahul had known this, but now he found it strange to share it with Mita. He said, "You were two-timing us, Samiran and me. I know this. Sandipan had hinted as much. Samiran was furious with you when he found you in my arms one evening behind the kindergarten park. He got hold of you later and threatened to kill you if you were unfaithful to him again. You challenged him to prove that he was as intelligent as me or he should forget you. Sandipan overheard this conversation from behind a pillar. Samiran threatened to kill me. You laughed audaciously and this made it all the more unbearable for him. He got hold of some crude explosives, possibly from one of his father's construction sites, and planted them in the laboratory containers, which were used to store dry chemical powders. He must have stealthily kept a watch on me for a long time before executing his plan. I must have used one of these spurious powders that day. "

Mita answered half-heartedly, "I think this is one of your crooked fantasies."

"No. I remember the reaction even now. I was to use a dazzling green coloured powder. Today as I see it in my mind's eye, there were chocolate nut-like granules in the green powder. They had no business to be there. Somebody must have put them there. Who could it have been other than someone who would want to hurt me, one who knew of my clandestine operations? At that age,

I was excited by the drama and overlooked all the perils. Well, what was to happen, happened and here we are recounting the tragic events years after they happened" Rahul said.

"Samiran was obviously crude and masculine. But do you think he could have done something so ghastly?"

"I'm glad that you're not disputing your role. It was simple. Samiran was overcome by rage. He had to avenge that insult by killing me. You suspected him, too, didn't you? Deep inside, you must have felt guilty for causing me irreparable harm, even if indirectly. Did you move away because of that?"

Mita was crying. "I don't know," she sobbed.

"By the way, do you still look like Parveen Babi?"Rahul asked.

"I don't know. I don't look at myself in the mirror anymore."

Nobody spoke after this. There was a great upheaval among the rapidly moving bodies of clouds in the grey sky above. Thunder crashed and a wind raged scattering litter and debris all around, piercing stone walls, crusty hearts and minds. It brought a cooling touch cutting through the hot spell. Then came the first rains of the season.

A Meeting in the Cafe

1.

Rahul gazed unblinkingly at his reflection in the mirror, looking for signs of a past that could provide him with subtle indications of the future. He wanted to know where destiny was leading him. He thought of the telephone call he had received a few days ago. An old man, on the verge of death, had begged to meet him. He was dumbstruck when the man introduced himself. He didn't know how to react. There was a void deep inside him. He was aware that he was talking to a man, whom he had always been very curious about. Enmeshed in the trappings of his own life he had forgotten this man in the last few years. But deep within him was a strain of curiosity. Rahul had finally agreed to meet him after deciding on a convenient date, time and venue.

When confronted with an overpowering turmoil in the depths of his soul, further intensified by the fear of dying a lonely and painful death, Rahul would immerse himself in the darkness of his study and look at his reflection in the mirror. Faint specks of light emerging through countless pores in the linen fabric of the curtains and tiny cracks in the panels of the doors and windows ensured that he could see his reflection. As his eyes adjusted to the darkness, the reflection that looked like an amorphous ghost took on a definite shape and he could make out the curved lines of his ears, his cheeks, his nose and lips.

Hours passed thus and then, overcome by disgust, he'd

fling the curtains wide open, and allow the light to rush into the dusty corners of his room. In that halo of light he imagined the scarred and ravaged face of his mother, her eyes sunken in the hollow sockets of her skull shrunk with age and disillusionment – eyes that were charming at one point in time. She warned him, in her feeble cough-worn voice, to run away and not to stare at her through the keyhole.

Rahul paced with a cigarette in his hand, inhaling the smoke as though it were the last drag of his life. As the pale blue rings of smoke emerged from his nostrils, he waved them away with his hands. He lost his balance and fell down on the marble tiled floor, now cracked and corrugated with lack of maintenance and disuse. He lay there looking up at the damp ceiling, devastated by the rainwater that had seeped in year after year making innumerable saline patches and ruining the carved designs.

Rahul smoked one cigarette after another till he was exhausted. His parched throat craved water. There was a raging fire ravaging his insides. But Rahul didn't make any attempt to quench his thirst.

Behind a screen of smoke he saw a dark adolescent with long tresses, walking through a forsaken mansion looking intently for something. The boy moved from one wall to another, pausing at the weed-infested doors, and the multi-coloured glass panels of the tall windows with their iron grilles. Lizards darted on the wet walls like streaks of lightning. The mansion was lit by sunbeams pouring through the openings in the walls, windows and glass panes. Between these patches of light were the frozen layers of darkness. The boy moved through the rooms, flitting through the rising smoke, light and darkness, hurriedly at times and sometimes slowly, looking furtively behind him as though chased by unseen djinns. On reaching one end of this empty mansion, he came across a spiral staircase without banisters, leading to the upper floors. He contemplated his next move for a while, and then moved on.

He crossed identical floors drowned in thick billows of smoke to enter a wide terrace strewn with moss, dead leaves, half eaten fruits and bird droppings. A look of happiness and amazement shone on his face as though his dream was suddenly realised. He saw a sunlit valley of violet flowers stretching out before him. There was a deep blue river flowing on one side, its surface gently rippled by a southern wind. Rahul thought of a caption for the scene, "If you dare to cross your fears you will experience absolute happiness." Rahul laughed. He knew that was not true. He was not sure how advertisements worked on human minds, or whether they worked at all. But the kind of money spent on advertisements of products and concepts amazed him.

A few months ago he'd been diagnosed with a critical illness; a spectre of impending death ticked inside his body. The pathological reports had made him laugh and it was a laughter that welled up from deep within. It was so wild that it created a prickling sensation in his hair follicles and struck the doctor and his accompanying nurses with undiluted terror.

2.

Rahul had set up the meeting at a nondescript café in a bylane of Hatibagan, once famous for its cutlets, non-vegetarian snacks and milky tea with little sugar. Now it looked like a sad cave with a faint smell of chopped vegetables and raw fish wafting out of its depths. However, the place soothed Rahul's soul. He loved the food, the tea and the loneliness, solidified as it were on the tables and chairs, on the walls, on the stoic faces of the waiters and the old man at the cash counter.

Debnarayan knew the place very well as he was almost addicted to its fish kabiraji. He used to frequent this joint every Saturday evening before he left the country. In the old days this eatery was frequented by the old and the young, by lovers and by the abandoned, by people who spoke Bengali and those who spoke English. It was 'home' to a community of people who relished good fish, chicken and mutton snacks fried in mustard oil. Today it was merely an obstinate reminder of the past. The ownership of the café had changed hands. The new owner was looking for an investor to turn it into a departmental store. Rahul shuddered to think that someday the eatery would cease to exist. He loved visiting this place every evening after office. After eating two chicken cutlets and drinking four cups of black Darjeeling tea, he'd puff away at his daily quota of fifteen cigarettes in a span of three hours. He'd watch the traffic and the thinning crowd as night set in. Sometime before midnight he'd return home with a burning sensation in his gut, a sour taste on his tongue and a damp heaviness in his heart. The eatery provided him with a critical vantage point where he needed to speak very little but could think for long, uninterrupted spells. He felt magically relieved yet tired by the time he left the place. This helped him get a good night's sleep and he could withstand the ordeals of meeting deadlines in office the next day.

The meeting was slated for a late winter evening. Rahul reached early and roamed about the packed thoroughfare. A spirit of festivity hung in the air with Christmas and New Year celebrations round the corner. Rahul was bracing himself mentally for the meeting. He tried to remember how Debnarayan had looked thirty-three years ago and how he might look now. That was a long time ago; he was a child then. Was Debnarayan dying? He sounded ill on the phone, "I've only a few days left, Rahul," he'd said. Was he seeking Rahul's companionship and attention? A few questions hovered in his mind. Should he ask them? He was not sure. Had Debnarayan re-married? He hadn't been legally separated from his mother. Could he have had other lovers? Had he fathered more children? Where was he all these years? Was he in need of money or shelter? Why was he so desperate to meet Rahul? Should he smoke in front of Debnarayan?

Rahul looked at his wristwatch. He was already late. He walked briskly and in five minutes he entered the eatery. It wore the look of a stoic forlorn widow. He couldn't see anyone except the waiters. Then, the old man who always sat at the cash counter walked up to him "Sir, there is somebody waiting for you in the last cabin.

We told him you preferred sitting outside with full view of the road. But he insisted on sitting there. He is a very old man, sir and is as tall as you."

Rahul walked into the dark cabin past the dirty curtains. An old man in a brown coat and old grey flannels rose to greet him. His hair was cropped short and his unshaven face was deeply tanned. Rahul looked at him carefully in the faint yellow light. The man was thin, almost skeletal, and seemed very depressed. Rahul said immediately, "Please don't get up. Are you comfortable here or should we sit outside?" Debnarayan didn't reply. Rahul understood that he wanted to remain inside the cabin so he took his seat opposite Debnarayan and drew the curtains again. The cabin was dark but gradually, he was able to see every feature, movement and twitching of muscles on the visitor's face.

Suddenly Debnarayan said, "Do you have a problem with darkness?" The voice was cracked, yet deep.

Rahul smiled. "No. I'm comfortable here. I hope you can see me properly."

Debnarayan replied, "Yes Rahul, I can see you properly." He looked at Rahul with a strained, distant look as if he was measuring him bit by bit, comparing him with the images of the past.

"When did you arrive? Have you been out of India all this while?"Rahul asked.

Debnarayan looked at him with his direct tranquil gaze, "I've settled down in Pondicherry, you know. I came back to India four years ago. I'm coming to Kolkata after a very long time. In fact, this is my first visit after my return."

Rahul couldn't stop himself from asking, "Anything special? Why did you come back here?"

Debnarayan looked away. He was toying with the soot-lined salt and pepper containers. There was a new flowerpot on the table with a large dahlia in it. The flower added a touch of brightness to the atmosphere in the cabin. Debnarayan touched the flower absent-mindedly, absorbed in his thoughts. "Have you heard of Bhabatosh Sanyal?" He asked.

Rahul was faintly surprised. "Of course, I've heard of him. He's a very powerful minister in the state government. What has he got to do with you?"

"He's one of the men who are changing the face of this government." Debnarayan replied. "It's said that he's responsible for most of the investors taking an interest in the state after a very long time."

"Could be", Rahul remarked, slightly irritated, "but I'm not interested in such things."

"It vexes me to know that one of the highest paid creative directors of a leading advertising company in the country could be an ardent lover of decay," said Debnarayan.

"I love decay and filth. Why does that bother you? I don't preach about this."

Debnarayan said, "I don't know whether you're aware that so much is written about you. You present a lifestyle that is contrary to what you create. You don't take advantage of the money that you earn or the power that you have."

Rahul exclaimed angrily, "Oh that's bullshit! Who told you that?"

"I don't know you. I'm only saying what I've read about you."

"Advertising is about trying to sell things. But it doesn't work in the long run. I'm sure about that. It's an obsessive invasion. You know, the visuals that you see, the humour and music that you hear are mostly pre-determined. They are later attached to the products by the oblique use of words. As such, they don't represent the intrinsic value of things. But advertising provides white collar employment and a channel for creativity."

Debnarayan asked, "Why would hard-nosed businessmen spend so much money on such endeavours?"

Rahul retorted, "I've no answer to that. But frankly did you want to meet me to discuss all this?"

Debnarayan fell silent and became meditative. Rahul said, "Would you like some tea and chicken cutlets?"

"I can have a fish kabiraji and a cup of tea. It's a long time since I ate here," Debnarayan replied.

Rahul called a waiter and placed the order.

He couldn't restrain himself any longer. "Do you need anything from me?" he asked impulsively.

Debnarayan didn't react.

Rahul was losing his patience, "I can't figure out why you wanted to meet me after all these years. By the way can I smoke?"

"Please go ahead. It's complex. Actually, I wanted to talk to you. I wanted to tell you something."

"Tell me."

It was a relief to be able to smoke. The food was served. Rahul and Debnarayan began to eat.

Rahul asked, "Do you like the fish?" Debnarayan nodded. "It's oily. But the fish is fresh. The mustard sauce is very good. I am in touch with my roots after a long time."

Rahul reminded him that he was supposed to tell him something. Debnarayan hesitated, as though he were buying time, "It's always difficult to start," he said.

Rahul chipped in almost contemptuously, "What is it? If you are trying to explain your running away, don't bother."

"Rahul, it has nothing to do with my explanation. I know it has been difficult for you. Your father abandoned you at an age when he should have been taking care of you. But did it ever occur to you why I did such a thing?"

Rahul replied dispassionately, "I understand family life is stifling, suffocating and boring beyond a point. Most people would like to run away but very few dare to do so. You were daring enough and you survived. I wanted to run away from Ma, too. She was sick, scarred by age, edgy and possessive. I saw her deteriorate from the fiery beauty that she was at one point in time. You couldn't match up to her demands and tantrums. I felt sorry for her. She was very insecure about losing her beauty."

Debnarayan said, "She was beautiful indeed, a rare specimen that every man wanted to conquer."

"These are just words. You can't conquer anybody. Not even a piece of land," replied Rahul.

"That's true. But you don't know these things when you are young."

"She loved being pampered by men – intelligent, good looking and powerful men. She destroyed many men. I've seen that with my own eyes. I understand it could have been hell putting up with her, day and night. A mistress like that might bring an exciting shade to your life, make you feel like you are riding against the wind. But a wife – oh no! I understand all that. I don't blame you."

Debnarayan did not expect this kind of maturity from Rahul. "You understand quite a lot, Rahul. After your Ma died of chronic liver failure, you married too, didn't you? I know. It didn't last long. "

Rahul was finding it hard to keep his cool, "Did you do research on me? My wife died in a road accident a few years after our marriage. I would have left her anyway."

Debnarayan chipped in, "She could have left you too!"

"Actually, she wanted to leave me because she thought I was perverse. She advised me to go to a brothel to satiate my lust. I took her advice and found what good sluts can do to your mind. They can open your heart. They can drown the pettiness and meanness within you. That's what good whores can do to you. You need to cultivate them over a period of time. You can face the world and its vagaries with a harem in your backyard. Don't you think so?"

Debnarayan said, "Your competitors say you got your wife killed because she was sleeping with your servant."

"Such stories make me laugh. How do you know so much about me? Have you been doing your homework for this meeting?"

"You became too famous too early for you and others to handle. Much is written about your personal life. It's quite fascinating. Your love for old buildings, monuments and old cities is legendary. Most of your work that I see on television revolves around this love. "

"I feel calmed by ancient settings. I detest the straight lines and angles of modernity. I abhor light and sterility. And I get turned on by fat women. Isn't this what's written about me? It's true. I confirm it." Rahul ranted.

Debnarayan said reflectively "You're a reflection of your mother."

"Is that bad? How can you run away from your mother? Do I have nothing that can be traced back to you?"

"Nilima didn't try to trace me, I know that. Did she ever refer to me? Do you remember anything?"

"She used to look at your photographs, specially the ones on horseback in Darjeeling. She was forgetting things as she grew old. She was a hard drinker and a chocolate addict. She was a chatterbox. She read a lot of intellectual stuff. She partied hard. She chased men, and men chased her. She was so busy running that she hardly settled down. But when she fell ill she abused you for all her miseries. She remembered you fondly at times, but that was very rare. "

"Did she take good care of you?"

Rahul gave him the complete picture. "Well I grew up among servants and maids. In a way, I'm grateful it happened that way. I learnt a few enduring life-skills and experienced unfettered pleasure very early on in life. However, it would have been nice to have a caring mother and father. I felt like an orphan, abandoned in a large mansion full of memories. A crumbling structure where a woman and many men played their games of sex and a group of servants and maids took care of this abandoned boy. But Ma never allowed me to go away or even move too far away from her. I had to be within sight. She returned to me at least once in the night and rested her tired face on my chest while I faked sleep. She listened to me attentively and didn't prevent me from mixing with our servants or for that matter, anyone else. In fact, she died on my lap. And I'm happy that nobody suggested that I killed her."

After a while Rahul asked, "Do you see anything of yourself in me?"

Debnarayan said reflectively, "How would that be possible Rahul?"

"Why?"

Debnarayan explained, "I've been away for so long. We've hardly known each other."

Rahul smiled faintly. "I thought genetic connections are stronger than matters of social association. Well, it confirms the fact that I'm not like you. I must clarify that this is not a sentimental issue with me but only a matter of curiosity."

Debnarayan looked pale and drained. His face seemed sinister as the purple veins below his pale skin jutted out like snakes. He was fidgety and ill at ease. Rahul feared that Debnarayan might throw up or suddenly get up and rush out of that claustrophobic space.

He sensed that Debnarayan was groaning. Was he trying to say something – a dangerous truth, which he had held within the recesses of his soul and now wanted to reveal to Rahul? He had been able to act nonchalant all this while but Rahul didn't think he could do so any longer.

Debnarayan was here on a larger mission that concerned him, and Rahul was apprehensive. He had survived so far by surrendering to a life of banality. He had a life that was glitzy, where he earned fame, money, and power. Memories of his mother enlivened Rahul. They also infuriated him. He didn't look at women's faces for too long, fearing that he might see his mother in them. So, he would pounce on them to erase any streak of that image. But he knew that his mother was deeply embedded in him, somewhere in the subterranean spaces of his being and he could emerge from that shadow only by continually hurting himself in darkness in a quest for salvation.

What did he say to excite such an agonising response from Debnarayan? Rahul put his left hand on Debnarayan's right shoulder and gently massaged his collarbones. There was hardly any flesh on his body. He said softly, "Are you feeling uncomfortable and hot? We can take a walk. The air should be cold and light at this hour."

Debnarayan removed Rahul's hand from his shoulder and whispered, "Rahul, Bhabatosh Sanyal wants to meet you in private. I've given him my word." If Rahul was puzzled, he didn't show it. "What has Bhabatosh Sanyal got to do with you and me?" he asked.

Debnarayan looked at Rahul, "He was your mother's closest friend at one point in time."

Rahul reacted aggressively, "That doesn't give him any rights over me. I resent this man and his deeds. You've made a grave mistake by giving your word without talking to me."

Debnarayan pleaded "He's your father, Rahul. He's a very powerful man today. But that's beside the point. He's married to a woman who could not give him a child and the thought of leaving this world without an heir is causing him tremendous agony. He wants to meet you and accept you as his son irrespective of what that might do to his political career."

Rahul was aghast. "Hold on, hold on, are you now telling me these sick stories to shock the shit out of me! I don't care."

"I've no reason to tell you stories. Unfortunately, I made a mess of my life travelling to various corners of the world. I was driven by my wistful youth. I re-married in Africa and had children. Financially, I was a shambles. I kept losing jobs before migrating to France. I met Bhabatosh there, a few years ago. He was on an official trip with a senior government delegation. I sought his help and he practically rehabilitated me with a job and a house in Pondicherry. I'm indebted to him in many ways. He didn't know about you. On one of his visits to Pondicherry we went fishing. He told me about his fate in a moment of weakness. Overwhelmed with gratitude by his kindness towards me, I told him about you. His desperation and childlike insistence were amazing. I gave him my word that I would get you to meet him."

Rahul's brow was furrowed in disbelief and his face seemed to shrink at the betrayal. "Can you tell me everything in detail?" he asked.

Debnarayan narrated everything to Rahul, "Bhabatosh was involved in Naxalite politics during his college days. He was an excellent orator and a popular leader. He had a massive fan following especially amongst women. Your mother and he went to the same college. She was his junior by two years. She accompanied him on his village treks working among peasants and guerrillas. The intoxication of rebellion and the company of a handsome man who lived dangerously thrilled her. They had a tempestuous relationship for three years till the police caught him. Well, your mother had very little interest in politics and didn't care for a lifestyle that was not comfortable. But she was absolutely in love with Bhabatosh and was pregnant with you when he went to jail. Your maternal grandfather was a famous barrister. Your mother pleaded with him to fight the case but he refused. I was an assistant to your grandfather and watched all this from the sidelines. Your mother slipped into depression and had terrible mood swings. Your grandfather refused to take her to a doctor lest it hurt his social standing and prestige. He was furious enough to think of killing her when he came to know that she was pregnant.

I rescued Nilima. It was not very easy to arrange for an abortion in those days. We came to an agreement and Nilima and I were married in a splendid ceremony. Gradually she settled down to a life that was quite beyond my grasp. I heard later that your maternal grandmother died early. She had turned completely mad by the time she took leave of the world. What I mean is madness runs congenitally in this family! Well, Nilima was normal in the conventional sense but the disillusionment after Bhabatosh's arrest aroused another facet of her personality. I felt imprisoned and caged but I was smitten by her beauty and hoped that she would return to me one day. I took care of you as though you were my own child, played with you and helped you with your studies. But Nilima didn't notice my loyalty and devotion for she was blinded by her love. There was a change of government after the Emergency. Political prisoners were granted amnesty and Bhabatosh was released. Your grandfather had died by this time. I was so insecure that I ran away. Once he was out of jail, Bhabatosh went into political hibernation for six years, travelling around the world and convalescing. He rejoined politics, this time with the ruling party, and rose year after year to a position of power and influence. He was married to the daughter of an influential politician, a minister in that government. Contrary to what I had expected, your mother never chased Bhabatosh again, nor did he make an attempt to find her. She was, by that time, surrounded by a group of fawning parasites who fed on her wealth and ageing beauty. Nilima and Bhabatosh were thus living two different lives – one was an embodiment of utter madness while the other was an epitome of cunning sanity."

By the time he finished his story Debnarayan was wheezing and panting for breath. He seemed exhausted by the effort. Rahul was caught in a whirlpool of emotions that shattered his calm. He had never heard his mother, or anyone else in the house, mention Bhabatosh Sanyal. He hated himself for having agreed to this meeting, thus jeopardising his control on his life. He'd had an ominous feeling that the meeting would churn up unpleasant memories but he hadn't expected this. After a while Rahul asked calmly, "Did he come to know of me from you or was he already aware of my existence?"

Debnarayan answered, "He told me he was not aware. I've no reason to disbelieve him."

"What do you think he wants from me, now?"

Debnarayan's voice had dropped to a whisper, "I feel it comforts him to know that he has a son. Maybe he wants to see his reflection in you, hold your hand and feel wanted. As you grow old you tend to feel distanced from the happenings of your own life. It's then that your grown-up children can affect you very strongly. It's like looking at the woods from the opposite bank. The jungle looks mysterious and you are struck with amazement how time can convert a single seed into such dense foliage. Bhabatosh is powerful and rich. But he is as lonely and sad as anyone else. He was moved when I told him the story and wanted my help to reach you."

Rahul was gaining some control of the situation, and said exasperatedly "I don't care who my father is. If I could live without him for so many years I can live without him now. What I know of Bhabatosh is that he's a ruthless man. He combines Marxist ideology with market economics. He believes in the culture of propaganda and champions a kind of artistic taste that calls itself socially relevant. He is a philosopher and practitioner par excellence in the sustenance of political power on the strength of a mafia that operates in the name of liberation. All this is an old-fashioned myth. It amazes me that he is willing to take a political risk by raking up his past. He has a sly motive, I'm sure. I won't meet him. I could use this information to destroy him but I won't do that either because I'm dying of a dreaded disease. If you knew this you wouldn't sit and talk to me. Tell your Bhabatosh, who wants to flaunt his fatherhood today, that I'm dying of a disease that you get in whorehouses. Will he give me shelter after knowing this? No! Cut this crap of parenthood and all that. I'm going. I can't stand this any longer. Well, now I'm sure of dying very soon. An early death at the hands of my father's goons. I don't think he can handle the truth and risk a live torpedo in his backyard. I bet he actually checked out the details on me before he wanted to meet me and sent you as his agent. He wants to finish me, tame me, domesticate me and send me to a distant sanatorium from where I won't be able to reach him or his myth, ever. This way, he gets to cleanse his past in one master stroke. Please get this clear, whatever I am; I'm not an easy catch."

Rahul darted out of the cabin like an arrow, stopped for a moment to pay the bill and rushed out into the night. Rahul felt comforted by the fleeting thought that he might be granted a swift death. If what Debnarayan had said was true, he might not have to worry about a long, painful battle with oozing infections, pus-filled ulcers, blood loss and ceaseless fever leading to a slow death.

Random Trial

1.

Rahul felt relieved on entering Radha's chamber. A quietness settled on his soul, the likes of which he had never felt before. Radha's chamber, with its colourful plants, moist green creepers, blooming flowers in shades of burnt red and orange gave it the appearance of a bright nook in a forest. A series of oil paintings of a Santhal woman in various moods, brightly illuminated by designer fluorescent lamps, was displayed on the southern and eastern walls. The high ceiling, resting on a grid of steel and timber beams, had floral designs embossed on it. Finely polished teakwood furniture and cabinets filled with hardbound books and journals gave it the appearance of a grand library. The soft yellow lighting and thermostatically controlled air-conditioning created a magical illusion of a cool evening breeze blowing across a tranquil sea. She sat behind a majestic table positioned diagonally between the southern and eastern walls, a soft smile playing on her lips. The chamber had a red-leather couch for patients by the northern wall and ceramic flowerpots filled with fresh jasmine flowers. It was from here that Rahul had recounted the stories of his life and responded to Radha's pointed queries and comments so many times. For Rahul this room symbolised uncanny symmetry, sublime design and a safe haven, as though it was not a part of the world that he knew with all its noise and dust. It fired in him a deep longing to return again and again.

Radha studied a dossier containing Rahul's history with great concentration while he sat on the couch and looked at her expectantly. A few minutes passed, Radha turned her gaze back to Rahul and said, "Rahul, I don't think you have any problem."

Rahul was a bit perplexed. "What do you mean?"

Radha replied, "You came to me believing that there was some problem with the way you think or behave. But from whatever you've told me I believe there is no need to be concerned. I can tell you middle-aged men exhibit such behaviour at times. It's important to get on in life."

Rahul reacted sharply, "Does that mean I needn't come here anymore?"

Radha smiled, reminding Rahul of a painting of brightly coloured sunflowers, and spoke in a teasing but guarded tone, "Why do you want to keep paying my fees when you don't require my services? Besides, you would deprive someone else of an hour of therapy; someone who genuinely needs it."

Rahul fell silent. After a gap he said almost helplessly, "You don't think my sleeplessness and obsession with death are problems that require medical attention."

"They do require attention, but not necessarily medical attention. You sleep less. I think that is because you worry too much about your ailments – some of them are genuine and some, imaginary. You admit that", Radha said. "I think this will pass. Something is happening deep inside you, something fundamental in nature. Let it be, for the time being. If the situation gets worse you can come back. At your age, there is a general disillusionment that results in such behaviour. With time it will pass. The trick is to remain immersed in work, family and leisure activities."

Rahul seemed a bit dismayed; "You know I've got used to your chamber and these weekly visits. I feel so relaxed here. Will you cut me off totally?"

Radha looked embarrassed. "Come back after four weeks. We'll talk then," she said.

Rahul walked back home that evening. It was a strenuous walk through peak-time city traffic and he hoped that the exertion would induce a good night's sleep. He slept for two hours, but when he got up he was nauseous and overcome by a fear of falling from the top of a skyscraper.

2.

Rahul's wife Putul was an excellent cook. She could make Bengali, Continental and Chinese delicacies with equal élan. She could cook for at least one hundred people without compromising taste. Though she was a poor eater, Putul loved toiling over food and enjoyed the appreciation showered on her for her cooking skills. All this good food had made Rahul and their daughter Ghungroo, quite obese. Rahul had become aware of this last year and often told his daughter to eat less. But Putul always said, "Eat as much as you can digest and work out as much as your bones permit." Putul's obsession with cooking made her object to using the services of a hotel or caterer even on formal occasions. Rahul found this rather irritating. If he suggested that they celebrate in a hotel or get a caterer to serve the food, Putul would say, "You can do that. But I won't attend your goddamned party." She would cry and add, "You're such a lousy brute. You can't even praise me for my work. You get jealous of the appreciation showered on me by your colleagues and friends."

Rahul would inevitably give in, "All right, have it your way. I feel guilty that you sweat over the arrangements while others enjoy themselves. You look so involved and worried. I want you to be free so that you can also have a good time and enjoy the moment."

"But darling I'm overjoyed when I see you and the others enjoying the food I prepare with such care and imagination."

It was Ghungroo's fourteenth birthday. Putul had started cooking since the early hours of the morning. Ghungroo's school friends, some close relatives and a few neighbours were invited to the party. Rahul generally invited his office colleagues on such occasions, but this year he said that most of them were travelling on work. When Putul insisted that their families be invited because a precedent was already set, Rahul refused. Rahul left office after lunch, that day, and walked aimlessly about the city for a couple of hours. He returned home sweating profusely, his knees throbbing in pain. He had a quick shower, slipped into freshly-ironed clothes and was ready to receive the guests.

There was a strange viral fever raging in the city at that time. It was featured in the newspapers, TV channels and everyone kept discussing it. Rahul was anxious as the fever had claimed a couple of lives in the suburbs. He ensured that all the windows in the house were open and the fans were switched on at full speed to keep the house well ventilated. He planned the movements of the guests in advance to reduce the chances of viral transmission. He tried to find out if any of the invitees or their family members had been suffering from any kind of fever in the recent months. He breathed a sigh of relief to know that they hadn't. Putul and Ghunghroo tried to ensure that Rahul would not get agitated unnecessarily. "Had any of them been seriously ill you would have known, wouldn't you?" he asked his wife and daughter. "Of course, darling," Putul replied instantly soothing his fears. "Of course, baba," said Ghungroo.

She wore a new, black skirt and a sleeveless cotton blouse that evening. Her long, thick hair was drawn back in a tight bun. Rahul looked at his daughter carefully and grew worried. She'd grown quite big and tall; she was still slightly overweight, despite being on a diet for some time now. In fact, she was an immensely charming and attractive adolescent, quite unlike her mother. A few uncomfortable questions crept into his mind but he brushed them aside.

Gradually, the house filled with guests. People were talking animatedly, children ran and screamed and loud music was being played in one of the rooms. Putul was looking for something, gifts were being opened recklessly and Ghungroo was calling her friends into her room. The smell of food, mingled with the smell of talcum powder and perfume hung heavy in the air. The balloons and crepe paper streamers hanging from the ceiling gave the house a festive look. Rahul went from one room to the other, speaking to the guests, making tentative gestures and moving on. Once the cake was cut and food served from a makeshift buffet, people settled down in groups. Putul was an amiable hostess. She saw to it that everyone was eating contentedly, and was flush with all the appreciation.

Finally a small group settled down with imported wine and tobacco and their conversation slowly meandered to the growing spurt of illicit relationships in every home. Gargi, one of Putul's friends, insisted that women were equally assertive of their sexuality and quoted urban statistics to prove her point. Everyone seemed to be enjoying the discussion and Rahul, standing slightly apart, was able to gather the drift.

"With excessive consumption relationships become fragile."

"Who is thinking of a relationship these days? Everyone wants a quickie, so that they can move ahead and then forget everything. Everyone needs more of everything."

"Craving for material things and building assets is what everyone wants."

"There is despair and desolation everywhere. Just see the news to see how gory civil society is turning out to be."

"There is war on TV. There are riots on TV. There are unreal reality shows on TV. Greed is being packaged and propagated like never before. There is nothing private or intimate anymore."

"Man is an animal after all. We are only getting what we deserve."

"And women?"

"They're worse!"

"A man experiences an orgasm and then forgets. What happens to a woman?"

"Doesn't a woman reach an orgasm?"

"A man is incapable of making a woman experience such bliss. As if you never knew that."

"We need mindless sex, athletic sex to forget things at the end of the day."

Rahul heard Putul's voice in the end. It was calm and composed. "But a woman's sexuality is burdened by menstrual cycles and maternity. A married woman experiences other complex losses. She changes her house. She changes her name. All these cast a complex shadow on her sexuality. Yet I don't know whether I realise what it is to feel uniquely like a woman, because I don't know what it is to feel like a man." Rahul was impressed by the sincerity in Putul's words. For a moment he wondered if he knew Putul enough to gauge her essence.

Soon the party was over. As Rahul was falling asleep he touched his forehead and was relieved that he was not running temperature.

3.

Three years ago, Rahul and his friends Sujoy, Shantanu and Raghu watched Satyajit Ray's *Aranyer Din Ratri* together in a multiplex. While discussing the film in a tea-shop, the four friends decided to take a short holiday together every year, like the protagonists in the movie. They planned a trip to the forest in winter to reconnect with the essence of their existence. They decided that they would not inform their wives about such outings, but would say that they were going on some urgent official trip. This arrangement had been continuing over the last three years.

This year they had gone to a forest on a mountainous plateau on the borders of Bengal and Orissa. They stayed in a dilapidated guesthouse belonging to the Forest Department and spent four nights there the week before Christmas. They had to cook their own food because the labour force and the peasantry in the area were involved in an agitation against the police and administration and had ceased work.

On the second evening they sat by a mountain stream enjoying the mellow sunshine and the chill. They smoked cannabis, which they had carried from Kolkata. The surroundings were wrapped in deep silence broken by the low humming of mountain insects.

Sujoy opened the conversation, lost in thought. "Do you guys want to live long?" he asked. It was not his voice but the intensity of Sujoy's question that aroused the others from the dungeons of their private worlds. They looked at Sujoy blankly, not knowing how to answer such a question.

Shantanu said, "I think we live much of our lives without knowing we are alive."

Raghu seemed to be in two minds. "Is it possible not to want that? Everyone wants to be immortal."

Rahul asserted, "We know we are not immortal. Yet, we aspire to be immortal."

Shantanu gave a different dimension to the idea, "May be not in the physical sense always, but at least we want a life beyond death, to exist even after we have perished," he said.

Sujoy sighed, "We exert so much to achieve that."

"But I wish to die at times," Raghu said.

"When?"

"When I'm sad and down. It's the same with everybody; I suppose."

"Maybe. But I've seen politicians, administrators and scientists take great pride in working towards prolonging man's life. Countries even display statistics to prove that various technological developments have made it possible for their people to live longer," Sujoy added.

Shantanu couldn't quite understand where the conversation was leading. "Yes, so?"

"Is it possible to live a happier life by living longer?" was Sujoy's question.

"Is it possible to live a happier life if life were shorter?" Rahul put in.

Raghu said, "That's a good counterpoint."

"I don't know. I suspect there is something fundamentally wrong with our natural instinct to live long."

"But there is so much death everywhere around us."

Shantanu asked, "You mean the deaths that we undergo while living, Rahul?"

"No, I mean real deaths – that is, when we cease to exist."

Raghu raised a relevant issue, "It's so paradoxical. Statistics show that we are living longer than in the past whereas you say there are deaths everywhere. What kind of error is that?"

"That could be unhappiness or being ill at ease with your own life," Sujoy interpreted.

Shantanu rephrased, "You mean boredom."

Sujoy elaborated, "It's like waiting longer. The longer you live, the longer you wait."

"Wait? But wait for what?" Shantanu asked.

It was Rahul's turn to answer, "For something magical to happen, to uplift us to a world of imagined happiness without our having to exert ourselves."

Sujoy asked an unexpected question, "Do you guys have secrets?"

Shantanu answered for everyone, "Everyone does."

Sujoy asked him, "Do you have any?"

There was a sudden spell of silence as though something was suffocating them. It was getting darker and colder. The humming of insects had grown intense. There was a strange mix of light and darkness settling on the jungle. They continued smoking one cigarette after another.

Sujoy asked again, "Shantanu, do you have any secrets?"

Shantanu answered, "Yes, I do."

"If you share yours I will share mine," Raghu said, trying to persuade him to talk.

"It's a good time to share secrets, by the way. The ambience is that of a confessional. Our faces are getting blurred, the darkness is our confessional veil," Rahul said.

Sujoy dared them, "Who will speak first?"

Shantanu asked, "What is a secret?"

Rahul defined it, "Something one attempts to hide from others, I suppose."

"Is there anything that we want to hide from ourselves?"

"Lots, Raghu," said Rahul. "We try to forget things quite often, don't we?"

"I repeat my original question, who will share his secrets first?"

Shantanu volunteered, "I will."

"Go on."

"In paper eight of our part two exams I copied all the answers from Ranjana's paper. She sat in front of me. But she failed while I passed the exam with sixty-one marks. I don't know how this happened. I have not told anyone this. Once the results were out, we quarrelled bitterly and Ranjana and I went our separate ways."

Rahul asked, "Do you feel guilty?"

"In a way, yes. I probably used the quarrel to walk out of that relationship."

Raghu queried, "Were you seeing someone else already?"

"No. Ranjana had grown bitter because of her failure. She was melancholic. I felt suffocated by all that."

Sujoy exclaimed, "You selfish bastard! ... We'll go clock-wise. Raghu, you are next in line."

Raghu began his story, "My father used to beat my mother. I had seen that a couple of times. It is good that he died before I grew into an adolescent, or he would have died at my hands. Whenever I used to see or hear my mother being mauled I would feel helpless. But I never cried. I used to wish that my father would die a horrible and painful death! But the day he actually died, I cried and felt weak, very weak and despondent. And that affected my relationship with my mother."

Sujoy asked, "Does she still remember that?"

"Oh yes, she does. Even when I go to meet her nowadays she rakes up the issue on some pretext or the other. Come on Sujoy, it's your turn now."

Sujoy shared his secret, "It happened long back in college; it was in the third year, if I remember correctly. I used to visit the Indian Museum, at least twice a week in the mornings posing as a guide. I would pursue young, female foreigners for I was convinced that these girls would be willing to sleep with me. At last after countless efforts I made friends with an ugly, hairy Polish female and had sex with her in a cheap Sudder Street hotel. She was very clumsy and awkward and dry. It was a bloody painful experience, my first ever. I was so randy at first but it was over within seconds because I was so excited. I was overcome by a terrible desire to kill myself and burn the world."

Shantanu pitied him, "Was it that bad?"

"It was horrible, man. She was smelly and her skin was dotted with ghoulish spots. But I was triggered by madness. I had feverishly imagined the darkness of a woman's insides – the shape, size, texture and smell – almost a billion times by then. In a way, this was a grounding experience; it made me quieter."

Rahul added, "Desire fogs our sense of balance and survival. It's good that this happened before AIDS became so widespread. "

Sujoy looked at Rahul and said, "Yes, that was a relief, of course. And, now the clock comes full circle. Rahul, speak up man."

Rahul began slowly, "I had once sneaked into my elder sister's study when she was supposed to be taking lessons from her tutor. I found her doing everything apart from studying. They were alarmed to see me there and my sister ordered me out. I was so furious that I pounced on her and began to strangle her. Meanwhile, that swine, the tutor, fled, fearing a public scandal. My sister started wailing. My mother rushed into the room. My sister was gasping for air and was terribly traumatised. We took her to the hospital but she was scarred for life. She lives in an asylum now."

Raghu asked surprised, "You have a sister?"

"Yes ... I think we should return now. It's very dark and cold out here."

They were intoxicated and disoriented from too much nicotine and cannabis. They got up slowly and walked up the steep incline pitted with sprouts of grass and moss. They felt dizzy with the effort but they continued talking as they moved through the dark moonless night.

Raghu broke the silence, "Do you think the elephants are roaming around freely now?"

Shantanu said, "They don't come out so soon. I am not so sure about the Maoists, of course!"

"The Maoists can't do us any harm. We're not against a classless society. We're not landlords or bank owners, either," Sujoy said.

"How would they know that? We look rich. They could kidnap us and ask for ransom from our families and employers." Raghu's mind was always filled with fantastic ideas.

Rahul quietened him, "Shut up man. Even trees have ears."

"Coming to think of it, there is so much poverty everywhere," Raghu said. "Do you think this war of the jungles can turn the tide for the landless and the dispossessed?"

Rahul asked, "Do you think a war can bring democracy to a despotic country?"

Raghu argued, "They are not similar wars."

Shantanu explained, "Yes, that's because they are fought from the two ends of the same spectrum. There are other wars being fought all the time."

"If you view from the top it's an eternal battlefront my dear. You can't adopt nature as it is because that would mean death."

Shantanu went on, "We, all through our lives, continue building our private empires. Our innermost desire is to have absolute control, a control that can run its writ even after our deaths. This starts all the battles."

Rahul made the final remark, "The longer you live, the longer you wait."

Silence followed. There were the hushed sounds of four men walking cautiously, through a rocky terrain. The whole area was dark and the scattered stars beyond the low clouds could not light up the earth. They reached the guesthouse at last. And arranged for some candles and planned to eat whatever was readily available. They finally settled for bread, boiled eggs and tea, followed by another round of cannabis which made their heads reel.

It was past midnight when Rahul went to bed. He dreamt of a young Putul sitting on a rock beside a lake. She was playing a cello and gazing at the mountain. He saw Radha sitting on a tree, listening to his stories about football matches played on water-logged grasslands. He saw a crowd of dark-skinned tribals chasing him with bows and arrows. His boss was puking in a conference hall, while Rahul was flying across the world. He flew over Agra, Cairo and Jerusalem, over Iceland and the Caspian Sea and then fell into the crater of a dormant volcano where he found a harem of the choicest whores from many lands. He smiled in his sleep because he had not parted with any of his deepest secrets. He also knew that Shantanu, Sujoy and Raghu hadn't done so, too.

4.

It was a lovely, Sunday morning in winter. Rahul and Putul were drinking tea and enjoying the bright sunshine and the view of the garden outside their living room. Putul reached for Rahul's hands and massaged them softly. "I want to tell you something," she said.

"What?"

"I've written a novel."

"A novel?"

"Yes, a novel. You asked me to start writing again, remember? You hoped that it would distract me and keep me from cooking, an activity that you dislike," Putul said.

"That's not true. I asked you to write because you write well and your narrative skills are first rate. Won't you show me the manuscript?"

"Of course, I will. You will be my first reader, my most important reader, Rahul. Always."

"What's the novel about?"

"I don't want to tell you, it will kill the suspense. Read it yourself."

"I will. Tell me the outline, at least."

Putul looked out over the garden summarising the novel in her head. "It's a story about a man and two women; one is a lady-chef and the other a psychiatrist. Both women are in love with this man, who is a marketing wizard. The man loves them both. Their relationship is divided into two parts – one, the first ten years when the man makes all the moves to win both women and enjoy their company and their bodies. And two, the last ten years when both the women, having reached the pinnacle of their careers, want to get married to him. He still enjoys their company but he doesn't want to marry either of them.

He is intoxicated by the progress he has made in his career and wants to establish himself as a marketing-cum-spiritual guru. He has, of course, been successful in keeping the two women unaware of each other's existence and conducts his amorous liaisons with both of them in a clandestine manner. He becomes an over-hyped guru among the rich and the famous over the years.

After ten years, in part two of the book, the three of them cross each other's paths in an international airport terminal that gets blown up by terrorists. The story ends there."

Rahul asked, "Do all three die in this attack?"

"Yes."

"It's a sad, yet interesting story. I can't wait to read it."

"All stories sound interesting when summarised."

"Who is your alter-ego among these three characters?"

Putul told him honestly, "I'm an outsider. I don't belong to the story."

Rahul was impressed. He said, "The story sounds much like a Pedro Almodovar film. How did you get to the core plot?"

"One morning many years ago, I was looking at a heap of vegetables lying on the kitchen table. I saw two capsicums and a tomato – their luscious bodies looked violent, in conflicting shades of green and red. That is when the first seed was planted in my mind. At first, it came and went, like a phantom on a swing. Later, I built a coherent story with detailed events. It happened over a period of time. Coming back to the inspirational vegetables – I sliced them neatly and used the slices to make a filling for one of your sandwiches. The terrorist attack was inspired by the destruction of the cooked food that occurs during the process of eating. I don't know if it sounds intelligent enough ..."

Putul sat very close to Rahul and kissed him passionately. This was happening after a very long time. Rahul felt that Putul had grown quite distant over the years. He was not very confident about her. The story of her novel flashed through his mind. He wanted to read it at once for he knew that shreds of evidence about her character were likely to be strewn in the text and this could help him unmask her real essence.

5.

Rahul finished reading the novel written by Putul. It was taut and racy and gripped him with such force that he completely forgot everything else. He was glad to find that the characters and events in the novel had little resemblance to her life. Yet, many questions welled up in his mind. Could she be leading a secret life? She had written the novel secretly, without his knowledge but it would be very difficult for her to lead a secret life. This clearly meant that she had a very vivid imagination. Was it possible to understand a person from the way she behaved? Rahul suddenly wanted to talk to Radha. He called her chamber. She came on the line finally and agreed to meet him in her chamber that evening.

As he walked into Radha's room Rahul was anxious and his stomach fluttered. Radha said calmly, "Tell me."

"I have a low grade fever."

"So? I'm not a physician who can cure physical ailments. You know that; don't you?"

"Thought I must inform you."

Rahul looked at the floral designs. Radha said, "You wanted to tell me something?"

"I wanted to ask you for your forgiveness. I mean this sincerely. I know this may not be enough."

Radha was taken aback by the sudden shift in the conversation. She exclaimed, "Forgiveness? What do you mean?"

"I know I violated you when you were young, very young, a minor," he said.

"I think you're getting mixed up. I've never met you before you came to me for treatment. So the question of your violating me does not arise." Rahul took no notice of what Radha said.

"Radha, I'm grievously guilty. Don't hush things up. You're a decade younger to me. When I was studying in college I used to go to your house. I was dating your elder sister Putul. One day, I saw you playing in the backyard. You looked like a wild puppy. You were thirteen. I remember. I took you in my arms, threw you up in the air and you erupted in gurgles of laughter. You smelled so nice and fresh that I rested my head on your bosom and felt like disrobing you. I kissed you but you ran into the house leaving me despondent with desire. I caught hold of you in your room, once. You wore a translucent green frock. I tried to lift the hem of your frock to look at your nakedness. You stood there crying helplessly. Someone entered the room and I couldn't proceed with what I had wanted to do. God was kind, in a way. You were saved and I was not caught. You kept quiet, out of shame and guilt. A few days later, you were packed off to a boarding school far away from the city. I forgot about this incident and went on with my life. You never talked to me later, except at social functions where you maintained a safe distance. You and Putul went your separate ways because of a family dispute. But frankly Radha, I've now been overpowered by an acute sense of guilt. Ghungroo, reminds me of you. She is very beautiful and I'm terrified at the thought that a monster like me can maul her and damage her innocent soul. That's why I thought of meeting you and seeking your forgiveness for what I did. Radha, will you forgive me?"

Radha tried to bring him to his senses, "Rahul, I'm your therapist and not your sister-in-law."

Radha understood that he was in a state of delirium and very depressed.

Rahul had a distant look in his eyes. He had difficulty focusing his vision. "Yes, you're my therapist. I got

confused by your name and your appearance," he said.
"Are you truly my therapist, Radha? You treat me as if
I'm a liability, a grave sinner. You want to throw me out
of your chamber, but I keep latching on to you."

Radha got up from her chair silently, and sat down
beside him on the couch. She took his hands in hers and
said in a sincere voice, "Rahul you're ill. I was wrong the
last time. I'll recommend you to a doctor who can treat
you properly."

Rahul's face turned pale. He said, "Am I such a sinner
that you can't even treat me? I know I've done something
very wrong, a grave sin for which no punishment would
be good enough. I'll rot and burn in hell."

Radha was crying. "Where is your sister-in-law now?"
she asked.

"Radha lives in New Zealand. I've not seen her for
years. Why are you crying?"

"It's difficult to explain. You've got me all wrong. The
day you first came to me I saw in your eyes a darkness,
which I don't remember having seen earlier. As time
passed, I was attracted to you. I have a family. You have
one too. Ethically and professionally, I can't treat a patient
with whom I get personally involved. So the first reaction
was to send you away. You wanted to come to me
repeatedly, not because of what I am but possibly because
I provided you with a pair of non-judgmental ears. The
intense darkness in your eyes reflects the turmoil in your
conscience. I fell in love with you almost instantly and I
still love you in spite of your offences. But I can't heal
you. I know that guilt causes acute depression which
manifests itself in other physical disorders and the
underlying cause is often forgotten. I suggest that you
write to Radha and tell her how you feel about the past. I
hope she understands you."

Rahul was doubtful, "Can she misuse this letter, show
it to Putul and destroy my family life?"

Radha said, "She can. But I don't think she will. Well,
I don't know her, so my answer is based on pure instinct."

"Radha, you're a marvellous woman. Putul is an
enigma to me till today. She is a very good writer and

storyteller. She has written a novel recently. I've not been able to understand her clearly to this day. At times, she is an angel and at other times a demon. She has been inconsistent all her life. I've always craved her attention and appreciation, but I've also been attracted to other women. There were times when I felt completely run down and suffocated by her towering personality. I could not attempt so many things in life because of her, so I constantly blame her for that. But in the end, I can't do without her," Rahul said helplessly.

"That's love, Rahul. It throws you ruthlessly against sharp outcrops of rock, makes you bleed yet you don't mind the suffering. Putul must be an amazing woman to have been able to captivate you for so long. I feel terribly jealous."

Rahul told Radha, "She is a good cook, you know. But I can't talk to her the way I talk to you. Can I continue coming to you?"

"No. I can't keep seeing you and not being in complete possession. I feel like being with you always. But that would hurt you further. It would hurt me too. I read somewhere that there are a few stories in life that never begin. Yet, they cast an impression stronger than the stories that get completed in a lifetime."

The intercom was buzzing. Radha said, "It's time for the next patient. I'll send you the name and contact details of a psychiatrist whom you should consult henceforth."

6.

Rahul and Putul were locked in each other's arms that night. They looked at a pale moon floating behind a patch of grey clouds. Rahul asked all of a sudden, "Putul, who are you?"

Putul was startled. "What kind of a question is that?" she asked.

Rahul stammered, "I mean, tell me which character resembles you the most in your novel?"

There was a twinkle in Putul's eyes. "Nobody. I

fabricated all of them; they belong to my imaginary world."

"You mean to say there are no real characters in your novel."

"There are. You are there, too. You know, I received two interesting phone calls today."

"Radha called from Auckland this afternoon. She is coming to India for some research and wants to stay with us for a week."

"What did you say?"

"I said she could stay for as long as she liked. What else could I say? She is coming with her South African boyfriend," Putul replied.

"That will be too much of a crowd, don't you think? I thought you two had parted ways forever."

Putul smiled. "Of course, not. Sisterly rivalry can't last a lifetime, my dear. Thank god it was not over a man. Radha's boyfriend is a publisher. I think, I can show him my manuscript and get his opinion."

Rahul said encouragingly, "Yes, you should. Who knows, he might even get it published!"

"That's expecting too much! Have you noticed how Ghungroo has begun to resemble Radha these days?"

"Maybe she does. I haven't noticed anything."

Putul seemed tense and worried, "Somehow, I remain very anxious about her. She attracts men and boys so naturally! Have you seen that Raghu chasing her? He even calls her his Lolita."

Rahul couldn't believe what Putul had just said, "Come on, that's an innocent joke, Putul!"

"You won't understand. I've asked Ghungroo not to pay attention to him. I've an eerie feeling about that guy. He has an eye for young girls. Just look at his eyes whenever Ghungroo is around, they're full of lust."

Rahul asserted, "That's, too much, Putul!"

"Won't you protect your daughter from a child molester?"

"Oh my god, you're trading serious charges!" Rahul exclaimed, "Well if he's one, I won't leave him, Putul! But I'm certain he is not what you think him to be."

"All right, next time he's in the house I'll show you how he behaves with her. Narayan called me today. You remember the boy who topped our batch in Presidency? His sister, also called Radha, is a renowned psychiatrist. She's married to the CEO of a multinational publishing company. I had told Narayan about my novel. He has not read it but it seems he has already talked to Radha and her husband about the novel. Narayan has asked for a copy of the manuscript and wants me to meet Radha and her husband."

"What did you say?"

Putul ran her fingers through Rahul's hair. "I said, let them read the novel first and if they feel, it is worth publishing, I will organise a multi-cuisine dinner in our house to celebrate the occasion with Narayan and his family. I have, of course, added a caveat: let this idea of mine be seen as jest and not as an attempt at emotional blackmail!"

"That's good. Very good!"

Putul put her head on his shoulder. "Coming back to your original question, who am I? Do you think you have any idea?"

Rahul kissed her lightly on her forehead before answering jokingly, "Oh yes. You're a cannibal of a warden in a god-forsaken jail. I'm the only inmate in its solitary confinement. Imagine!"

Putul whispered "There's hardly any respect in your voice for your jail warden. That's too bad. Your warden takes good care of you, no? She can't consider sharing you with the world. That's a crime; she doesn't mind committing over and over again."

Rahul kept quiet and slowly slid his right hand between the soft confines of her legs. Putul made sounds of delight and pleasure. The night was still and airless. Rahul saw the disconnected events of his life floating around like cotton balls, unable to fathom their significance.

The Reunion

1.

Rahul was reading the newspaper at the breakfast table while munching on cucumber sandwiches, a bowl of fresh fruit and home-made curd. Sana had left for school; in summer her school started at 7.30 in the morning. Leila was eating fat-free corn flakes with curd and sipping on a glass of chilled milk as she read a literary journal. Rahul and Leila spent most of their time reading. They rarely spoke to each other these days, except when they were fighting.

Rahul was a chartered accountant and a senior partner in a financial consultancy firm owned by his father's friend. Leila was associate professor of education in the oldest university of the city and a regular columnist with an English daily. She wrote on serious political and moral issues. She was a controversial writer because of her unconventional views on war, terrorism, family, industrialisation and education.

Sana, their daughter, was eleven years old. She studied in an English-medium missionary school famous for churning out movie stars in the past. Sana was very talkative, smart and well-informed for her age. She surfed the Internet, watched television and constantly overheard the maids, servants and drivers gossiping amongst themselves. She had already been in and out of love a number of times. She loved being admired for her beauty and exceptional cycling skills.

"I'll be late today. We have a conference at a client's place. I'll have dinner there. Don't wait for me," Rahul said as he finished his breakfast.

"A client? As far as I know, you have only one client. That soul-corrupting lifestyle company, headed by Gargi, who wants to jump into bed with you at every opportunity!" Leila said curtly.

"Don't start this all over again. For god's sake, stop spying on me. Gargi would never sleep with me. She has film industry hunks at her beck and call. Why the hell would she fancy me? Our firm advises her on investment matters, you know that, and I'm doing my job on behalf of my firm," Rahul snapped.

But Leila wouldn't let go so easily. "Don't lie, Rahul. Naren*kaku* said that he had initially assigned the work to Biren. But it was Gargi who insisted on having you manage her affairs."

"What the hell am I supposed to do if my client prefers me to that smart-ass Biren? If Gargi insisted on me it's because I'm a better accountant and financial consultant than he is."

Leila said mockingly, "Lots of people in your office have seen you and Gargi in compromising positions when you are having those one-to-one meetings with her in your chamber. Your secretary Sankar as well as Biren have confirmed this. Now tell me, are they wrong?"

"I don't need to tell you anything because you are a nymphomaniac yourself and so you believe that every other woman is like you," Rahul said disgustedly. "You are able to get nasty things out of people's mouths, which are invariably against me. They know what you want to hear so they speak accordingly, plying you with lies. I agree Gargi has style and an aggressive way of doing things. But, I think it would be below her dignity to behave like that."

Leila's voice was scathing, "Your springing to her defence shows what you guys have cooked up over the years. By the way, what moral authority do you have to call me a nymphomaniac? I told you very clearly I need unconventional sex, didn't I? You just failed to satisfy me because you are a bloody accountant and not an artist. Artists know how to handle a woman's body. Only they can make a woman scream with pleasure."

"All right. I have never objected to your seeking unconventional sex with artists. Why are you so possessive about me, then?"

"I'm not possessive about you, Rahul. I get mad at you. You've systematically deprived me of pleasure. It's something you've kept reserved for your girl friends and one-night stands. When your intentions became clear, I sought pleasure from others and got it."

"Get it and now get out. I've got to go to work. I don't have time for your twisted justifications. Let's get this straight. You don't like sleeping with me. I don't like sleeping with you. But we have a daughter, three houses, four cars, a solid bank balance and other assets. We can behave like responsible adults and get on with our individual lives in peace, can't we?"

Leila stormed out of the house. "Come late, very late tonight because after Sana goes to sleep I'm going to call Amit and Sekhar, the two young artists who are doing my nude study in oil and woodcut. Their exhibition will travel all around the country very soon. I hope, you'll care to visit the Kolkata chapter, this time."

Rahul kept quiet and finished his breakfast. He took a pair of scissors and cut out a small news item on page seven. He folded it neatly and placed it in his shirt pocket to read it in detail in the car.

Ever since Rahul read the news in the morning paper he had been vexed and anxious. His face clearly revealed that he was in a dilemma. He took out the newspaper cutting and read it again:

A WOMAN KILLS HER DAUGHTER AND HUSBAND
IN A FIT OF RAGE IN NORTH KOLKATA

A woman named Bimala Sen, from a lower middle-class quarter in the northern part of the city, was arrested late last night on charges of murdering her husband and daughter. The woman, in her mid-fifties, is reported to have lost her mental balance and was prone to aggressive and hostile behaviour with her family and neighbours. She has confessed to her crime during the preliminary interrogations in police custody. The daughter, in her early thirties, was found in a thick pool of blood, with multiple wounds inflicted by a sharp knife on her chest, abdomen and face. It is believed that the girl was in a compromising position with an accomplice of her father (an alleged pimp), when her parents barged into the room. According to eye-witnesses, the man fled the scene leaving the dazed girl and her father who was immediately attacked by Bimala Sen in a fit of rage. The murder weapon has been recovered from the scene of the crime. Bimala Sen has been remanded to police custody and the lawyer provided to her by the State is likely to apply for bail soon. The extent and motive of pre-meditation is likely to be a matter of deliberation among the investigating officers and lawyers in the days to come.

Rahul considered the newspaper report for a long time and wondered whether this was the same Bimala Sen he had known some twenty years ago.

2.

It became increasingly difficult for Rahul to concentrate on his work in office. In the mornings he was usually busy in analysing share market reports and estimating the resultant gains and losses his clients had endured the previous day. Accordingly, he would issue instructions about subsequent transactions that were to be made on behalf of his clients during the day. In the afternoons, he generally reviewed the profiles of upcoming IPOs but Rahul was fidgety and restless today. He downed ten to twelve cups of coffee in quick succession and this resulted in a painful burning sensation in his upper abdomen.

He called Gargi and asked, "Are we meeting this evening?"

"I prefer to meet you for lunch. I want to discuss the financial structure of the new company," Gargi replied.

Rahul said hurriedly, "All right, I'm coming over."

Rahul wanted to leave office at once. He wanted to be on the move to get over this feeling of restlessness. It subsided marginally once he was out of office but it did not die down completely. He read the newspaper report again.

*****

Gargi was the only heir to her father's business empire. She had lost her mother when she was fourteen and her father had died of a massive heart attack while he was playing golf, four years ago. She had taken charge of the business and guided its operations with an instinctive flair for the job and achieved a reasonable degree of success. In the four years since she'd taken over the original business, which dealt with spice and leather, had been sold off. She had forayed into eateries, retailing, and lifestyle-stores, and was planning to launch an entertainment company. Her father had been a close associate of Naren*babu*, Biren's father, and Naren*babu* wanted her to marry Biren in due course. So his firm provided financial advice to Gargi's companies free of cost.

Gargi took advantage of this arrangement in the first two years and even slept with Biren, occasionally. But one day she told Naren*babu* that she was not willing to marry Biren though she didn't mind continuing with his firm as her financial consultant. She would pay twice the regular fees if Rahul looked after her company's assignments, or, she made it amply clear, she would scout for some other firm. Rahul was a senior consultant, famous in his own right in accounting circles, and a star asset for the firm. Naren*babu* agreed to the proposal on account of the fees. He could understand that Gargi and Biren were temperamentally different, she enjoyed confrontation, whereas, he was mild-mannered and followed her instructions faithfully and that bored Gargi. Rahul made her sell the businesses set up by her father and use the cash thus generated to set up the new ventures whose requirements and ambience she understood instinctively. She was able to grow as a leader and enjoyed her work. Rahul also helped her develop a well-knit team of brilliant co-workers. Naren*babu*, meanwhile trebled his fees, but

Gargi didn't mind because she was enjoying multiple benefits from the association.

Rahul in the deep recesses of his mind loved dark, exotic sex, which he could never attempt with Leila, although there were very few women who were as confident, brilliant and sexual as Leila. Leila was fair. In his fantasies he always saw himself sleeping with dark women. Gargi was wheatish in complexion. Rahul wove elaborate sexual fantasies involving Gargi. However, he conducted himself in a professional manner in his association with her for a very long time.

After two and a half years of professional association, on a hot and humid night when they were returning from a business dinner, Gargi suddenly said "Will you kiss me, Rahul?" Rahul froze. He did not get down though they had arrived at his house.

"No, not now. Or I will feel like sleeping with you. I won't be able to control myself. Can I tell you something?"

Gargi went crazy with desire "Tell me, Rahul" she whispered.

Rahul said, "I have a recurring dream of making wild love to you: unshackled and unfettered! Will you let me do that, Gargi?"

Gargi was shocked. She turned the car at once and drove home with Rahul. He threw up his arms in mock protest, pleasantly amazed at the turn of events, "What's this? What do you want to do to me now? Kill me? De-list the services of our firm? What?" He exclaimed.

Gargi seized him by the collar, "I want you to come inside and do exactly what you have been dreaming of doing to me, you asshole!"

The sex that night was terrific, but clumsy. Rahul could not have imagined the rigours of anal sex had he not experienced it earlier. He felt a terrible closeness to Gargi after the act was over. He realised Gargi withstood severe pain only for his sake. He lifted her, like one would lift a baby, for she had became immobile with pain and pleasure and washed her and made love to her repeatedly like a hungry animal as she whimpered and moaned in pleasure. They collapsed in bed and fell asleep in each other's arms

drenched in sweat and saliva. What happened as a result
of this escapade was that Gargi became pregnant. She got
the foetus aborted in a private nursing home later. Rahul,
meanwhile, developed painful warts and had to consult a
venereal disease specialist. He took a course of antibiotics
and the doctor counselled him about anal sex.

Rahul and Gargi became lovers after this, grasping
moments of togetherness anytime anywhere. They loved
each other's bodies. Gargi loved chaining Rahul and
making love to him. Surprisingly, this sexual stress
improved their professional performance and they
performed well in business as well as in bed.

*****

Rahul reached Gargi's office in an hour. He was
distracted and ate his lunch without speaking much. He
was totally withdrawn and when Gargi, after repeated
attempts, could not attract Rahul's attention, she slapped
him hard. Rahul slapped her back with such force that
she tripped and fell to the ground. "How do you feel
when somebody abandons you, Gargi?" Rahul screamed.

Gargi was perplexed. "Are you planning to leave me? I
won't let you go. I've shared you with Leila and god knows
how many other women but, no, you have to come back to
me. You belong to me! You belong to me!" she exclaimed.

Gargi had cheated on Rahul three times since that
raunchy night a year ago but she still believed that he
was the epicentre of her life. She believed that Rahul was
her destiny and the key to her happiness so she
surrendered to him without caution. Her flings with others
were more the result of her needs to be desired by
attractive and powerful men.

Rahul said, "You've misunderstood me Gargi. It has
nothing to do with you. I need some rest. I must leave."

He slammed the door and went out without looking
back.

Gargi screamed, "Get lost! Do whatever! But I won't
accept a delay in the financial closure of my new company,
you bastard!"

*****

After her classes were over, Leila rushed to Amit and Sekhar's studio which was on the fifteenth floor of an apartment building. They had taken the flat and the terrace on rent and converted it into a studio. The pungent smell of turpentine oil, linseed oil, colours, fresh canvasses, wood and soil was all-pervasive. Canvasses that had not been completed and sculptures in wood and stone were scattered in all the rooms. The master bed was crumpled and untidy with stains of semen, blood, wine and sweat. A strange smell hung in the air.

As Leila entered the flat, she found Amit and Sekhar working in the main section of the studio that overlooked a multitude of newly constructed buildings. They were jointly working on a cinemascope canvas that was divided into two adjacent frames. The left frame depicted a skyscraper in flames (in long shot). The other frame captured a modern bedroom in one of the flats within the skyscraper (in mid-long shot): the threatening glint of flames, a hint of smoke and soot in the background and two naked men (modelled on both the painters) and one naked woman (modelled on Leila) caught midway in a ferocious sexual scene on a large mediaeval bed. Their supple bodies, muscular curves and the descending rivulets of sweat were distinctly visible and the contours merged to form a frozen scene of intense energy. The men's eyes were locked on the woman's face, but her eyes were closed as though she was cut off from gravity and time.

Leila announced her arrival jovially and went into the master bedroom where she undressed and began to smoke. As the rings of smoke wafted towards the ceiling, she found Amit standing by her side looking at her with burning eyes. Amit brought a bottle of shaving foam and dabbed some on Leila's pubic hair. Sekhar approached the scene with a shining razor in his hand and deftly shaved off a cloud of bushy hair to expose cream-coloured skin and the blooming petals of a rose locked between Leila's legs. Amit softly applied a golden coloured silky lotion on the skin. Leila anxiously anticipated a rush of cream flowing from within her belly. As the duo started licking her hungrily and pierced her, an ocean moved inside Leila. She fell unconscious.

In the invading darkness she saw two brief films:

- Rahul and Gargi were making love passionately on a giant wheel. All the other seats (barring the one where she sat, diametrically opposite to them) were empty and swung freely in the air as the massive wheel went round and round. Her eyes were locked on to their movements and as the wheel went faster, she lost her balance and fell into the truss of steel bleeding profusely while the lovers remained oblivious of their surroundings.

- Sana dropped to her knees from a toilet seat in pain, shocked at the blood oozing between her legs. She screeched soundlessly and from the movement of her lips, Leila realised Sana was calling her.

As the images faded, she opened her eyes to find Amit and Sekhar naked, both having pierced her crevices and when she realised that the motions were causing no further sensation of pain or pleasure, she started crying. Silver drops of tears flowed from her deep black eyes, like mountain streams abandon the heights of glacial peaks in desolation and solitude.

3.

Rahul drove around listlessly for some time. As the fog in his mind settled, he was pleasantly surprised to feel an action plan taking shape. Gradually, his car crossed Alipore Central Jail, the Race Course, Esplanade, Mahajati Sadan and Girish Park. About half a mile from Girish Park he turned into a bylane on the left and tracking a complex loop of narrow, dirty, lanes, he was suddenly in front of an ancient, fissure ridden mansion of bricks and mortar. He was amazed at his memory for he had not visited this part of the city in the last twenty years. The air was heavy and laden with gloom. The people on the streets and in the openings of the buildings seemed impoverished with years of neglect, their faces devoid of any emotion, their eyes blank.

Someone asked Rahul if he was looking for any specific location, but Rahul avoided these queries. He knew where he had to go. As he re-entered a world that he had traversed long back with longing and hope, he was saddened by the infinite decay it had undergone over the years. For a moment he felt as if these shadow-like structures would collapse and crush him to death. He could see a patch of gray sky that was dotted with crows. As he stood before the mansion he was suddenly overcome by a desire to flee from the scene. He returned to the main road, had a cup of tea in a tea stall and determinedly proceeded towards the police station.

The police station was filthy and smelly and strewn with thick files containing jaundiced papers and fat, metallic trunks. He started panicking when the OC told him that Bimala was locked in a cell in the backyard and he was free to meet her. He had introduced himself as a distant relative and having read the news in the morning paper he had come to help her with the legal proceedings. The OC scrutinised Rahul's face; he advised him in a matter-of-fact manner that he should contact the lawyer provided to her by the government, and he gave Rahul, the lawyer's details.

"Rahul*babu*, Bimala*debi* is an under-trial, charged with murdering her daughter and husband; she is poor, wretched, abandoned by fate and society, and debilitated by insanity and ill health. She was once a sparkling beauty, true. How come she suddenly attracts a not so young, rich, relative ready to offer strategic help but not wanting to meet her? I feel there is something wrong, somewhere!" he said sarcastically.

Rahul left the police station in silence and drove to the lawyer's office. After introducing himself briefly he came to the point.

"Sir, I want you to take an interest in this case. I want Bimala*debi* released on bail as soon as possible and then we can see how to build up the case so that she gets a light sentence. I'll do anything to get this done. I know this can be managed if the public prosecutor and the concerned judge co-operate. Please don't think you are constrained by resources." Rahul said, with a rush of adrenalin coursing through his body.

The lawyer smiled and said, "I can try. But first tell me your story, Rahul*babu*."

Rahul laughed sadly, "My story, sir, is one of abandonment! It started when I joined the best Commerce College of this city some twenty-three years ago ..."

Rahul narrated his story over the next three hours. After three rounds of hotly debated hearings and some quality backdoor lobbying, Bimala*debi* was granted bail under the following conditions:

a) A surety was required to be provided by way of a personal bond concerning absolute restrictions on her movements very similar to house-arrest and attending further court proceedings as per requirement from such confinement. Rahul provided this.

b) A surety was required to be provided by way of a personal bond that all along she would be kept under approved psychiatric and medical monitoring protocol and the developments regularly briefed to the court. Rahul provided this too.

The main obstacles in getting bail were the gruesome nature of the killings and Bimala's mental condition. Rahul and her lawyer prepared a detailed case for bail on the basis that the murders could not have been pre-meditated but were caused due to a momentary lapse of reason (on encountering her daughter being forced into prostitution by her own father because of abject poverty). They argued that this required immediate medical attention and rehabilitation of the accused. A detailed report on the qualities and strengths of her personality and the gradual deterioration of her mental health was also submitted.

Bimala Sen was finally released on bail and brought to a bungalow that Gargi had gifted Rahul on his forty-first birthday. Rahul wondered whether he had become a different person. Leila, Gargi and Sana, the three women in his life, retained their sense of calm and dignity through the whole process and were amazed by the whirlpool of events surrounding them.

4.

When Rahul joined the best commerce college in the city twenty-three years ago he had many options. He could seriously pursue his studies by attending classes, listening to lectures, taking notes, delving into reference texts, attending additional tutorials, and leaving nothing to chance.

Or, he could pursue his studies reluctantly, kill time sitting in the college canteen with a group of awkward boys and girls. He could write conceited poetry intermittently and fall in love with one of the better looking girls who would listen to his poems and in time, offer him sex.

Or, he could pursue his studies reluctantly and simultaneously pursue some childhood hobby of collecting stamps or coins or flower petals or performing theatre. He could drink cheap alcohol, smoke grass and wander about the city and its suburbs. He could stop his studies and immerse himself in student politics aligning with one of the established political parties – revisionist left, right or centre.

Yet another option was to immerse him in some other kind of meaningful work, joining revolutionary leftist politics to be an integral part of the de-classification process, future armed struggle and establishing the rule of the dispossessed and the proletariat.

He could be nonchalant about his studies and participate actively in a nascent brand of thinking, which advocated going back to the past, adopt ecological lifestyles and work towards evolving a zero development society through seminars, conferences and world travel.

He finally decided that the option of joining revolutionary leftist politics was best suited to him.

He began to bunk classes, wore tattered clothes, grew a long unkempt beard, and kept his hair uncombed. He smoked unfiltered cigarettes and carried hard-bound copies of books by Karl Marx, Engels, Lenin, Mao Tse Tung and Saroj Dutta in a cloth bag. He didn't read them in detail but memorised the prologues, epilogues, and a few critical passages in them. He attended inner circle debates and processions, protesting against government policies and atrocities. He read leaflets carefully and expanded the issues, with additional material collected from other sources. Rahul's unconventional looks, sound assimilation of thoughts, efficient organisational and oratorical skills attracted the attention of the leadership and a few beautiful female comrades. He was tired of talking about revolution with these women and dreamt of sleeping with them.

Slowly, he became frustrated with his non-existent sex life and focused all his energies on becoming a revolutionary and a committed political worker. He stopped reading the works of creative writers whom he had admired all through his adolescence. He was advised against reading such ambiguous stuff as these writings rarely inspired or uplifted the soul. He didn't argue or do anything to show that he was a less committed soldier in the upcoming human battle of emancipation from the tentacles of capitalist and feudal extortion. He distracted himself by reading histories of the Bolshevik uprising, the Cultural Revolution in China and the Vietnam war. On repeated readings of such texts, he experienced sorrow at the tales of suffering, misery and collective human effort to rise above the most depraved of conditions. He asked himself what was lacking in him that distracted him from such heroic and time defining acts to the selfish demands of satiation of his body. He decided to change his life.

About this time he was introduced to a fascinating person in one of the study circles. Ashesh*da* was in his early fifties, bespectacled, dressed in loose white pyjamas and kurtas. He was a chain-smoker of bidis, soft-spoken and had a curly tuft of greying hair and a beard. Ashesh*da* worked in the peasant unit of the Party in a village in Birbhum, among landless peasants. He had been with the Communist Party since the mid sixties. Finally, he joined the Naxalites when the party was divided for the second time. He had been to villages all over the country on political work and was an authority on matters related to

Indian agriculture. His life of renunciation and his ignorance of the practical matters of day-to-day life were genuine. He had been to prisons on charges of anti-state activities and undergone extreme levels of torture. Rahul was comfortable with Asheshda. He remembered a conversation he once had with him:

Rahul said, "Asheshda to me you are more of a saint than a political worker."

Asheshda seemed pleased, "I'm happy that you think so. But sainthood is hard to achieve in political life."

"Frankly, I don't get the motivation to carry on even today. But when I think of what you've gone through despite the factionalism, millions of interpretations of state character and theories about the nature of revolution floating all around, I think you are made of different material."

Asheshda answered at length, "The turbulence of the ocean is on its surface. Inside it is calm. I don't work on the surface. I work inside. I see so much of man-made deprivation day in and day out that it revolts my soul. Actually, my deepest wish is to run far away, but where can one go? Besides, this is the only craft that I've learnt; I would be practically useless in any other vocation at my age. My only focus wherever I work is to create an understanding among the systematically deprived people about the perpetuator and how to dislodge such forces in an organised and structured manner. We must save land, water and people from the expanding city line, which symbolises the very essence of human greed and consumption. I strive to build enduring individual relationships in the process and participate in personal stories of fear and suffering. But I don't think I should talk like this. There is a dangerous trend of creating magic and lyricism with words, a magic that doesn't last for long. "

Rahul asked him naughtily, "Were you never distracted in the initial period? Didn't you want to sleep with some beautiful girl?"

"Well, I would love that even today. But yes, it was different in the beginning. I was in love with a very attractive girl in college. We started doing revolutionary politics together. She left me when I migrated to a village and married a bright doctor. It's a pain I never got over. I wanted to show her what it truly means to be committed."

Rahul concluded, "So all that devotion that we see is, in one way, a melancholy way of taking revenge on your girlfriend. Isn't that true?"

"True."

"Have you never fallen in love after that?"

"I went through two brief relationships in a south Indian village but they were complicating my political life. I had to make a choice."

"What about your sex life?" Rahul asked hesitantly.

Asheshda didn't hold the truth from him, "My sexuality got dysfunctional after my first stint in prison."

"I've got it, Asheshda. Motivation in revolutionary politics depends on two things: one, a betrayal in love and two, a dysfunctional sexual system."

Asheshda looked at Rahul kindly and laughed. "Rahul, don't do anything out of pressure. It is important to see things for yourself. I'll take you to a few labour colonies of the jute mills that are shut down, and a few labour movements on the fringes of the city. See things for yourself and make up your mind. Somebody was telling me you are good at English and Mathematics; can you, my dear, teach these subjects to an unfortunate brother and sister? They are the children of a young comrade. He was an Office Superintendent in a jute mill that closed down. He was into trade union politics earlier. Although, he has strayed away from the movement, we are trying to bring him back. I don't think you have ever seen such a family from close quarters. This will give you some first-hand experience and they will be immensely obliged as well."

"Where do they live?"

"In a tiny rented flat in North Calcutta. I will give you the address and directions," Asheshda said. Rahul agreed instantly and started work the very next day. The shabby buildings with large doors and grilled windows and the heaps of soil excavated during the construction of the underground railway in north Calcutta did not leave any immediate impression on Rahul. He wanted to concentrate all his energy on becoming a revolutionary, a guerrilla and gain practical experience to go to the roots of human suffering. He was conscious of a tremulous feeling of entering a different world, an unknown world, as he climbed up the stairs engulfed in a magical darkness, a few split arrows of day light piercing through random holes in the walls and roof. The smell of damp bricks and mortar, stains of red and green on the walls and trickling sounds of leaking water stayed with him as he reached the modest third floor flat where Kalyan Sen, Bimala Sen and their two children Mamoni (aged ten years) and Biresh (aged eight years) lived. There was one bedroom, an antechamber, a small kitchen and a tiny toilet in the flat. There was no furniture except for two stools. There were two trunks and two almirahs and a few mats on which they sat during the day and slept at night. The ceiling was high with exposed timber girders and the stained plaster was peeling off the brick walls. The walls were solid, thick and damp and Rahul could feel a chill going down his spine.

Once inside the flat he was left with a feeling of entering a bunker and being isolated from the outside world. The whole building was dissected into tiny flats by thick ancient walls. It was inhabited by grim-faced men and women and indifferent children; people spoke in whispers, but at times, the heavy atmosphere was punctuated by screams of women and children.

Mamoni was bright and intelligent but distracted, while Biresh was eager but rather dull. They went to a municipality school nearby where the teachers were quite irregular. Rahul continued his efforts to educate them for Asheshda's sake. He bought them new books, paper, pencils and stationery and gradually, they gained interest in their studies and interacted with Rahul excitedly on various matters. Rahul told them stories of Cleopatra and the Greek wars, which they enjoyed very much. He worked to a well-planned routine and ensured that the brother and sister, apart from learning what was in their curriculum, were exposed to matters of wider interest like literature and sports. He never saw Kalyan Sen in the house. Mamoni said that her father came very late at night and he looked very tired and never smiled or talked to them.

"*Kaku*, whenever I see him I feel like crying. He looks like a defeated and a dejected man."

Rahul rarely talked to Bimala. He tutored the children in the bedroom, while Bimala remained in the kitchen – except while serving tea and biscuits to Rahul mid-way through the lessons. Rahul never looked at Bimala straight in the face. He would look at her from the corner of his eye as if he was looking at something else. There was a black and white photograph of Kalyan and Bimala probably taken in a studio just after their wedding. One day Rahul looked at this photograph intently but stealthily and realised that this Bimala Sen was a woman of rare beauty and charm. Rahul marvelled at the fact that she hadn't tried to escape from these unhappy circumstances despite being so beautiful. He felt that she could have eloped with someone who was better off.

Rahul yearned to look at her closely but made tremendous efforts to remain aloof whenever she was around.

On a rainy day in autumn, Rahul was stranded in a traffic jam and reached an hour late. The door to the flat was closed and when he knocked on it, it was opened by Bimala. She looked straight at his face and exclaimed, "Oh my god, I thought you won't be coming today. So I allowed the children to go to the sixth floor flat to play. I'll call them just now."

Rahul breathed heavily from the excitement of finding Bimala alone in the flat, but he tried to hide this. "Kindly sit down, sir. You're panting. You must be tired coming up the stairs," she said.

"No. I don't plan to teach the children today. I have some work. I'll make a move."

Bimala replied, "It's all right, sir. But can I offer you some tea and biscuits? In any case, it's raining now. You won't get a bus."

Rahul faked reluctance, "All right, if you insist. I want to tell you something. I don't like you 'sir-ring' me, okay. You are at least ten or twelve years older than I am."

Bimala smiled and went inside. Rahul sat down on the mat. He was terribly excited. Bimala was dark and had clear skin. She was wiry and athletic and had a fine profile. Her eyes were deep and black and made Rahul think of a pair of mystical islands lost in a foaming ocean. They reminded him of a photograph of rain forests he had seen in his geography book way back in school. She applied coconut oil to her hair. The most interesting feature was her smell. She smelt of a mixture of spices, fish and mustard oil – the aroma of her kitchen from where she ran a tiffin counter for working men and school children. It was a commercial venture that she operated from her flat after Kalyan's mill had closed down. He sat straight again as Bimala entered with tea and some snacks. The flickering image of her suddenly exposed navel nearly stopped his breath and he wondered how Bimala would taste if he ate her.

Bimala said, "I've never been able to offer you any snacks earlier because everything is made to order. I keep the surplus to a minimum. Today, because of the rains two plates of vegetable rolls have remained. Please eat."

Rahul ate the vegetable rolls. "You're a wonderful cook, Bimala*debi*. The rolls are marvellous."

Bimala said politely, "I'm not a goddess. Don't call me *debi*; you can call me Bimala*di*, if you like."

There was a fresh rush of blood pumping in his veins. "Can I call you Bimala if you don't mind?" He asked.

Bimala didn't react immediately there was fear and concern in her eyes. "Please call me Bimala, if that pleases you," she said.

Rahul asked, "Don't you feel like getting out of this cage?"

"I don't know the world outside. This is the place where I belong. Every place has its limits, its dimensions. Nothing can be boundless. Except the sky. Any place, except the sky, is a cage."

"What's Kalyan*babu* doing nowadays?"

Bimala suddenly looked in pain. She said, "I don't know. He tells me nothing. Earlier, when he was in the movement he would tell us fearful stories of his battles against the owner and his cronies in the mill. I never felt insecure then. He had a body language, used words and laced his lines with warmth that uplifted us, gave us hope. And then suddenly the movement was crushed by the insiders. This shattered him more than anything else. He reacted to this betrayal with vengeance. He stopped meeting people who are his well-wishers in the Party, even today. He mixes with a different set of people nowadays. This he does in rage, in defiance of his past. He wants to erase his memories of working in a revolutionary organisation by leading an anarchic life. He tells me he is investing money in a business whereas I know he regularly gambles on the street, loses money and even recovers small amounts by selling his own blood."

"Do you believe in the revolution, Bimala?"

Bimala smiled, "I've no views on such things. But, yes, to me Kalyan was a loveable and a loving person when he talked of the revolution. To start with, it's hard to believe in light. Light, to me, is transient. Darkness is permanent. Maybe, talking about the revolution and creating a perception of working against the permanency of darkness is soul uplifting, although it may not be true because life is a defeat in the long run."

Rahul choked. He suddenly said, "No, life is not a defeat, Bimala. I can't withstand this pain and agony you are going through. I'll get you out of this horrific dungeon. I love you, Bimala."

Bimala got up, shock and disbelief in her eyes. She said sharply, "What are you talking about? I'm a respectable woman, Rahul. We're poor, all right, but I'm not a loose woman."

Rahul got up too, like an automaton, in reaction to Bimala. He stood dangerously close to her and caught hold of her hands. An electric sensation passed through his body. He said, "You have not understood me, Bimala. I love you. I want you to come with me out of this hell."

There was a sudden gush of wind and a shower of rain sprayed on their bodies. Rahul lost his balance as the sari fell off from the upper portion of Bimala's body exposing her abdomen and a glint of saliva streaked on her lips. He tore open Bimala's sari, blouse and petticoat and entered her like an advancing wave. After a few gushing savage-like motions, he exploded for the first time in his life within the warmth of a woman and felt like dying, unable to handle this unknown pleasure, as though he were falling from a peak into a moonlit ocean.

When he returned to his senses he heard Bimala sobbing and urging him to get out of the flat in panic. In the next two months Rahul tried to get Bimala to pay attention to him, but received no response. Bimala sometimes murmured, "What we've done is a sin. My family is in peril. I don't want to aggravate the situation. If you don't want to teach my children under the circumstances, so be it. You may stop coming from tomorrow."

Rahul kept on saying, "I love you, Bimala. I love you. We can work this out together. I know for sure, that what you are saying is not what you feel. You don't want to face the truth. "

Bimala would say, "I don't know what love is except what I feel for my children."

At one point Rahul felt like slashing his wrists or banging his head against a wall or jumping off a rooftop. But he did nothing of that sort. One day he reached Bimala's house late in the morning when the children had gone to school, to talk to her and take a decision about his life based on this final interaction.

When Rahul stepped into her flat against Bimala's wishes, she said, "How many times do you want to hear the same thing, Rahul?"

"One last time. Your answer will decide my fate."Rahul said helplessly.

Bimala looked at Rahul. She gazed at his face, his eyes, his hair and then, into his soul. She asked softly, "Where's your mother, Rahul?"

Rahul was taken aback. He replied, "Why, she died when I was two years old."

Bimala moved towards him; she held his hairy head in her hands and thrust it within the crevice of her bosom. Rahul felt that he was diving into endless layers of flesh – soft and drenched in sweat. He burst out crying. They didn't talk for a long time and stood there holding each other, each immersed in the blackness of their own worlds.

Bimala undressed herself. Rahul threw open his clothes. Bimala took Rahul in her arms and rocked him like a baby, kissing him all over, feeling his hardness with her tongue and hand. He knelt down and motioned Bimala to lie down on the mat. Rahul kissed her between her legs and as her smell penetrated him, so did the sensation of wetness of a peppery cream on his tongue as it pushed against her burnt red lobes. Rahul felt like a wild demon on the prowl. When they were locked in each other's arms between sleep and wakefulness, Rahul heard Bimala saying, "I love you too, my savage."

Rahul asked, "Do you sleep with Kalyan? Will you sleep with him ever after this?"

Bimala whispered in Rahul's ears, "We've not slept together for years. I won't be able to sleep with him anymore."

Rahul felt happiness flowing inside him like an avalanche. Slowly Bimala told Rahul about herself. She hailed from a refugee family that had moved out of East Pakistan during the Bangladesh war. Her father, who was a small time trader, lost everything in the war and was forced to work as a clerk in a British company in Calcutta. When this company closed down after two years he did menial work for people who took advantage of his difficulties and rarely paid him.

Bimala had been forced to give up her studies but she was a good swimmer and had swum across the Hooghly under the Howrah Bridge several times. She could climb coconut trees and often dreamt of becoming a sports woman. One day, while riding a neighbour's cycle, she had fallen down by the side of a drain. A good-looking young man helped her up and said, "I work in a jute mill. I'm an honours graduate in physics. I'm the son of refugee parents, but they are dead. I stay in a bachelor's hostel in north Calcutta and come here to attend study circles of the Party of which I'm a member. I do revolutionary politics. I've been watching you for the last six months and find you very attractive. I earn a salary with which I can take care of you and your parents. I want to marry you. Will you marry me?"

Her marriage to Kalyan was like a fairy tale. Sometime after their marriage and a move to a rented flat, her parents died. Kalyan's constant attention and support and the stories, fables, novels and poems that he read out to her helped her overcome her loneliness. Gradually Bimala started going out with Rahul. They went to the Zoo, the Indian Museum, Victoria Memorial Hall, the Planetarium, and Jorasanko. They went to the cinema, too. He remembered seeing two films with her. One was *Blade runner* in New Empire. She fell asleep during the course of the film but he liked it immensely. When he explained the story to her later, she liked it too. The other was *Ghare Baire*, a story, she had heard from Kalyan. She was excited, but she did not like the film. When she explained why she was disappointed Rahul was amazed at her understanding of the complex nuances of the story, the latent shades in the characters of the protagonists and the filmmaker's vision.

One day she declared "I won't go out with you again."

Rahul was shocked. "But why?"

She said, "I don't want to deprive my children. Second, I've seen the look in people's eyes when they see us together. It's shameful, Rahul. I can't bear that. Please try to understand."

A few days later Rahul noticed that she was very anxious, "What's the matter, Bimala?" he asked. She started crying uncontrollably. "I'm pregnant, Rahul. I'm pregnant."

There was a sudden sound of thunder in Rahul's head. He seemed lost in a deluge. He felt his world spinning as though he was caught in a whirlpool. He felt trapped within the walls of Bimala's flat.

Where was the sunshine, where was the sky he had seen after a fierce round of lovemaking? Rahul looked at

Bimala carefully and found an ordinary girl beneath the veil of beauty.

Rahul said, "Bimala, I need cigarettes. I'll go down, and buy a pack. I need to smoke as I think, my dear."

"Come back soon. I need you by my side," Bimala pleaded.

Rahul went down the stairs counting each step. After descending ninety-six steps he reached the road and ran to the bus stop as if a bunch of killers were chasing him. He never returned to Bimala's flat again.

5.

Leila had taken Sana and gone to stay with her parents. She wanted to be alone for a few days to reconnect with her life. Sana was at an impressionable age and the scandals involving her father that were being published in newspapers and discussed on TV chat shows were bound to affect her. However, in her own heart Leila wanted to understand Rahul one day. He was the only man she knew who could torment her soul.

Gargi was furious to see Rahul drifting away. Her instincts told her it was essentially a mid-life crisis that Rahul was experiencing. He would get over it soon but he would not find another woman who could satiate all his animal instincts like Gargi did. She was convinced that Rahul would return so she found no reason to delay the financial closure of her new company as she was accountable to her banks, debtors, shareholders and stakeholders. She spoke to Naren*babu* and Biren was brought back to complete the assignment.

Rahul had employed the best nurses working in two shifts to attend to Bimala. Consultations were made with the best psychiatrists and medical practitioners in the city. He soon realised that Bimala was recovering very fast because of the wholesome nourishment, care and the rest that she enjoyed. Bimala didn't talk to anybody, but she didn't resist the rehabilitation process, either. She behaved as though she had surrendered herself to the physical process, but her mind was elsewhere. Rahul went to meet her on a Sunday, three weeks after her release on bail. He had seen her from a distance in court. She was old and wrinkled and her bones stuck out on her skeletal frame making her look like a starving ghost. Rahul was shocked to see her in this state. Only the faint sparkle in her eyes still remained.

As he entered her room he was pleased to see that she had gained some weight and her skin looked soft. She wore clean, starched clothes. The ravages of time were still visible on her face and her eyes stared into the distance.

Rahul said emotionally, "Do you remember me, Bimala?"

No answer.

Rahul was overcome with guilt. "I know it's difficult for you to pardon me. But I'm repenting my actions, I want to repent further. I will do anything to make you happy."

Bimala said nothing.

Rahul coaxed her lightly, "Bimala, we have to prepare your defence. We need to hear your side of the story in detail."

Bimala turned her head slowly and looked into his eyes. He could not face her gaze. "What happened to our child, Bimala?" he asked.

There was a hint of a rising mist in Bimala's eyes. Rahul repeated his question.

Bimala said, "It got killed in a fist fight with Kalyan. He came to know since I was missing my periods. I took ill for seven to eight months. He was completely crushed. He took revenge on me by ruining the future of my children. He started beating his son every night. The boy was injured in the head and lost his sense of comprehension and memory. He was killed in the crossfire between two rival gangs when he was loitering in the street. My daughter was smarter. She took her father's side in order to save herself. She started watching cheap films to learn the dancing styles of vamps and started dancing in shady hotels and shows organized by her father. I tried to prevent her but she told me that her father and I were dependent on her income so I should keep my mouth shut. She always reminded me that I was the first whore in the family and I had brought ill luck. She went to many places with her father and earned lots of money. Her father snatched the earnings away. God knows what he did with it. I remained in that hole forever."

Rahul could sense her anguish. "But why did you kill them, Bimala and add to your burden?" he asked.

"There is no point in discussing these issues. How are you?"

"I've led a wasted life, Bimala."

"You're a big man, capable of changing the fortunes of people."

Rahul sighed, "That's how it seems from the outside. But truly, I've wasted my life. It's been a life spent in trying to forget things."

"Why do you say that?"

For years Rahul had not spoken about this but he couldn't contain himself any longer. "I've slept with so many women; I have done all this in an animal-like fashion. It bothered me to remember the simple ways I made love to you. I wanted to run away from those memories. But I didn't know how to run away."

Bimala asked, "Did you desert the revolution immediately after deserting me?"

"I was never a part of the revolution. I got caught up in circumstances more dramatic than I was capable of handling and got defeated."

"I don't know whether you will understand. I had been planning to kill Kalyan for the last ten years for ruining my children's lives. He wanted me to see this destruction a million times and die every second. I didn't have the courage or means until then. That day, I had gone to a doctor because I was suffering from heaviness in the heart and a shooting pain in the head. When I returned, Mamoni was dancing merrily in our flat to satisfy a man as old as her father, a man who had been his friend for a long time. Can you imagine this was happening under her father's nose? For a moment I felt comprehensively cheated by life: how could life be as harsh and cruel as to deny a shred of happiness to a piece of my own flesh and blood, my daughter? We were abandoned by fate. Actually, I had meant to kill that man and Kalyan but ended up killing my daughter, blinded by fury and the urge for revenge. I struck the dagger many, many times with all my strength. I don't need any defence. I want to die. Do you have any children, Rahul?"

"I have a daughter," said Rahul, "She has gone with her mother, to stay away from me."

"You're trying to save me and risking your own life in the process."

Rahul knew what was coming and braced himself, "Well, yes. Is that wrong?"

Bimala said almost disinterestedly, "I'm not the right person to answer this. I don't need your lawyers to defend me in court. I don't want to stay in this house. I want to surrender and return to jail."

"Are you rejecting me, Bimala? Are you still so angry with me that you don't mind destroying yourself when you can rebuild your life?" Rahul asked, hurt.

"There is nothing left to destroy. In retrospect, I feel you've been good to me. You, like so many other people, were an important part of my life. I stay away from interpreting life. I can't afford to do that. Please, release me, Rahul."

At last, Rahul said with a heavy heart, "I can't do anything against your wish, Bimala."

6.

That night after a long cold shower Rahul jotted down the following questions on a piece of paper:

■ *Why is it that I could never stay committed to a single woman?*

■ *Why did my chase of every single woman start with the fundamental motivation of a conquest? Why did my interest cease mid-way making me run back?*

■   *Do I perennially swing between the purity of love and impurity of lust, purity of meaning and impurity of meaninglessness, with a secret blinding attraction for lust and meaninglessness?*

■   *Why was I never capable of pursuing any great idea or being a part of it like the revolution?*

■   *Was my act of bravado another sophisticated way of wooing back Bimala in the evening years of her life? Did I pursue immortality at last? Did Bimala pursue immortality by refusing me in the public glare?*

■   *Where is Asheshda today? Is he dead or alive? Is deprivation increasing or withering in this complex maze of technologies, revolutionary parties, political systems, NGOs and rights group lobbyists pervading the entire landscape?*

■   *Why is it that I never got bored with too much sex and still want more of it? Is the pursuit of pleasure a hidden pursuit of death or running away from dying? Can this be a sin ushering me into hell?*

■   *Should I kill Leila for modelling nude for a painting? Will Leila come back to me? Does she remember me when she is in bed with others? Why don't I want her to be seen as a nude model?*

■   *Should I confront Gargi with the evidence of her cheating me three times? Should I destroy her by working with her competitors and disclosing all her trade secrets?*

■   *Has Sana started menstruating? Will she ever like to bed a man like her father?*

The Lie

1.

Rahul was seated on a leather couch in the living room surfing television channels in a disinterested manner. He was dog-tired. Once home from office, he would take a shower and then sit like this for hours, munching roasted puffed rice flakes and changing channels. He was hardly aware of the colours flashing on the television screen or the noise and chatter coming through the loudspeakers. It was as though this cacophony of images and sounds carried him to a zone where his nervous system became dysfunctional.

Rahul was flushed with a numbing sensation of immobility. He came back to the present when his wife Kokil called him to have dinner.

His attention was drawn all of a sudden by a flickering image on the television screen. It was Ishita Sen being interviewed on an entertainment channel.

*****

Ishita was a celebrity. She was the leading lady of the Bengali film industry, having reigned as the number one heroine uninterruptedly for a decade. She had, in recent times, surrendered that position to the pampered daughters of cine-stars of yesteryear. They themselves had faded into oblivion, but were investing their time and money – in manipulating the careers of their untrained and often badly groomed offspring. Ishita was also involved in a much larger controversy that began when her career took a downswing – She was separated from her husband and daughter and allegedly was enjoying multiple raunchy affairs with two leading men of the industry. The men were reported to have fought over her after downing a couple of pegs at an awards ceremony, threatening each other with dire consequences. One of them could have been killed that night had a sane journalist not intervened in the nick of time. Everyone believed Ishita was reckless and loved playing with men.

The next day the vernacular newspapers went berserk with highly exaggerated versions of the story and it took many months for the scandal to die down. The incident caused a dent in Ishita Sen's career. The producers felt that the audience, comprising elderly men and women, sentimental unemployed young men, college dropouts and the underprivileged in urban and rural settlements would be reluctant to accept someone who lived such a flamboyant life in the frigid and unidirectional roles she was required to play on-screen. They refused to sign her for their subsequent ventures. The two suitors, whom Ishita had deserted after the public brawl, also added fuel to fire. They raised questions about her morality and initiated a slander campaign against her, emphasising that she was neurotic. This impression was supported by Ishita's husband and her own behaviour in the intervening period when she became exceedingly edgy, temperamental, and depressed. The journalists took advantage of the situation and fabricated tales that were not refuted by Ishita. She had started suffering from major psychosomatic problems and consulted various doctors who prescribed anti-depressants. This made her sleep for long hours and her work suffered but naturally.

One day, she moved out of Kolkata without informing anybody and shifted to her sister's place in Trivandrum. Ishita, in spite of her ill health, had planned her moves meticulously. She was a crowd-puller. However, the sudden exposition of her controversial private life made her a talking point in intellectual circles. She had created a niche market for her persona in the minds of the intellectuals at a time when the film industry was on the threshold of a critical change. A few directors were attempting to tell a story differently, without any moral and ideological prejudices influencing their vision. They were seeking actors and crew members with requisite sensibility and sensitivity to give shape to such a vision. These ventures were supported by financiers because market demands were changing. It was necessary, therefore, to make films catering to the needs of an emerging market and to go back to the lost world of aesthetics and storytelling.

Some of these directors cast Ishita in roles she had never done earlier. She played a female pimp, a call-girl in a mofussil setting, a college professor in love with one of her students, a rabble-rouser in a home for destitute women and a mentally challenged woman physically traumatised by one of her uncles. These roles were a test of her acting skills. These films had fewer song-and-dance sequences and were shot according to completely bound scripts, so detailed script-reading sessions, rehearsals and workshops for the difficult scenes became a part of her life. Earlier, she was used to producers calling the shots, directly or indirectly. Slowly, she saw directors take over. It took her some time to get adjusted to the new environment, but she gradually started liking the flavour of working in this new set-up since she felt more involved and connected to the entire filmmaking process.

Ipsita Sen was not a trained actor, dancer or model. She happened to land in the film industry by sheer chance. After she completed her master's degree in International Relations she was offered a cameo role in a film by one of her father's acquaintances. She did a mediocre job but was impressed by the glitz and glamour and the money she could earn. She was beautiful, spoke well and dealt with people intelligently. She avoided unproductive confrontations, was patient in approach and style, and was a fast learner. She had a flexible body and knew the secrets of associating with the right people. With time, everything fell into place.

While shooting for her first film she was betrayed in love by an elderly man, a few years junior to her father. She had been involved with this gentleman, a widower from an aristocratic family, for many years. She was bowled over by his flamboyant personality and debonair ways.

They had met at a family get-together. This man had vowed to marry her but warned her against joining films, in fact, he didn't want her to work at all. When her first film was released her small role was appreciated by the public and the producer declared that a new era had begun in Bengali films. She was hailed as the most beautiful star to have emerged after Suchitra Sen left the industry, and the producer expressed his desire to cast her as the leading lady in his next film. That night, however, her lover spat on her and hit her in a fit of extreme jealousy. She was asked to choose between him and her career. Ishita was intelligent enough to choose her career although she cried her heart out. She focused her energy on learning the tricks of survival in the blatantly commercial film industry and mastered it with unmatched élan. Later, she was to unlearn this process when she did art-house films and needed to acquire a different set of skills although the networking skills required for survival were similar in both worlds. Ishita's work received coveted national and international awards. Gradually, she secured her position in the hall of fame of the Bengali film industry.

Ishita had started a production house recently with the help of an NRI investor and roped in a promising Institute-trained director to do a few films. The first film was a straight lift from an American bestseller. They did this film without acknowledging the source and thereby, avoided contingent costs on account of copyright laws. The story of the film had already generated substantial controversy in the city, much to the liking of its producers. They only ensured that such popular controversy thrived in public imagination by conveniently taking use of the media. In the week before the release of the film, Ishita, the other major actors and the director of the film were busy giving a series of publicity interviews to various television channels: both vernacular and national.

*****

It was one such interview that attracted Rahul's attention that evening. Rahul listened to the interview with concentration.

The anchor began, "Don't you think the story of your film is targeted completely at the multiplex audience?"

"We expect the urban audience to react positively to the film. It has a sleek and racy finish. We plan to release the film in the suburbs and smaller towns shortly. If we find the response to the film in the suburbs and one-screen halls encouraging, we will release fresh prints in the next couple of weeks. The film is also being released simultaneously in all the metros in India, London and New York with English sub-titles."

Rahul found that Ishita had aged. The folds on her neck and the texture of her skin revealed this fact despite the makeup that had been applied. But her eyes flashed occasionally as in earlier years. On closer scrutiny he concluded that she looked tired and unwilling to proceed.

The anchor continued, "Don't you fear that the international release could get jeopardised by allegations and charges of plagiarism?"

"You must understand that it's impossible to create original storylines in today's world. Similar ideas inspire creative minds across continents and different spans of time. For me the idea is not at the core of things; what I, like many others, am concerned with, is the interpretation and visualisation of these ideas. Well, if we get mired in controversies, we'll cross the bridge when we come to it. However, we don't see any reason why we should face such a situation."

The next question was shot at Ishita. "Apart from you, everybody else in your film works primarily in the Mumbai film industry; was it a conscious decision to cast more known faces? Does it not cast an indirect aspersion on the dearth of local talent?"

Ishita said firmly, "No. That's a very cynical way of looking at things. Casting is done according to the actor's ability to fit into the characters and their inherent

behavioural and attitudinal patterns. The next film that
we're planning is likely to have an all-local cast. What do
you have to say to that?"

"Oh, it means you're already working on the second
film! Is this an inspired film too?"

Rahul wondered whether he should call Kokil who
was busy with her needlework in the bedroom and Joy,
his son, who was doing his homework in the study to
watch the interview. Kokil and Joy knew about the film.
They were intrigued by its unconventional storyline.

"Since you raised the issue of our second film let me
tell you this. I had gone to visit a friend of mine who was
recuperating from a leg fracture. I found a tattered, moth-
eaten, badly printed book of poems by someone called
Rahul Guha in her husband's library. I read a few poems.
I would not say they were of great quality, but there was
something in them that deeply affected me. There was a
poem about a woman who jumps into a river in a bid to
kill herself. She finds a new lease of life in the depths of
the ocean where she is carried by the river. She encounters
fishes, whales, eels and a set of people who were lost
years back when their island got submerged. I want to
construct a fantastic fable out of this idea and make it
into a film."

It was as though Rahul was struck by lightning at the
unexpected mention of his name. He was rummaging in
the bylanes of his memory and could see a faint sign of
smoke but he couldn't see what existed beyond this veil
of smoke.

The anchor asked curiously, "Do you know this Rahul
Guha?"

"Actually, no. I asked my friend and her husband but
they had no idea. It is possible that someone had given
them the book. "

"Will you be looking for this gentleman?" the anchor
asked.

Ishita was saying, "I don't know. It may be daunting,
you know..."

Rahul switched off the television. He had moved
beyond that phase in his life when he wrote poems, was

careless about his future and wanted to become an established poet. He was lazy and timid and had never stood up for himself. He had charted a course of life that offered him the least resistance. Being a drifter, he had moved into a life that was invisible because of its ordinariness. He couldn't imagine that he could have done anything that would create an impact on anyone. He felt a sense of sadness on reminiscing about his life, which had no action or drama in the real sense. Kokil called him softly from the dining room asking him to join them for dinner. He didn't know whether he should tell her and Joy about what he had just heard on television. Finally, he could not muster the enthusiasm to do so, so he had his meal silently and went to sleep.

He dreamt of an ocean regaining its calm after a violent storm. He, Kokil and Joy were standing far apart on the rain swept shore against a backdrop of swaying coconut trees. The sky looked fiery like an orange canopy wavering against a blowing wind.

2.

Rahul raked his memory to reconstruct his past in a coherent manner. Was he forgetting things because of the painful occurrences in his life? He had very little memory of himself and concluded: he must have forgotten a few chapters of his life. He could remember his parents from the photographs. He remembered his school building and the small patch of thorny bushes in its backyard where they would often play hide-and-seek. He remembered an evening when he had discovered a piece of bone amidst the dust and dried leaves and emerald coloured butterflies were flying in the air. He had stood there for a long time not daring to touch that piece of bone. He studied economics because his father had asked him to. He excelled without much effort. In college, he had fallen in love with Pablo Neruda and Samar Sen.

He had started writing poems in college but was dismayed to find that all of them were copies of either

Neruda or Sen. He did not give up easily; he started refining them to impart his own identity and style. Most of the time he remained dissatisfied with his efforts and wallowed in gloom until his mind wavered to any other streak of happiness that he would find by chance. He read out these poems to a bunch of enthusiastic friends who appreciated him spontaneously like a court poet was applauded in public in ancient times. This made Rahul happy. He yearned to write volumes: the sequence of images continuously taking birth in his consciousness initiated by the words of Neruda and Sen. He wanted to publish books and make a name for himself and secretly desired to be nominated for the Nobel Prize one day. However, he planned to refuse it as a mark of protest against the economic and military atrocities inflicted upon poor nations by the rich ones. He had even drafted a refusal speech, which he rehearsed day and night in his bathroom, looking at his reflection in a mirror. He imagined an animated audience clapping at the end of his long speech.

Sanjay, another poet in his college, was so impressed with his work that one night, over a few glasses of country liquor, he declared that he would edit and publish fifteen of Rahul's poems using his own savings. The collaboration was an instant hit and the book was published. Three hundred copies of the book were sold at rupees two per book in a single day in college. Rahul harboured dreams that night of lecturing at Oxford, Princeton and other places on exotic subjects related to poetics.

A few days later, a girl came up to him in the college canteen and said, "Rahul, my name is Kokil. I have bought a book of your poems."

Rahul replied, "I've seen you in class. I didn't know you were interested in poetry. Thank you for taking an interest in my book."

There was amazement writ large on Kokil's face. She said, "Why? Do you need to have something special to be interested in poetry?"

"No, no, nothing of that sort. You're so studious and look so prim and proper. How did you like the book?"

Kokil was candid in her reply, "It has been printed very badly. There're so many spelling mistakes. Your proof reading should have been better to say the least."

"And, you've nothing to say about the poems?"

What Kokil said tore Rahul apart. "There is a lack of intensity in almost all the poems. As if, these are not your words. As if, these are not your ideas. You do not lose yourself in what you write. The words seem to have been strung one after the other to make an impact of sound. But are they born out of a sincere wringing of your soul? They are just not authentic enough."

Rahul was speechless. He felt he was being punched squarely and brutally on his jaw and then on the solar plexus in front of a live audience.

Kokil added, "I'm sorry to have said such things so harshly. But I'm on your side. I think you will make a better economist than a poet, Rahul. Why don't you attend your classes regularly?"

Rahul felt like a rickety boat which had been damaged in a hailstorm. His sense of shock remained for a long time. He seemed to have forgotten the details of this period.

From the second year onwards he attended his classes regularly. He still read poetry intermittently but stopped writing poems. One day, Kokil came up to Rahul in the college canteen and said, "It's nice that you've started attending your classes regularly. You've done so well in the first year exams, too. But why do you look at me like that? I feel so awkward. Are you still angry with me?"

Rahul didn't know what to say. They started meeting quite often after this and were soon married. On the wedding night, Rahul asked Kokil, "Did you find my poems that bad?"

Kokil had replied smilingly, "No, my love. I would not have fallen in love with you had you not published those poems. But I didn't want to get married to an impoverished poet. I wanted a poet for myself and an economist for the outside world. So I planned this move, which was ultimately successful."

Rahul felt his life shackled forever with Joy's birth.

He felt tied down, chained. He had not wanted to father a child. Gradually, as years passed by, he became superstitious, because deep inside he believed he was a sinner. He pondered over his actions to see if they could have an adverse impact on Joy. He was devastated whenever Joy fell ill. As Joy grew older and stronger Rahul, much to his bewilderment, started enjoying the companionship of his son. When Joy was nine years old, he stood first in his class. Rahul felt happy and got deeply involved in his studies. When, Joy was twelve years old and could not earn a place for him in the junior football team, Rahul was devastated. Kokil understood his silent agony and soothed it with her words and love.

Twelve years ago, Rahul's parents died in a road accident while returning from Belur. After three months they shifted to the large three-bedroom apartment in Tollygunj provided by the company. Rahul sold off all the belongings in the old house, except the master-bed and dressing table used by his parents and the photo albums. Kokil wanted to keep the box containing Rahul's old writings, but he chose to burn them. Kokil was scared by Rahul's decision to destroy his past, but she didn't intervene. Rahul had invested a lot of money in designing their new home with murals, wallpaper, teakwood furniture, modern fittings and lighting accessories. The house evolved into a modern affluent home with excessive amenities. Rahul knew that such a home would help its occupants age comfortably without expectations from each other.

Kokil had stopped working after Joy turned six and refused to be fed, clothed and made to sleep by nurses and ayahs. He would create a scene everyday at lunchtime and Kokil would have to rush home to drown her anxieties. Rahul had insisted that Kokil should continue with her job and they should send Joy to a good boarding school and not give in to his tantrums. Kokil did what she felt was best for Joy. Initially, she felt miserable, spending the whole day with Joy and the servants. There was nothing to challenge her mind. Slowly, she got so involved with Joy that she dismissed the two ayahs who were employed to look after him. Rahul was happy with the way Joy was shaping up under Kokil's supervision. He was promoted to the position of Chief Economist in the company and advised the management on future strategic investments, diversification and planning. Rahul had stopped reading anything not related to his work, though he watched films at times. He was unhappy because he felt that he had not pushed himself enough, but he didn't dwell on this emptiness for long.

As he came back to the present he was more or less convinced that he would not find even a trace of his poems or a single copy of the book. He couldn't think of anybody who could have retained a copy of the book, the manuscripts were burnt and Ishita did not care to disclose the identity of her friend during the television interview. A link to his past that had sparked momentarily like an incandescent filament tripped into absolute darkness.

Rahul wanted to write again. He sat down with pen and paper but his mind was blank. He had been writing serious management notes with numbers, charts, graphs, analysis and conclusions for so many years. He knew nothing of the mysteries that governed life and existence, that could have inspired ideas and made him write. As he failed in his attempts to write anything, except that which was connected with his profession he felt depressed. Filling up even a page of his small diary would have given him unstinted satisfaction but he felt the hood of failure engulfing his soul, like a conspiratorial demon, a deadly curse. He wondered what his life would have been if he had not succumbed to Kokil's strategic move years ago. He felt torn, bitter and willing to revolt.

3.

Rahul was to visit Trivandrum for a four-day business conference. The conference was scheduled at a super deluxe hotel by the sea and designed to be a digression from the daily routine of work. He was to read a paper on the third day of the conference for which he had prepared well in advance although his excitement had gradually waned. He had read his paper a couple of times and found it to be a subtle concoction of manipulated data and pre-conceived fashionable jargon. He found that the views expressed were not his own, but belonged to someone else who had taken mystical control of him over the years, like a weed that grows unhindered in a mass of wood.

Rahul was overwhelmed by oblique thoughts: Did he believe in anything at all? Did he believe in the sanctity of public services the way the leftists did? Can a man's actions be interpreted and judged based on his economic identity? If a man is a combination of various identities, some of them contradicting each other, how is he to be judged? Kokil's action of alienating Rahul from the world of poetry had meaning if one believed in love. If love itself had no meaning, Kokil's actions would appear to be motivated by her blind desire to conquer Rahul.

Rahul wanted Kokil and Joy to come with him to Trivandrum. But Kokil refused because Joy had school. Moreover, Sanjay was coming down from London on his spring vacation. Sanjay spent a fortnight in India every year; the first ten days were spent with Rahul and the rest with his aunt in Shantiniketan. Sanjay taught at the School of Oriental Studies, and had become a famous poet and novelist over the years. He had not got married because Kokil was the woman he had loved, but she had chosen Rahul. Rahul felt happy that he had something which Sanjay did not have. He envied the name and fame that Sanjay enjoyed, but most of all he envied Sanjay's carefree life. He took care not to display this envy in his words and attitude. Sanjay and Kokil were like playmates. Rahul encouraged their friendship and secretly relished the thought that Sanjay did not have a woman, in his life, who would guard his family with endless love, care, finesse, patience and charm.

Kokil bade him farewell as he set out for Trivandrum. "I'll see that Joy completes his homework in the next four to seven days. I'll also ask Sanjay to spend the first few days in Shantiniketan this time so that we can visit the

Sunderbans and have a good time once you're back. Present your paper well at the conference, for god's sake. Don't lament or stutter like a philosopher and don't look burdened by the most ambiguous questions of life, my dear!" she said.

At the end of the first day, Rahul hitched a ride on a fisherman's boat to see coral deposited along the shoreline. He wanted to see how boats and nets were made and maintained. He collected starfish and had a strange desire to eat them raw. He visited a coconut plantation and saw the sudden burst of rain splattering in the sea. He viewed the transient interplay of indigo, black and orange in the sky, and quivered at the tingling touch of sharpness in the wind laden with scents of salt and fish. Suddenly he noticed gadgets, strong lights, reflectors, and hordes of men and women dangerously balanced on a large steel platform against the backdrop of the sea. The platform was supported on steel columns anchored to the rocky table land like gigantic scaffolds. A film shooting was in progress and a passionate love scene was being picturised with dramatic effect.

"A film shooting is in progress, sir,"someone said.

"Is it a Malayalam film?"

"Yes. Actually, the heroine is from Bengal. The hero is the number one actor from Kerala, sir. It is a dramatic inter-religious love story based on local folklore."

Rahul was surprised. "Of course, I've heard of this hero, but you said that the heroine is from Bengal? What's her name?"

The man looked confused. "I don't know, sir. I've actually heard this from the other hotel boys. She is also staying in this hotel."

Rahul sighed deeply. He went closer to the parapet and focused his gaze on the shooting. But it was difficult to recognise faces from such a distance. He went to the reception area and talked to the man standing at the counter. Rahul asked, "Is Ishita Sen, the actress from Bengal staying in this hotel?"

The man checked on the computer and said, "Yes, sir."

"You see, I'm staying in this hotel too. I'm Rahul Guha

staying in room number 1025. I have some work with Ms. Sen. May I know her room number please?"

The man replied affably, "Sir, as per the privacy rules of our hotel we can't disclose information about our guests. You can ask the operator to connect you to her room on the house-phone, if you like. Or, you could leave a note which we can forward to her."

Rahul decided to write a small note and leave it at the reception. He wrote, "Madam Ishita Sen, it's a strange coincidence. I'm Rahul Guha staying in this hotel (room number 1025) in connection with a business conference. I understand that you are here in connection with a film. You had recently referred to one of my poems in an interview. Please let me know if I may meet you in this regard. Thanks and regards. Rahul."

Rahul read the note thrice, folded it neatly and marked the envelope 'Kind attention – Ms.Ishita Sen' and left it at the reception. He didn't expect Ishita to call him immediately, but when there was no call at the end of the second day he was sure that the note had not reached Ishita. He felt a little embarrassed at having thought that Ishita would be compelled to talk to him. He tried to concentrate on his paper but he felt bored with its contents. He escaped to a deserted beach and watched desperate waves spraying their ire against jagged edges of rock. He saw the lanterns on fishing boats, like tiny dots of light, spread across the black waters of the night sea like random fireflies. The moonlight illuminated the coconut trees swaying with the wind, the lonely fishermen and the advancing waves. He was filled with melancholia, a deep sadness for the fishermen out there on the boats waiting sleeplessly for a bounty of fish to land within their nets and the loneliness of fishermen's wives. He wondered whether the wives slept at nights or during the daytime with their husbands after they returned from work. There was a worn out, decaying lighthouse at a distance in the north with its moving torch of light voicelessly communicating with sleepy navigators on ships from some other world. The lighthouse in a strange way reminded him of an ancient, ghost like phallus that had lost all its glory.

He had a light dinner and returned to his room around midnight. Suddenly, the telephone rang. A soft male voice on the line said, "Is this Mr. Rahul Guha?"

"Yes."

The male voice continued, "Sorry to disturb you at such a late hour, Mr. Guha. You had written a note to Ishita Sen. Madam wants to know if you're free now and would you mind dropping in at the roof top coffee shop to meet her?"

The timing of the proposal perplexed Rahul, but he remained calm. "All right, I will be there in ten minutes." Rahul sat on the bed and wondered how to proceed. He was excited, but he was also hesitant.

Rahul reached the open-air coffee shop that was magically lit by the soft moonbeams. It was deserted and he had to strain his eyes to see the lonely woman sitting at a corner table sipping from a large porcelain cup. The woman was looking fixedly at the sea. When Rahul approached the table, she turned her head abruptly and greeted him with a smiling face. She was wearing a maroon gown and her hair was loose. She was thin and pale and looked as though she could do with some sleep. It felt strange to be face to face with a celluloid star, who could draw people's attention and generate fantasies in people's minds. He was aware of Ishita's clout among a coterie of powerful people.

Ishita said, "I'm having hot chocolate. Would you care for a cup, Mr. Guha? By the way, why are you standing? Kindly have a seat."

Rahul sat down. Ishita said politely, "It was nice of you to have written that note. I couldn't find time yesterday. My sincere apologies, Mr. Guha."

"Thanks Ms. Sen. You're a very busy woman. I understand that."

"It's not that. Our shooting schedules are so erratic. You wanted to talk to me. What was it about?"

Ishita ordered a cup of hot chocolate for him. Rahul sipped the drink slowly. It felt good.

Ishita asked, "Do you see my films, Mr. Guha? You don't look like one of my fans."

"I've seen some of your recent films. You've done a good job."

"Thank you. But what is it you wanted to talk about?"

"You had mentioned a poem of mine in a recent interview. You said you would like to make it into a film. Is it true?"

"What is truth by the way? Is it not an illusion? And, is there anything that is not an illusion, Mr. Rahul Guha?"

"You're asking very serious philosophical questions, Ms. Sen."

"Rahul, do you remember me?"

Rahul was taken aback. He said, "I don't understand."

Ishita told him, "We've met once before: you and me, briefly, one passing inconsequential moment."

"I don't remember really. Where? How?"

Ishita gave him the details, "I got my first national award five years ago. The officers club in your office invited me to a show where your Managing Director felicitated me. Later, at the dinner you praised my performance and said, 'Madam, you have a face and eyes that are pregnant with sadness and intensity. They expose the soul of your character replete with hopelessness, longing, compassion and the forces of survival and guilt battling out their primeval wars in the mansion of her heart. You've sketched a wonderful role. My compliments are with you, madam.' It was such a chivalrous and elegant way of appreciation that I could never forget those words. I requested you to write whatever you had said and give it to me. You said you would send it by post if I gave you my address. I did. "

"What happened after that?"

"Don't you remember anything?"

"I really don't. Tell me, what happened after that."

"You sent me your book of poems, a skeleton of a book really, with a note of appreciation for me on its cover page. Those were the words you had uttered at the party. There were a few more lines - 'You've perfected the art of deception. Acting is the art of masking and unmasking. Acting is life. Do we know a way to live without our masks?' A very heavy thought, I must say."

"Hold on; hold on ... where would I get a copy of this book five years ago? Even the manuscripts were burnt approximately twelve years back," Rahul looked tense and thoughtful.

Ishita exclaimed in disbelief, "Burnt! Why?"

"I don't want to discuss all that with you."

The lights were turning dim and the sea breeze was turning cold.

Rahul said softly, "There's something wrong with what you're telling me."

"There's nothing wrong. There was a handwritten inscription in the book that read 'Our copy - Kokil and Sanjay'. There was also a handwritten conversation between two people at the back of the book, as if they were playing a game. Instead of talking they were writing out their thoughts in silence."

Rahul asked, "Do you remember what was written?"

Ishita was positive, "I do. It was something like this:

■ *These poems were originally copied from the ideas of Pablo Neruda.*

■ *I don't believe you. Show me which ones.*

■ *It's difficult to identify today because it was I who introduced the stamp of original identity by styling on the basic imitation.*

■ *You mean to say he copied and you styled.*

■ *Yes.*

■ *The appreciation that was due to the stylist went to the copier, is that it?*

■ *That's the most tragic part of it.*

■ *Are you sad because of that?*

■ *Yes.*

■ *But you've ended up becoming a famous poet and novelist. You've got fame, name and immortality. Whereas, he's saddled with the burden of a mundane, domesticated life.*

■ *But I don't have you. This book was originally meant to impress you. I tried to explain to you that the credit for the beauty of these poems should have come to me and not to him.*

■ *You've got me in the long run.*

■   *I didn't want you as my mistress. I wanted you to be my queen.*

■   *Damn you, you conman! The ending of your second novel* Swordsmen *was copied, in part from the poem 'The lighted den'.*

■   *That's because both were written by me."*

When Ishita had finished Rahul asked, "But didn't you say you had come across the book in your friend's house only recently?"

"That was a lie."

"A lie! But, why?"

"To create a dramatic effect in the interview. To keep people guessing. To throw a seed of thought that might grow into a tree. I also felt that if you saw the interview; you might want to meet me. A remarkable coincidence, indeed."

Rahul asked with a sense of resignation "Do you think I have a pathetic destiny?"

"No. Look at me. I've been obsessed with myself all my life. It comes naturally in our profession. As I'm aging, losing all control on my beauty, I am filled with a combative edge to deal with the outside world. I'm filled with nostalgia and want to return to my daughter. But it's not possible. Her guardians feel I'm a fallen woman, someone with loose morals."

Rahul said frankly, "You've betrayed so many men, Ms. Sen. Is it fair?"

"I've been betrayed many times too. In the heat of desire I lost all control over logic and rational thought, Mr. Guha. I never believed I would grow to be ugly, weak and nondescript. I've seen enough to understand that the seeds of betrayal are sown in the flowers of desire. That's a dirty trick nature plays on us."

"But I can't understand what made you desert your own daughter. What could it be? Money, fulfillment of sexual desire, a sense of being unshackled, or all of these? I don't need an answer from you. I would never have done such a thing, Ms. Sen. Thank you for your time."

Rahul came out of the coffee shop abruptly without

looking at her again. He didn't feel sleepy so he wandered around listlessly on the road running parallel to the coastline. He walked for hours till he was no longer able to walk because of sweat, thirst and a nagging pain in his knees. It was already morning and he was having difficulty looking at the sunshine and the azure sky.

His phone was ringing. It was Kokil.

"Hello. How're you? You present your paper today, no? I thought I'd wish you good luck early in the morning. I hope you had a good night's sleep. Do your best."

Rahul didn't want to talk but forced himself to reply calmly, "Yes. I'm almost ready."

"I can hear the sound of waves. Are you standing close to the sea?"

"Yes."

Kokil could sense the chill in Rahul's voice. "Are you feeling well, Rahul? You sound so odd."

"It's nothing. I was just looking at the sea ... foam everywhere!"

"Joy wants to go to his aunt's house tonight. Is it okay if I send him there?"

Rahul was bored with the conversation, "Why, is there any problem?"

"No, I just thought of asking you, first."

Rahul suddenly asked, "Kokil, do you remember my book of poems?"

"Yes. Why?"

"Did you have a separate copy of the book marked in your name and Sanjay's name?"

There was a spell of silence that continued for a long time.

Rahul asked emphatically, yet again, "Can you remember anything, Kokil?"

There was an attempt to conceal something in the way Kokil answered, "No. I mean there was no such copy. And, why do you think Sanjay and I would have kept one copy for us? It's ridiculous. We don't stay together. We don't even interact except during the few days he is in India. It's you who burned all your work. Why are you asking this now?"

"It's nothing. Somehow the thought just crossed my mind. Don't bother about it."

"You shouldn't be thinking about all this today, Rahul. You should be getting ready to read your paper in the right frame of mind. Goodbye, darling and best of luck," Kokil hurriedly disconnected the line.

Rahul felt very tired.

4.

Joy had gone to his aunt's house. Kokil was lying naked on her bed. Sanjay made delicate hillocks of cheese and cream around her navel and licked them savagely.

Kokil said lustily, "Where do you learn all this? From your French mistress and Turkish brothels, I suppose. They teach you and you make me do all these gravity defying feats during these tiny stolen moments of pleasure. My heart is constantly pounding in fear. Nowadays, I find your fire for me is dying out. You are no longer as excited as you were before."

Sanjay didn't respond. He went on doing what he was doing.

Kokil held Sanjay's head by his hair and spoke to him looking straight into his watery eyes, "I must tell you something, Sanjay. This morning, Rahul asked me on the phone if you and I had retained a marked copy of his book of poems."

Sanjay replied reluctantly, "You told me five or six years ago that you had lost that secret copy of yours. Didn't you get it back?"

Kokil said, anxiety showing on her face, "I lost it suddenly one day. I used to keep it in an empty packet of sanitary napkins thinking nobody would touch it. Whenever I touched that book I felt so close to you, looking at your handwriting and remembering what lengths you went to show that the poems were actually your creation and not Rahul's."

Sanjay didn't speak a word. He licked Kokil's neck devotedly like a hermit at work. In other times, Kokil would cry in pleasure as Sanjay's tongue wandered over her skin.

Kokil nearly screamed, "Sanjay, please listen to me, I'm scared. I'm terribly scared. Suppose Rahul has that copy and charges me with being unfaithful and throws me out of the house; what will I do, Sanjay? Listen to me, you brat."

Sanjay looked at Kokil with disinterested blood-shot eyes and said, "What?"

Kokil repeated, "What will I do if I am caught?"

Sanjay said calmly, "Do nothing. Come with me to London and be one of my sex slaves."

Kokil slapped Sanjay and started crying. Sanjay took her softly in his arms, "Come on, baby. I'll take care of you."

"If matters take a turn for the worse will you take me to London?"

"Yes. Do I have to write this in blood? Will you cook for me? Will you take care of my home the way you do for Rahul?"

"Only if you agree to get all your writings routed through me to your agent, editor and publisher."

Sanjay said, "Done."

A sudden wave of sadness rushed through her body. "But what will happen to Joy? What will happen to Rahul?"

"I don't know. I can't take care of them."

Kokil said sharply as if willing to bite off Sanjay's ears, "Don't you have a soul, Sanjay?"

Sanjay sprang back, "Stop this crap, Kokil. Don't expect a soul in a writer or an artist for he is required to be as cruel as God."

Kokil knew she was neither a writer nor an artist. She was desperately in love and lusted for these two men who were bound to their individual fates. She fell silent. She felt as if her being was on fire. She began to cry.

In moments of extreme guilt with the inferno of torment burning inside her, Kokil withdrew to her private island, surrounded by an unsurpassable ocean, with the innocent face of her adolescent son hanging like a bright star in the winter sky: his soft and gentle rays of light keeping her warm and protected.

The Last Plunge

1.

Three years ago, just as spring was coming to an end, a lethal virus invaded the city of Kolkata. It spared no one, causing high fever with aching joints. Unresponsive to any medication, it progressed without remission and resulted in heavy nasal bleeding, brain haemorrhage and subsequent death. As soon as the monsoon began, the virus magically vanished from the city. In the intervening period of two and a half months it claimed three thousand and five hundred lives. The doctors, the state-of-the art private hospitals stashed with life saving drugs, the state-run dispensaries and the government machinery were of no use. The suddenness and ferocity of the epidemic had thrown life out of gear. By the time the epidemic subsided there were huge losses. A pall of gloom settled over the city and suspicion hung in the air.

Rahul lost his wife and two sons to the epidemic. They fell sick and died, one after the other, and he had to go to the cremation grounds thrice within a fortnight. While returning from the burning ghat the last time, he had seen rain clouds threatening to burst any moment. He knew he was next in line – may be the fever would come that evening. He had waited, expecting the fever to rage in his tired body and kill him in no time. But nothing happened; instead, the city was flooded with rainwater in the next few days. The grave face of his elder son, as he witnessed his mother and brother dying painfully one by one, loomed large on the screen of his mind. As he saw those menacing rain clouds while returning from the burning ghat, he wondered what saved him from dying and why. Did his wife and sons die to protect him from death? Did nature use them in a cunning way as human shields, to prolong his life? He never believed these three deaths could have happened at random. He felt there was a pattern.

2.

Rahul walked to distant parts of the city and saw the impoverished neighbourhoods of Rajabazaar, Watgunj, Salkia, Posta and Shyambazaar. He saw the rich localities of Alipore, Ballygunj and Salt Lake. He went to the old style markets of New Market, Maniktala Bazaar and Hatibagan and then to the new shopping malls on Camac Street and City Centre. He travelled through the port areas of Kidderpore, the crowded railway stations of Howrah and Sealdah and the airport in Dum Dum. He visited Nakhuda Masjid, Saint Paul's Cathedral and Dakshineshwar Temple. He saw the Indian Museum, Victoria Memorial, Race Course, Eden Gardens, Princep Ghat, Jorasanko and Belur. He spent time at the cemeteries, the fast vanishing wetlands, the ship building yards and dined in the restaurants on Park Street, Elgin Road and street cafes on College Street and the Esplanade.

He studied the faces of people during these travels, often reaching the same place after long intervals, at different hours of the day or night, travelling by different routes. He stared directly at the faces with his soft gaze, exploring signals in unknown eyes. He realised the face was the most essential and mysterious part of the human body, which contained an army of conflicting signals beneath its sheath. The unmasking of the human face required clear observation and extraordinary skills of decoding difficult riddles. But he found no calm or peace. All that happened was that he lost weight and got a tan.

3.

Rahul was a senior professional. He approached his work with diligence, sincerity and passion and this made him successful at work. He earned a lot of money, acquired vast material comforts thereby ensuring social prestige for his family. The owners of the company where he worked were pleased with him because his presence meant dividends and profits. He had set high standards of professional excellence under trying circumstances.

But now, shrouded in solitude, he found no joy in success. There was nobody at home to share the unprecedented increment or the premature letter of promotion, or the appreciation he received in office. As he saw faces and more faces he understood work was not worship but an escape to a world where one could hide from the meaninglessness of life and the burden of coming face to face with oneself.

Rahul stopped exerting himself but the owners of his company, did not react negatively to his growing apathy for work. Instead, they invited him to their home to attend various religious recitals and discourses. Rahul attended these functions but found them boring.

Rahul was, in due course of time, transferred to a department where there was hardly any work. So he had plenty of time for his travels and walks. He was not growing in professional stature any more but somehow felt more contented, although he was restless. The questions kept coming back to him like arrows dipped in poison.

4.

One day he walked past the university where he had studied. It was in the late afternoon when the crowd of students and staff had thinned. He walked past the libraries, playgrounds, conference halls, canteens, hostels, union rooms, and gardens, searching for clues from the past. He found none. He couldn't remember much of the four vibrant years of his youth that he had spent in these confines. He met nobody who was familiar. As he went past one of the canteens somebody called out to him. He stopped and turned around to see an old man walking towards him. When he was very close he smiled innocently and asked, "Rahul, do you remember me?"

Rahul felt embarrassed at not being able to identify him. The man said, "It doesn't matter. You are a big man now. Remember the hunger strike you and your friends went on in solidarity with our movement? The contract staff of the university canteens was struggling to be recognised in the permanent staff list; this would improve their economic condition. That was a long time ago, of course. We won. Your ideas were crucial in the final stages of the movement. Do you remember me now?" Rahul felt shaky.

"Aren't you Bula*da*? Of course, I remember you. How is life?" He asked. There was a glowing smile on Bula*da*'s face, now. Then he suddenly turned wistful and said, "Life is cruel, my son. I lost my wife and grandson in the epidemic. I feel lonely nowadays. I want to die."

5.

Rahul read the newspapers at night. He didn't read much these days, just scanned the headlines. The American war in Iraq was intensifying. There was other news pertaining to Indian companies taking over European companies, the Indo-US nuclear deal, and the food shortage all across the globe. The world was full of terrorists, it seemed. They killed innocent people. Or, was it the State killing its innocent subjects and staging the killings as the handiwork of terrorists? This would increase expenditure on defence budgets, legitimising political force that at times turned to violence.

There was propaganda everywhere in the name of peace and development. The Maoists had taken over the jungles in India. Oil prices were shooting through the roof.

The UK was tightening its immigration laws. North African countries were in a constant state of civil war. Rahul had two questions to ask: were people getting richer or poorer and was that of any consequence? Were people getting happier or sadder and was that of any consequence?

One night, he saw a strange news item in the city section of a newspaper, which read as follows:

A UNIQUE FINDING IN NIoV SURVEY

The National Institute of Virology (NIoV) is conducting state funded research on the epidemic that had broken out in Kolkata and its suburbs three years ago. The main objective of the research is to examine and determine the source and nature of its causative virus and analyse how defence mechanisms could be built in humans to inhibit multiplication of the virus post-infection.

To collect exhaustive data, the Institute has planned to visit homes in the areas worst affected by the epidemic on a door-to-door basis to hunt for survivors. One would recall that this virus was reported to have caused death every time the symptoms of infection had manifested themselves in a person. The Head of the Institute, in a press conference declared yesterday, that they have identified a lady by the name of Rekha Dutta Gupta during one such survey. The lady, reportedly, survived the high fever and bleeding quite miraculously without any medication barring a few analgesics. The Institute has now planned to conduct a thorough medical examination of this lady, including all blood and gene related tests, to unravel the mystery of her physiological defence mechanism. Scientists are hopeful that through such a detailed study they will be able to look for an effective antidote to this mysterious virus and devise suitable protection for the future. The question to be answered is: what does this lady have in her, which is so different from the other citizens of the city?

6.

In one dark and dwindling part of the city there was a stone-lined street with rows of butchers and tailoring shops on either side. The tailoring shops were not doing good business but the meat shops had long lines in front of them. The street was filthy but after a spell of rain it looked clean, and almost welcoming to the occasional visitor.

On one rainy day, Rahul walked down this street to watch the meat chopping operation at length – the butchers and their assistants who made *keema* meat meticulously and the people who came to buy meat in starched clothes. He witnessed an agitated procession on the street. As he looked at the people in the procession he was overwhelmed by the older intellectual faces, the baby-faced young students, the hollow-cheeked faces of peasants and the dark faces of provincial women. They were shouting slogans vigorously against the government's industrialisation policy and the recent land-grabbing tactics for setting up car factories and chemical hubs in the suburbs. There was an intensity and clarity in the slogans, which affected him. He thought of joining the procession. Suddenly the area was cordoned off by the police. He felt afraid of being beaten up and slipped away, almost hurriedly.

That night he remembered the face of his elder son. Tears came to his eyes and a poem welled up in his soul. He sat down and wrote the lines that resonated in his soul.

When I entered the prison I was wearing a blue shirt.

At night, a few stars slipped into my dungeon, snatched the blue out of my shirt and made it colourless.

Morning, I rushed to the faceless Warden and reported the stars.

This warden then looked at me and my colourless shirt and tore the clothes off my body.

When he saw my frailness trembling,

He spoke in a whisper –

Tonight, I will ask the stars to come and prick all the flowers out of your body and leave you flowerless, my boy.

When I entered the prison I had a dahlia and a lily growing on my shoulders...

Having written the poem, he felt an unknown happiness and calm surging inside him. He titled the poem 'Enter the

Dragon'. Before going to sleep he read the poem a couple of times. A question leapt into his mind: Is it possible to achieve true happiness by living a solitary life or is it important to lead a community life where one instinctively believes that one's own desires are insignificant compared to the desires of others and one works towards fulfilment of their desires as if they are one's own?

7.

One evening, as Rahul was walking back home, he saw a tall veiled man walking past him in slow motion illuminating his mind with a flash of light. He saw, in the theatre of his mind, his look-alike, falling peacefully inside a gorge filled with flakes of snow (although it was hot and humid on the road). He was suddenly transported from the chaos on the road to the overpowering silence inside the gorge and the fiery orange-tinged black sky filled the solitude of his soul with a sense of pride as if his loneliness had a unique meaning and a purpose.

When he reached home he had tea and snacks and tried to remember the women in his life. It took a long time for the images to appear. He saw three images. One, a small woman, with a pale leaf-like face and dark grief struck large eyes, wearing a white sari, standing by a lake. Was she a widow? Then, he saw a tall dark woman with kohl-lined eyes, dark brown painted lips and diamond-studded ornaments on her ears, neck and hands. Was she a seductress? Third, Rahul saw a plain rustic woman wrapped in a length of cloth with her head covered in a hood. He saw her tearful eyes and her sombre face. Was she crying for her own grief or did someone else's sadness make her sad?

Studying these images carefully Rahul saw a part of his soul reflected in these three faces. Many questions crossed his mind. Did he secretly crave to believe in god? Was he looking for a god to deflect his loneliness or was his loneliness actually a sense of pride, which was an obstruction between him and his god?

8.

Rahul was not a voracious reader but when he read, he read three or four books at a time forming a complex web of time, events, characters and storylines in his mind. Although this style confused him he enjoyed its intoxicating impact. Just after the epidemic he had read three books at the same time, over a period of one month. The books were: *Anna Karenina* by Leo Tolstoy; *Immortality* by Milan Kundera and *My Name is Red* by Orhan Pamuk. He kept a diary of his jottings from the books he read. At times, he read this diary and thoughts flowed freely in his mind. One day, he conducted an elaborate search for the diary to check the notes he had made from these three books. He found the diary in a locker, under empty cardboard boxes. There were three sets of notes, one from each book.

The quotation from *Anna Karenina* belonged to one of Anna's internal dialogues in the end (Part VII/Chapter XXX) and it read as follows:

"My love grows more and more passionate and egotistic, and his dwindles and dwindles, and that is why we are separating," she went on thinking. *"And there is no remedy. For me everything centres in him, and I demand that he should give himself up to me more and more completely. But he wants more and more to get away from me. Before we were united we really drew together, but now we were irresistibly drifting apart; and it cannot be altered. He tells me I am unreasonably jealous, and I have told myself that I am unreasonably jealous; but it is not true. I am not jealous, but dissatisfied. But ..."*

The quotation from *Immortality* belonged to a reflective description of the author in the opening scene (Part 1/ The Face/Chapter 1) and it read as follows:

"She passed the lifeguard, and after she had gone some three or four steps beyond him she turned her head, smiled, and waved to him. At that instant I felt a pang in my heart! That smile and that gesture belonged to a twenty-year-old girl! Her arm rose with bewitching ease. It was as if she were playfully tossing a brightly coloured ball to her lover. That smile and that gesture

had charm and elegance, while the face and the body no longer had any charm. It was the charm of a gesture drowning in the charmlessness of the body. But the woman, though she must of course have realised that she was no longer beautiful, forgot that for the moment. There is a certain part of all of us that lives outside of time. Perhaps we become aware of our age at exceptional moments and most of the times we are ageless."

The quotation from *My Name is Red* belonged to a monologue of a dog (Chapter 3/I am a Dog) and it read as follows:

"Allow me to remind you of 'The Cave', the most beautiful of the Koran's chapters. I'm reminding you not because I suspect there may be those who never read the Koran among us in this good coffeehouse, but because I want to refresh your memories: This chapter recounts the story of the seven youths who grow tired of living among pagans and take refuge in a cave where they enter a deep sleep. Allah then seals their ears and causes them to doze off for exactly three hundred and nine years. When they awake, they learn just how many years have passed only after one of them enters the society of men and tries to spend an outdated silver coin. All of them are stunned to learn what has happened. This chapter subtly describes man's attachment to Allah, His miracles, the transitory nature of time and the pleasures of deep sleep, and though it's not my place, allow me to remind you of the eighteenth verse, which makes mention of a dog resting at the mouth of this cave where the seven youths have fallen asleep. Obviously, anyone would be proud to appear in the Koran. As a dog, I take pride in this chapter, and through it I intend to bring the Erzurumis, who refer to their enemies as dirty mongrels, to their senses."

Rahul read the extracts a number of times trying to remember the circumstances under which he had read these books. He tried to decipher the underlying signals which these lines communicated to him, softly yet most intensely like the silent rush of falling snow. Slowly, he recollected Anna's lamentations reminded him of the depraved life of his sister; the scene described by Kundera brought the shadow of Rangamashima's sad smile to his eyes and the last monologue sketchily erupted the images of his storyteller father who was repeatedly cheated by women and loved to sleep for hours to glide through all the sadness in his life.

9.

A few days back Rahul visited a remote mountain station, covered with cedar, cinar, maple and deodar trees. He stayed in a small cottage surrounded by brightly coloured wild flowers. The sunshine was pale. The sky was a mixture of colours – ultramarine and grey. At night he walked through the dimly lit alleys, searching for something but he could not remember what he sought. He was perplexed and vexed.

During one of his nocturnal expeditions, he came to a playground lit on all sides. It was crowded with people sitting in zigzag rows, looking attentively at a raised podium where a play was being enacted by a group of young energetic men and women dressed in strange colourful clothes. He could see that the play was serious in content but it was entertaining, too. Once the play was over, a serious-looking gentleman in traditional mountain clothes announced in a deep baritone, "Now, ladies and gentlemen, we've come to the last part of our programme. We proudly present before you a woman who survived death in the most infamous epidemic that ravaged the eastern parts of our country a few years back. She is presently under rigorous medical investigation by the National Institute of Virology. Doctors and specialists believe she could be holding secrets in her blood, secrets dealing with life and death. The medical fraternity is spellbound by the way she has defied death. She is a poet of great merit and has agreed to read out one of her earliest poems. . Ladies and gentlemen, I present Rekha Dutta Gupta!"

A few seconds later Rahul saw a small woman on stage. She wore a white sari with a cobalt blue embroidered border. She had large black eyes set in a beautiful face. She looked at the audience almost reluctantly for some time and then began in a low, soft voice.

"There was a man who was in love with me. This was a long time ago. While I was deeply moved by his silent love, I was helpless. I was already engaged to another man who was a friend since my college days. However, I was so touched by this man who loved me silently that I followed his life closely. A few years later, when I was already settled in my married life with two sons and a creative career I wrote a poem titled 'Missing Rahul'. Ladies and gentlemen, I'll read out this poem to you now."

Rekha paused briefly and then recited the poem.

"This mask will go away this year
That mask will go away that year
These are the words Rahul's ma remembers Rahul had said
when he left home two years back.

Where has Rahul gone two years ago never to come back home?
His ma says – "Rahul did not talk to me after those words."
Between this year and that year
There are other years.
Between this mask and that mask
There are other masks.
Between years and masks Rahul has held –
The scents of his ma's bosom
The simmering shadow of a gun
Nanu's fragile fingers
The yellowing photograph of Rupa who never
Came back after making it in tinsel town
Rangamashima's spasms between his legs
The Krishnachura tree where they played hide-n-seek
Fried malpuas dipped in jelly on a cloudy
                              Autumn afternoon
And then tired of holding all these
Rahul withdrew his hand one night and let
                    Matters fly and
                         Fall....
I could not meet Rahul even in oblivion.
One evening, as I opened my e-mail box
I found a message from him that goes like this –
"Nanu, you believe the sky is blue.
I believed the sky is blue.
              But, Nanu, sky is space.

And, space has no colour.
When the masks are gone, the man does not exist for you.
You do not see him though he is
Breathing down your neck.
Only silently, unrelenting space falling
From within the cups of your palms."

Once the poem was over there was a huge round of applause and everyone got up to gather around Rekha to ask her how she had survived the epidemic. Rahul moved out of the area dazed. He walked, immersed in his haphazard thoughts, till he reached the edge of a deep valley, which in the darkness of the night looked like an expansive gorge opening its secret doors to the center of the earth. He was suddenly taken over by an overwhelming desire to feel the depth of the gorge.

He jumped like a thunderbolt, Rekha's voice ringing softly in his ears.

The Last Plunge

1.

Rahul remembered it vividly. It was on 23rd November that Ipsita Dutta had come to their office. Her employer, a management consulting company (engaged by the owners of Rahul's company), had deputed her as a senior consultant to work closely with the senior managers in his office. Her brief was to help them improve their interpersonal and communication skills. This was because the management was of the opinion that the senior managers were unnecessarily at loggerheads with each other over every possible issue and they communicated poorly amongst themselves. The financial experts believed that their company was losing substantial revenue on account of this squabbling. This behaviour, in spite of being criticised, never really died down but, like an endless fountain, continued to enjoy the tacit support of the sources that mattered.

Six senior managers (who oversaw the functions of engineering, finance, sales and marketing, operations, IT, HR and administration) were shortlisted to go through a specially designed orientation-cum-counselling session with Ipsita. Rahul was one of the six senior managers.

At first sight, she looked pretty, peppy and chirpy, an audaciously fake smile hanging on her face like an oscillating chandelier. Rahul was amazed by the efficiency of her jaw-breaking, round-the-clock smile. On the first day, Ipsita rounded up the six of them in a conference room and introduced herself tendentiously and got to know them conversationally. She informed them that they would first have to sit with her individually for personal interviews so that she could know them as individuals and only then would she be in a position to deal with them more effectively in a group. She allowed the men to talk about them at length. They were also informed about the personal interview schedule with details of the time and agenda. Rahul's happened to be the last interview, two days later, in a post-lunch session. Was this move to keep his name at the fag end a deliberate one, he wondered. There was no way to find out.

In the night, he tried to remember Ipsita's face. He couldn't recall it even after several attempts. Her face, somehow, had blurred mysteriously in his memory. As he tried harder, he conjured images from his childhood birthday celebrations, as he often did. Rahul's birthdays were celebrated with pomp and grandeur. After the guests left, the house looked like an abandoned battlefield, the depleted balloons lying on the dusty floors like the severed heads of soldiers.

Unable to sleep, he went to the terrace room in search of his childhood diaries. In these he had written down (long ago) in great detail some magic tricks he had learnt from various sources, especially from his *kaku*, who was a magician in a circus troupe for some time. He unpacked the diaries and dusted them off. When he opened them and saw the yellowed, at times eaten away, pages and the old diagrams, equations and steps neatly jotted down with a pencil, he was amazed by the distance he had travelled in his life.

*****

Two days later, on 25th November, when Rahul was face to face with Ipsita, he wanted to look at her closely. With this intention, he positioned himself so that he did not obstruct the soft light emanating from a corner in the false ceiling. Her eyes were kohl lined. She had generously applied rouge on her cheeks. Her lips were painted a deep brown. There were coloured streaks in her hair. She was wearing a navy blue business suit and laced soft leather black shoes. He wondered what Ipsita's original complexion would be. Her breasts were cleverly padded to mask the sharpness of her nipples. She had a remarkably sharp nose and chestnut eyes. Looking at her carefully, he had a feeling he was talking to a masked woman shrouded in a phantom-like dress or veil. She was not smiling like she was the other day. *Was she in a bad mood?* The absence of the smile made him curious about her. *Was it because of him? Or, was it something to do with her?*

She asked politely, "You're Mr. Rahul Roy, Vice President (Operations)?"

"Yes," he answered.

"Do you mind if I call you Rahul?"

"No, and what should I call you?"

Ipsita said, "Call me Ipsita. We encourage people to address each other by their first names. That's a positive start to building intimate professional relationships."

Rahul was impressed. He said, "Can I call you Ipsy?"

She was surprised but hid it behind a half-smile. She remarked, "Ipsy! What's that supposed to mean?"

"Nothing. But it sounds good to the ears and is easy on the tongue. What do you say?" He expected her to raise an alarm based on his experience.

Ipsita didn't pay any heed. She said involuntarily shrugging her shoulders without a trace of emotion in her voice, "Okay. Tell me something about yourself."

"About what?"

Ipsita sensed Rahul's reluctance in going through the whole exercise. "Something about your professional life. Something about your personal life."

"At office I'm responsible for achieving time, cost and quality targets. At home I have one wife, a pair of sons and a set of parents."

Ipsita started with her usual questions. "Are you the only child of your parents?"

"No. I have an elder sister who lives in Australia."

"Do you feel you're in the right kind of job?"

"As a mechanical engineer of my calibre I think it's all right, I'm doing pretty fine," Rahul answered thoughtfully.

Ipsita quipped, "But otherwise?"

"I can't say."

"Why? Didn't you want to become an engineer? Were you forced to study engineering?"

"No," Rahul answered in a dry voice.

"Then?"

"I can't explain."

Ipsita was persistent, "Did you want to become something else? Were you good at something else that you did not pursue?"

"No, no, nothing of that sort, really."

"Are you unhappy with your present work?"

Rahul put his foot down. "I won't answer that question."

"But that's important to know, Rahul. We're here to structure a pattern of working that will make you guys satisfied and more involved in your work. That's not possible without knowing the real issues of concern both at the individual as well as the collective level."

Rahul answered firmly: "Please carry on with your job. You can't force me to answer any of your questions, Ipsy."

Suddenly, Ipsita looked at her watch and said, "Rahul, we'll do this tomorrow. I've got to go. My daughter was taken ill from school this morning. I hope you won't mind."

Before he could answer, she had left, absent-mindedly. In the night he wanted to remember her face. He could. But the make-up distracted his thoughts.

*****

Next day they met again in the interview room in the morning session. He asked her about her daughter. She said her daughter was afflicted with a bout of viral fever. She had shown her to a doctor and was advised a mild dose of paracetamol, analgesics and bed rest. He wanted to know a few things, but he refrained from asking. She looked less made up today. She was wearing a green salwar kameez. It was clear from her eyes that she had not slept well.

She asked, "Where were we yesterday?"

"I think I refused to answer your question about whether I'm unhappy with my work."

"Which, clearly means you're unhappy with it."

Rahul kept quiet.

Suddenly, Ipsita asked, "What makes you happy, Rahul?"

Rahul rephrased the question for her. "You mean what makes my soul burst with joy?"

Ipsita looked at him with wonder-struck eyes. She seemed bewildered and pleased with his expression. She said, "What a beautiful choice of words!"

"What?"

"Soul bursting with joy, because that's what happiness is all about. What makes your soul burst with joy, Rahul?"

"Well, frankly speaking, when I've had a solid round of shit with all the dirty stuff and gases out of my belly early in the morning. It is usually followed by a vexing emptiness crawling in my stomach. When I've partly fuelled it up with lemon water, a leopard-like hunger gradually springs into action, recoiling like a python inside me and yes, that makes me damn happy."

Ipsita nodded as if she understood and then went on. "That's one kind of happiness. There's another kind of happiness as well, I believe. What about your achievements – don't they make you happy?"

"But when did I achieve anything in life?"

Ipsita didn't seem to believe him. "Of course you've achieved quite a lot. You're the youngest Vice President in this company."

"Do you consider that an achievement? Frankly, I'm working amidst a bunch of duds. That makes me look smarter but that doesn't mean I'm very smart." Rahul was blunt to the point of being offensive.

"Are you trying to impress me or pass judgment on your colleagues?"

"Actually I was trying both."

Ipsita brought up the topic she wanted to discuss with

Rahul. She told him, "There are issues about your being brash, arrogant and judgmental. There are serious concerns that you are highly individualistic and at times anarchic in work. Don't you think that to achieve a goal a team is more important than an individual?"

"I have nothing to say. I can tell you I don't like those dames – Shailaja, who is heading the finance department and Maitreyi, head of the engineering department. They must have told you something potentially dangerous against me because they want to show me down all the time. They try to create obstacles in my work."

"Since you've raised the issue, it's better I tell you their side of the story. Shailaja feels you make commitments to vendors on payment terms, etc., without considering her opinion. Maitreyi feels you buy or get machines fabricated from outside contractors without consulting her on technical matters. If these are correct then you're clearly breaching certain fundamental principles of collective working. Are these accusations correct, Rahul?"

Rahul was flabbergasted. "Looking at them from the outside they are stated all right. But by relaxed payment terms I've reduced cost. On technical matters, I've used my years of knowledge of operating machines, which Maitreyi is incapable of understanding. I don't blame them. The game is clear. First you put an instinctive bugger like me in charge of operations, make me responsible for all the critical things in the world and then transfer the noose through my bloody ass and hand it over to these dumb females to control me like a puppet on behalf of the lazy morons at the top. On top of that you ask me to be a team man. If I get these assholes involved in decision making , they will only see to it that the entire process is horribly delayed, on grounds that will look damn right, only apparently of course. I would be chewed up in the end, the company would have lost substantial time and money and I would be blamed for somebody else's actions. These dames would be giggling all the way at this joker of a mega carnival, yes, that's me. I have a point to make. I'm not concerned with goals and collective working. I'm just passionate about my work."

"But there are serious concerns; I am told you handle these women like a ruffian and not a professional. If they go public with sexual harassment charges against you, the management could be seriously embarrassed in the media and it could dent the image of your company. Don't take this lightly, Rahul," Ipsita warned him.

"Let's stop this right here, Ipsy. I think this whole goddamned exercise has been designed to goad me with rubbish lectures. Excuse me, but Shailaja showed me her boobs one evening after office hours, to tell me how our top man beats her during violent sex when she travels with him on foreign tours. I thought this to be a signal that she wanted to sleep with me. Otherwise, tell me, why would a woman suddenly bare her bruised boobs to her not-so-good-looking colleague without any related perspective or forewarning? I was only too eager because my wife never really allowed me to touch her after our second son was born six years ago. She got entrapped in some holy shit. Good for her. In any case, sex between us was sparing even earlier. I was like a hungry animal. So when I stated my intention to Shailaja in a straightforward manner she slapped me and threatened to tell the boss and get me thrown out of office. I was scared and, believe me, I had to pay her to keep her quiet. At times she still threatens me with her looks. But I don't give that bitch a damn nowadays. That serves her right, you know." Ipsita asked, "What about Maitreyi?"

"One day, during a meeting, I was vacantly looking at her (she was sitting opposite me), engrossed in some other thoughts and could have winked accidentally. She was short of raising hell and warned me not to look at her with such animal lust or she would blind me with a hot spike."

Ipsita looked at him strangely and said, "Don't you respect women, Rahul?"

"What is that supposed to mean, Ipsy?"

She was clearly at a loss of words. The silence was becoming unbearable. He thought he should say something.

"Didn't you sleep properly last night?"

"No. My daughter was running temperature. I had to sponge her, pour iced water on her head at regular intervals."

Rahul commented, "I don't know if I'm being too nosy but what was your husband doing? Snoring?"

"I don't have my husband living with me. I'm fighting a divorce petition. I live with my mother. She helped me throughout. But she too is not quite well."

"I'm sorry, Ipsy."

"What's there to be sorry about? I'm just fighting a case and living my life on my terms."

They parted after some time, not able to speak any further.

At night Rahul thought of her. He was filled with an aching desire to be in bed with her.

2.

It was November 29th and Rahul hadn't been to the office for the last three days. He felt dizzy; he knew he was crossing an invisible border. His deputy took care of work in the factory pretty well. Sometimes he consulted Rahul over the phone. Rahul provided him with tips and leads wherever required. He rested in phases during the day. For the rest of the time, based on the instructions encoded in his childhood diaries, he constructed and put into place multiple accessories required to perform various magic tricks and practised them one by one.

He rarely spoke to anybody in the house. His parents were sick, dying. His wife was mostly in the kitchen or in her *puja* room. She rarely looked at him. Even if she did, there was pure disdain in her eyes to indicate how he had ruined her life. She silently blamed him for her fate. His elder son was studious. He kept cramming something or the other or writing and copying from textbooks like a calligrapher the whole day. His younger son painted well. He spent most of his time drawing sad landscapes and abstract faces of women.

One morning, Rahul went to his parents' room to watch

them sleeping from up close, but they were already awake. His father had swollen like a balloon over the years and looked terribly pale. His mother had shrunk to half the size she used to be when she was young. They were ailing from a number of complex, age-related diseases and were able to avoid death only by the intervention of life-saving drugs and the incessant care of their daughter-in-law. He was a bit scared the way they both gazed at him with fixed eyes and a mysterious halo around them made by the sunlight streaming in through the east-end window.

His father said breathlessly, "Rahul, there are wrinkles on your forehead. Your hair is greying. You're getting older, my boy."

His mother intervened in her wheezing voice, "He looks a fine young man still. But he needs to go on a voyage. He has to take care of us. He's worried if anything should happen to us. He needs to go out without worries."

His father said, "That's not possible, Nilima. Even if we're gone he'll be worried about his wife and sons. Come here, Rahul. If you have some time, sit down here beside me. I want to hold your hands."

He sat down at the edge of the bed with one hand in his father's hands and the other in his mother's lap. They both rubbed his hands delicately and started crying silently. He was struck by an intense attack of claustrophobia.

Rahul never went to the *puja* room, but today he went in to check what was happening there. There were spiralling ribbons of smoke, the sandalwood fragrance of incense sticks and the melody of Meera's bhajans Mita sang in her deeply sonorous voice, floating and rising above the overpowering cleanliness in the room. The room had been insanely sterilised, the rows and columns of decorated apparatus and the shining idols of marble, brass and silver. Mita hated Rahul going inside the *puja* room. He was barely inside the room when she got wind of his coming (he couldn't fathom how), stopped singing and said to him, "Don't you enter here without taking a bath and changing your night clothes. This is my only refuge. You know I don't like this place getting polluted in any way. Please respect my wishes if you can."

He came out. He looked at her. She had aged. But she looked fresh after her bath. Her hair was still long and charcoal black; it had not greyed. Her skin glowed with magical light. She had an intoxicatingly tragic face and the sad, lovelorn eyes of a devotee. He loved looking at her slender fingers and lips, which glistened even without makeup. He was painfully overcome by a desire to hold her like a bandit, tie her hands and legs to the grilles of a window and make love to her.

The second night after they were married he had undressed her hurriedly, against her wishes. He was amazed by the small tuft of grassland over the swollen mound between her legs. It looked like a beckoning mountaintop. He had gone mad looking at it for the very first time in his life; it was very different from what he had imagined. She had put her hands over her eyes in shame and embarrassment. After he had rolled down his underpants, she stealthily saw his erect thing through the gaps in her fingers. She gave out a gasping wail as if he had gagged her. She had pleaded like a beggar, "No, Rahul, don't do this to me. I can't take that monster of a snake inside me. It will kill me. It will break my insides." He entered her like a bull. She fainted. He made love to an unconscious, quasi-dead piece of flesh. He could never enter her fully. There was surmounting resistance between her legs. Much later, her gynaecologist had advised him (after their second son was born) against such invasive sex. The doctor said that he had already damaged her vaginal passage almost irreversibly.

He moved out of the *puja* room silently and went into the study. His elder son was writing an essay on James Watt. Rahul asked him, "Have you ever seen a steam engine in real life?"

The boy dived inside the lake of his thoughts and replied reflectively, "No. I've only seen them in photographs and movies."

Rahul said, "Do you love steam engines?"

"Yes, I love watching the smoke rise above the world,

listening to the whistle and rhythmic sounds of its motion. It gives me a strange sense of enchantment and brings tears to my eyes unexpectedly. Baba, can you tell me when and where the first railway service was established in the world?"

Rahul replied, "If I remember correctly, it was in France in 1829 from Lyons to St. Etienne."

His younger son was doing a pencil drawing of his mother drying out her hair in bright sunshine on the terrace, her eyes locked to a portrait of a man held in her hands. He looked at the portrait of the man and shuddered at the emerging talent and skill of his son and the resemblance of the man in the drawing to somebody he knew long ago. He masked his feelings. Rahul asked him, "How did you draw this?"

His son replied gleefully, "I saw Ma like this one day, exactly as it is in the drawing and copied it on paper from my memory. Is life like this, *Baba*?"

Rahul did not reply. He went to the terrace room to practise his magic tricks. He practised them ferociously like a madman chasing a fantastic dream of becoming a magician overnight. Somehow, his hands, fingers, body movements, eyesight and reflexes worked in perfect coordination.

There was a call on his hand phone. It was Ipsita. She asked excitedly, "What's this, Rahul? Are you deliberately skipping the orientation programme?"

He said, "No. I'm not well."

"What happened?"

"I'm feeling dizzy. When I walk I feel I may fall."

Ipsita asked with genuine concern in her voice, "Are you all right now? Have you shown yourself to a doctor?"

"I'm improving. Don't worry. How is your daughter?"

"The fever is gone. She's a bit weak but she has joined school. I want to tell you something."

Rahul said, "Tell me."

"You look silly when you use foul language. Why do you want to constantly portray someone you're not?"

Rahul laughed. "Is this a devious way of coaxing me into your orientation programme?"

"If you refuse to co-operate and participate, your bosses could hold this against you and disrupt your career."

"You're a management expert, aren't you? Can you tell me what really bugs my bosses about me?"

There was hushed laughter at the other end. Rahul said, "Why are you silent? Tell me."

Ipsita answered, "I don't know, but my assumption is that entrepreneurs feel threatened by entrepreneur-like managers in their system. They feel insecure by the possibility that their business will be hijacked by another independent mind. So they prefer top-class, educated professionals working like slaves – which you clearly refuse to do."

"So what's your prescription for me?"

"Nothing really, except that it would be nice if you go through my orientation programme and participate without rebelling."

"Let's see. But I don't think that's likely to happen."

3.

Rahul had not been to office for almost a week. It was December 7. He had been rigorously confining himself to the terrace room, practising the magic tricks to perfection.

Barun, a school friend from a business family, had recently built a modern eatery on Park Street. Barun had informed him casually about this when they met at the last school reunion. The eatery had a live band to entertain its guests in the evenings. A few days earlier, Rahul had called Barun to know if he would be interested in a magic show performance in the eatery. He had answered in the affirmative but was curious to know the details of the magician – was he famous and a star attraction by himself or only a debutant?

Rahul said, "Don't you remember, Barun, I used to show you guys tricks in school during tiffin hours? Remember how you used to adore that trick of infusing life into a stuffed bird and asked me to repeat it over and over again?"

Rahul's proposal shocked Barun for a moment; he stuttered badly in response. However, he remained extremely warm in approach and called him for a preview the next day. Rahul showed Barun, his wife Tanuja, his twelve--year-old son Bivash and the rock band musicians five of his most difficult tricks. The magic tricks that he showed them were:

a) In an empty cardboard box he put in five marbles in full view of the audience. In two to three minutes of hypnosis, the five marbles multiplied hundred times. Bivash was called upon to open the box and count the marbles. He went bonkers counting the five hundred marbles and by the sight of so many red, green, violet, scarlet, mauve, turquoise and sky blue marbles.

b) He hung a canvas copy of Leonardo da Vinci's 'Mona Lisa' on the wall and covered it with a red scarf for a few seconds. When the scarf was removed with a flourish, Mona Lisa's mysterious smile had changed to boisterous laughter. Tanuja clapped animatedly.

c) He brought out two packs of cards and displayed them to the crowd. He asked Barun, Tanuja and Bivash to pick one card each, remember their respective cards carefully and return them to the pack, which he energetically shuffled thrice. The cards were placed upside down on the adjoining table in full view of the audience. After carefully considering each of the cards from a distance in a saintly trance, Rahul suddenly picked up three cards and gave one each to Barun, Tanuja and Bivash. He asked them to look at the cards. Their jaws dropped: they were holding the cards they had picked. From the look in Barun's eyes, Rahul could safely conclude that Barun was spellbound.

d) Rahul placed five tennis balls on the table and covered them with an empty box (shown to the audience beforehand). When the box was lifted, the five balls had vanished and in their place was a football. Bivash was enormously pleased when Rahul gifted him the football at the end of the trick.

e) He placed three stuffed parrots on the table. Each parrot was shown to the audience separately. A black silk cloth was spread over the stuffed parrots. The cloth was then blown away by a strong gust of wind created by the robust pedestal fan behind. The stuffed birds suddenly came to life and the parrots went up in the air flying.

The show ended to a round of wild applause and hearty cheer. Barun was visibly moved by the performance and said excitedly, "I'll draw up a year's contract with you, Rahul. It's fabulous. Please get started from tomorrow if you like. We'll do the most aggressive marketing and publicity in the city. You'll be a star overnight, my boy. Tell me your price. By the way, are you quitting your job?"

Rahul said, "All right I'll start from tomorrow. Meanwhile, let me think over the price part. I'll let you know. I don't know about my job. I have been bunking for the last few days now. I'll have to decide. Let's see." He walked out of the room, satisfied.

When he returned home, he saw a few missed calls from Ipsita, his deputy and a long sms from his sister in Australia, which read as follows: "Do you roam around with your two young studs? I'm with my young boy whose teary-eyed darling face amazes me. It reminds me of the grief of a harbour – a huge ship loaded with wine, men, women and loot is about to depart this harbour; it reminds me of a cloud, which is about to burst into rain. There is so much ambiguity in the faces of young boys, aged concubines, sleeping eunuchs and faithless evangelists. I look at these faces tirelessly. I understand nothing of their meanings and keep getting endlessly attracted to their silent hooting."

He replied to his sister. "*Didi*, does it make you happy to know that I'm on my way to becoming a full-time magician?"

After midnight, Rahul saw a blink of light on his phone. There was a message from his sister. It read: "It's magic to be a magician. I'm very happy for you, my baby."

*****

On the morning of December 15 there was a call from Mr. Pasricha.

He started in a crisp, business-like tone, "I'm calling from Delhi. Is it true that you're not coming to office for over a fortnight?"

Rahul answered, "Yes."

"There is also some talk of your becoming a magician in some restaurant on Park Street. Is this true?"

Rahul answered in a brief yes, again.

Mr. Pasricha lost his cool, "What's this all about, Rahul?"

"I just wanted a change of scene, Mr. Pasricha."

Mr. Pasricha almost barked into the phone: "You just want to change the scene, Rahul. Do you know the significance of what you're saying? We take care of you all these years in the best possible manner. And you put us in a lurch at the worst time, when we're up against stiff competition, increased input costs and a drop in demand! How much are the Kapadias paying you to damage us in this manner? If you needed money or anything else you should have talked to me directly. When can we meet to sort this out?"

Rahul did not prolong the conversation. He disconnected the line.

4.

Rahul completed a week of his career as a magician. It was gaining a momentous rhythm of its own. The tricks were made catchier and elegant by the use of background music, colourful props and dresses, smart stage management, choreography and dramatic pauses. The crowd response was exceedingly encouraging. Daily revenues doubled in the restaurant and Barun expanded publicity through billboards, television and radio.

The restaurant was now open up to 2 am. Rahul's remuneration had not yet been fixed.

A week later, around midnight, he saw a woman entering the restaurant escorted by a tall man. He recognised Ipsita instantly. They sat in a corner eating, looking at the magic show in rapt attention. When he moved backstage for a break, he saw Ipsita coming round the corner smiling brightly at him.

Ipsita said, "I could have never dreamt of a magician hiding behind the garb of a sullen, rebellious middle-aged manager!"

Rahul asked, "Did you like the show?"

Ipsita answered, "It was great. It de-stressed me completely. I've been calling you but you haven't been returning my calls. I need to talk to you about something, Rahul."

"Tell me."

She asked, "Are you done for the night or have you another round to perform?"

"I have to pack up and leave. Why?"

"Then pack up. We can talk once we are outside," she suggested.

Rahul packed up and changed his clothes. Half an hour later, they were walking along the deserted Park Street. It was cold and foggy. She had no make-up on today. She was pale wheatish in complexion. She had big watery eyes under long, curved eyelashes. She had unkempt hair. She was wearing rugged clothes and looked very different from the day they had met. She resembled a fragile, elegant relic of an ancient clay statuette Rahul had seen in the Indian Museum.

They followed a scarlet trajectory hanging in air tirelessly illuminated by the weak street lamps, advertising signboards and security lights from empty office buildings, shops and bars.

They took no heed of the roaming dogs, fox calls from an old cemetery in the distance, the dark St. Xavier's campus, pavement dwellers sleeping in huddles and heaps to beat the biting cold, the alertness of guards in the Park Street police station, the sudden screeching of a black car and the melancholy traversing slowly in the Muslim dwellings in Park Circus area.

Rahul started the conversation, "Was that your boyfriend?"

"Who? In the restaurant? No, he's my lawyer. We were discussing a few technical points related to my divorce case. He left after we were through with our discussions."

"You said you wanted to tell me something."

Ipsita said, "Mr. Pasricha feels all this magic stuff is a hoax, a front to work on behalf of the Kapadias. He plans to sue you. He has asked the company solicitors to prepare the necessary papers through a senior counsel."

Rahul was not bothered. "Let him do what he likes."

"But this will damage your time and money."

"I can't avoid it at this stage. I've not as yet firmed up my contract with Barun. I can ask him to cover the legal expenses; over and above that, I can take a small salary, too. How is it going with your divorce case? Why do you want to divorce your husband, by the way? Am I intruding by asking these questions?"

A cloud of sadness crossed Ipsita's face before she began. "I'm not divorcing him, Rahul, I'm fighting the divorce. My husband wants to marry another woman. She is a famous singer. If we split, I've asked for hefty alimony, besides a settlement amount on which arguments are going on. Working women with decent salaries have difficulty getting alimony. But I'm not letting it go easily. Now my husband and his lover are sending goons after my daughter and me. Imagine!"

Wondering at the strange twists of fate, Rahul said, "Love is indeed strange."

"Have you ever fallen in love?"

"Frankly, no, Ipsy."

After a pause she said, "I like your calling me Ipsy. How are things with your wife?"

Rahul answered cynically, "I think she has been devotedly in love with another man for years. I could never understand that really. A few days back it was revealed to me. It was shocking in a miserable way. But this pursuit of becoming a magician has cured me, soothed me and made me realise what we have ended up doing to each other in all these years. It would still wound my ego extremely to let her leave my home. At times, I wonder if everything could vanish and come back differently."

"Do you want that magic to enter in your life?"

"Coming to think of it, I would say no. But it would be nice to work some magic on this city."

"Like?"

Rahul said dreamily, "Like the roads to be lined with cypress and fig trees. Like these modern apartment buildings to be converted into minarets, cathedrals and vaulted spaces where souls can rest and mix with each other. Do you wish for any other magic?"

There was a distant look in Ipsita's eyes. "Yes," she said. "Snow falling on the leaves of trees, domes and roads and a grey screen languishing over everything, the way you look at the universe through a film of falling teardrops."

"I'll think about this, Ipsy, and let me see if I can do something to perform magic on such a large scale some day."

The Prank

1.

Rahul woke up to a cold, frosty morning. Lying in bed, he saw the condensed mist dripping from the northern window glass panes. The view of the garden was thus hazy, as if a fresh dab of watercolours in shades of red, light green, pale yellow and white had intermingled and mistily refracted the shapes of the garden foliage into a mass of an incomprehensible cloud.

For a few moments, this rush of colours and the black and white texture of his dreams conflicted with each other and made him forget where he was. It took him some time to realise that he was in his duplex apartment in the residential complex of the company campus where he worked.

The company, a premier engineering and manufacturing organisation, had been built in the suburbs, away from the strains of the main city. There was dense vegetation, a lake and wildlife, creating an impression of serenity: a perk for slogging to meet time and cost deadlines. The British had started the company in the late nineteenth century; it moved into the hands of local private investors in 1969. It was doing quite well, in spite of fluctuations in the market, because of its strong engineering back-end with innovations and technological advancements.

The needles of diffused sunlight penetrated Rahul's bedroom, making the morning look like dusk. He got up with reluctance, still sleepy. The image of a woman in his dream last night came back to him. He had dreamt he was running after her on a wet railway bridge, the menacing landscape of a wide river in flood looming large in his vision. The deathliness of the swell in the river was in stark contrast to his carnal chase of a voluptuous woman whose face he could not see but whose ripeness of flesh and pure black hair reminded him of somebody he had known long ago. As he reached the middle of the bridge, the sky thundered and the clouds exploded like bombs. Torrents of rain drenched everything in thick columns of water. Then he heard a monster like, thumping movements of an approaching train behind him. He lost sight of the woman and was brought back, as if by the stroke of a magic wand, to the dark confines of his bedroom.

His mother died the previous year after leading the life of a ruthless monarch for years. His older brother and his wife with their two children lived in Delhi. They had moved out primarily because his mother could not stand anything about his brother's wife. She would torment her daughter-in-law without any provocation in the most uncouth manner, bordering on physical assault at times. His brother left home one day shouting the choicest abuses at his mother and cursing her, much against the wishes of his wife. He abandoned the city and took up a new job in Delhi never to return or meet her.

He did not attend her funeral or the subsequent ritualistic ceremonies. Rahul had been left with no choice but to take care of his mother. Although she had become quieter after his brother had departed, it was only marginal because her tantrums continued, targeted to gain attention and perverse degrees of fidelity.

Considering the unhappy sequences of his brother's family life caused by his mother, Rahul had decided not to marry, a fact she was secretly pleased with. She was always tutoring Rahul against marriage directly or indirectly, citing numerous examples of how petite young women turned their innocent husbands into warring generals against their mothers. Rahul rarely protested against his mother because he considered her a pathetic, neurotic and soulless woman beyond redemption. But he also loved her in a strange way. Rahul would not be alive but for his mother.

One of Rahul's kidneys had become dysfunctional when he was three years old. Doctors in Calcutta had given up hope and had declared that anything fatal could happen any time, when his mother, already insane with the surmounting agony of her son's impending death, had intervened and volunteered to donate one of her kidneys for transplantation. This was successfully done by one of the renowned renal surgeons in India. Unfortunately, the transplant resulted in a few post-surgical complications that once again drew a battle line between life and death. His mother single-handedly took round-the-clock care of her son without a moment of respite. By the age of seven Rahul had reached some degree of consistency in his health and thence his mother diverted all her attention to his studies. These intense moments of togetherness in the throes of life and death cemented their bond irreversibly. However, in the process, his brother who was only four years senior to him was alienated from his mother. As a result, his brother became fiercely independent and aloof. Rahul's father was an outsider to the family. He remained one all his life and died silently by the time Rahul was a teenager. Rahul's mother was the only daughter of an aristocratic family – its only surviving heir. She had inherited large sums of money and property. As such, the family did not face any financial hardship at any point in time.

The cloud cover outside had disappeared by now. The universe was lighted by pale sunshine. Rahul proceeded to the dining room to sip his staple morning drink of lukewarm lemon water. His servants were busy with their respective jobs. He remembered it was a holiday. After breakfast, as a routine on holidays, he would go to the club for a few hands of auction bridge. He was a lonely man and was riddled with the greatest puzzle of the living world: how to pass time. He was saddled with another problem of late: having to deal with sudden attacks of monstrous erections irrespective of any external influence or provocation. This caused a nagging strain on his nerves. He started suffering from spells of nervous tension in anticipation of the next attack. It was not something for which he could consult a doctor easily; he felt embarrassed. At the same time he realised that a normal round of masturbation would not cool off such erections. It was as if his solid shaft stood in protest of his life, lustily screaming for the touch and care of a real woman. He had never had any sexual experience barring various kinds of masturbation – slow, fast, rough and smooth – in differing mediums of coconut oil, mustard oil, butter, cheese, honey, milk, soap lotion, toothpaste, shaving foam and fruit pulp, applied generously for lubrication and effect.

In these moments, he would invariably envision Purnasree. Purnasree was his neighbour when they lived in his mother's inherited home. Rahul was in college those days. Purnasree was an accomplished Bharatanatyam dancer. She practised classical dance rituals early every morning in her house, in a room opposite to Rahul's. The room had a window, panes of which were always kept half-open. Rahul's gaping, sleepy eyes could get a complete view of what was happening inside through the space between the window panes. Purnasree would be clad in a colourful silk sari, with flowers in her hair, deeply immersed in her graceful movements carved within the grammar of an ancient dance form, of which Rahul understood nothing. The scene aroused in Rahul a deep sense of longing and desire, poking him like dowels of steel. This silent duet of performance and appreciation connected by a low scale torment and rapture of hearts went on for one and a half years.

One day, Rahul got to know from his brother that Purnasree was getting married to the man she had loved since her school days, a ravishingly handsome young man, an upcoming criminal lawyer, from an elite family. Rahul felt a nagging pain in his heart; an army of ferocious ants hungrily chewed at his nerves. Rahul could not look at any woman straight in the eye for a very long time thereafter. He lost his life gradually to an imaginary jungle, building up his career and providing single-minded companionship to his mother.

Five years ago, his brother left for Delhi. Meanwhile, Rahul got a job in a company that provided him luxury accommodation away from the heart of the city. That suited him fine. Rahul's mother decided to sell off her inherited house and invest the money. Rahul had no opinion on this. She didn't leave a single penny for his brother, her first son. Rahul, after his mother's death, contacted his brother and expressed his wish to share the inheritance in a rightful manner. His brother refused. He said he was not keen on maintaining any relationship with Rahul in the future. The seed of poison that was planted in his brother's heart in his adolescence blinded him; he disregarded and failed to recognise the anguish of a lonely younger brother yearning for affection. Rahul remained dignified, preferring silence to speech under the circumstances.

The morning erections were, moreover, painful. As the day progressed outside, Rahul conjured up an uncanny vision of his two escapades from a run-down brothel; his colleague Rajesh had taken him there, years ago. Both the times, once to a swarthy, elderly, fleshy woman and the other time to a pale-skinned thin young woman, he could not bring himself finally up to the act of penetration. In fact, after so many years (he was not sure whether his memory was playing tricks) what he clearly remembered was that he had not touched their bodies; he was not even aroused. On both the occasions, he sweated profusely (while others felt he was melting in the heat) seeing dotted porous skin from extreme close-up, turned nervous by the prevalent smell of lavender mixed in sweat, punched with pungent stench of urine. He was finally overcome by a howling churning of his intestines to shit and buy peace with the disquiet burning in his gut. He ran away, chased by sharp sounds of smutty giggles, spitting betel leaf juice from stained mouths and the thunder of taunting claps emanating from a procession of ghost-like women trailing him.

Rahul drank successive glasses of warm lemon water. This relieved him substantially. He had vowed to get a woman within the next year by hook or crook but didn't know how. At his workplace he had no interaction with women. The few women he met at social gatherings and the club were wives, daughters and relatives of his colleagues and friends. He was not flirtatious by nature and was completely at a loss when it came to conversing with the wives in the noisy, opulence-driven, smart and superficial parties. He was sure that unless he adopted certain unconventional methods, there was no chance of finding any woman in the near future. He knew instinctively: it was not possible for him to find a virgin anymore. He refused to resort to Internet chat rooms, matrimonial portals and advertisements – he found them exceedingly boring and laborious. In fact, he was not pursuing marriage seriously; he craved companionship and sex. After days of racking his brain, he concluded: there was no other option but to become a hunter to get the right catch. It's not as if he didn't face moral battles within his soul. The choices were between: leading a normal life with adequate sexual fulfilment irrespective of the methods by which he achieved such fulfilment barring paid sex or marriage, and oppressive abstinence replete with the overburden and unnecessary weight of morality leading to sickness.

In the last ten days he had shortlisted six women among the wives of his thirty-seven colleagues and decided on a dramatic channel of communication with them. These six women were Nilanjana, Nandana, Chaitali, Kakali, Bakul and Shruti. He collected their cell phone numbers from the company colony directory. These women lived in various parts of the colony within families of their husbands, children and in-laws (who visited them once in a while); he met them daily perfunctorily at some point in the day, masking his intention carefully. They were married to his colleagues Samar, Pradeep, Sagar, Manab, Amit and Sandip, respectively. He knew them quite closely, interacted with them regularly in the office, club and at social gatherings.

While short-listing these women, he had applied a certain yardstick, conversely meaning that these women shared a few common properties. One, they had all been married for more than ten years (it was a good enough time to get disillusioned with marriage and try out newer, unconventional relationships), second, each had one child in the age group of seven to ten years (once again, a time span suitable enough to sustain that mystical sense of responsibility in a mother without destroying her natural instinct for wildness), third, they were homemakers and self-employed on a part-time basis (a combination of experience in two kinds of organisations: one that glorified labour in the name of money and the other that glorified labour in the name of love). Another trait was that they were all melancholic, withdrawn and aloof in most parties (perhaps demonstrating their disdain for superficiality and love for a deeper sensibility to the complex aesthetics of existence). And, lastly, they were a part of a nuclear family (this ensured a limit to adjunct irritabilities and engagements, thereby ensuring a physical space for amorous ventures).

It took him ten days of arduous labour and a couple of sleepless nights to make a comprehensive list, interspersed by his ruminations of the colony wives – their behavioural patterns, styles of make-up, dresses, inner-wear and attitudes towards male strangers. Rahul first wanted to check the response of these women by sending them an interesting short message on their cell phones. He had bought a new cell phone the previous week solely for this operation. While getting the network connection he had to submit a proof of identity. This made him anxious. What if one of these women went berserk upon receiving his message and immediately sought the services of a nearby police station to get an investigation instituted? The police would no doubt contact the network company, obtain his identity from their records in a matter of seconds and catch him. Rahul fought these thoughts and after hours of internal struggle decided to go ahead with his plan, attracted by the piquancy, perceived thrill, danger and drama, which were hitherto missing in his life.

He went to the toilet. Before entering, he asked his cook, Anil, to prepare his breakfast. On holidays he loved to eat poached eggs and croissants followed by three to four cups of steaming black Darjeeling tea with honey. He prayed sincerely that his rectum would get evacuated in one shot so his bowels would not nag him during the day with bubbles of anxiety swimming discomfortingly in his gut and colon. He knew the situation was now far beyond his control. To bring the tiring outbursts of prolonged, uncontrollable erections under his control, there was no option in the long run but to park his throbbing missile in a cave that was real and flushed with flesh and fluids. The image of Purnasree dancing to a classical raga in a white Kanjeevaram silk sari, fresh cream-white flowers in her black hair popped into his mind's eye for a split second and vanished.

He planned the text of the message he would send to these six women to pull them out of their familial hibernation. He wrote various drafts on his mental notepad. He edited, erased and added. He was once again brought back to the real world by Anil's warnings that his eggs were getting cold.

After breakfast, he sat down in his living room with the new cell phone and typed out the draft he had finalised in his mind. He enjoyed the growing anticipation and a flutter of excitement in his chest.

Anil asked, "Will you have lunch at the club or at home?"

Rahul didn't answer. He was engrossed in typing the message. Anil repeated his query. Rahul looked at him as if he had woken up from a reverie and continued looking at him absent-mindedly. Finally he asked a bit dazed, "Did you ask me anything?"

Anil said, "Yes, will you have lunch at the club or at home?"

Rahul replied, "At home maybe. In any case, cook something light."

Rahul finished typing. He read the text silently a few times and then aloud a few more times to check the impact of the words. A smile of satisfaction formed on his face.

He genuinely liked what he had written. He had copied the contact numbers of the six women in a separate diary. He got the diary and entered the numbers in the contacts list of his new cell phone one by one. He sent the text message to all the six women; once the delivery reports were received he gasped with a sense of relief and release; he felt as if he had crossed a critical milestone of his life. He expected immediate replies. There were none.

He could not go to the club with his new cell phone – he knew he would spend the hours there in a trance of cautiously guarded excitement. The text he sent read: "This is a signal from a lonely planet looking for an inhabitant. Do you feel lonely? Do you drown your loneliness in work, routine and family? Will you look up in the night sky for this planet? It looks like a crystal of greyish blue. There's no mist surrounding this planet. It's so lonely."

There was a call on his regular cell-phone. The call was from Manab and Kakali's residence. His heart pounded. He felt his breath choking. Was he caught so early? How was it possible? Where did he bungle up? Terrified, he took the phone call. He heard Kakali's frothy voice.

"Rahulda, this is Kakali. How is life? Manab and I are throwing a party tonight."

Rahul released his breath as if he had escaped the fall of a guillotine blade on his neck. A wind of happiness blew inside his chest. Rahul asked, "What's the reason for the party, Kakali?"

Kakali sounded excited. "Just to meet and chill, of course. When did we require an excuse for partying! Why don't we do a play on Poila Boishakh this time? We can discuss the details tonight. You have to come. Don't make any excuses, Rahulda."

Rahul replied in a faked tone of resignation, "I'll come. Who all are coming?"

Kakali answered, "The gang, of course."

This meant he would be able to interact with all the six women for quite some time tonight. He felt good. He declared, "Anil, no dinner for me tonight."

2.

In the club Rahul made a desperate attempt to concentrate on the game; he sipped his morning drink slowly. Rahul loved his morning drink on holidays. It made him feel as if he was swimming inside an aquarium. It slowed down the world for him. He liked this effect. One or two drinks in the morning helped him infest his siesta with peppery dreams.

He played auction bridge with Manab, Pradeep and Sekhar. Manab was his regular partner. Everybody observed that Rahul erred while calling as well as playing the cards. Manab got irritated as the game was played with stakes of cash and the carelessness of one partner caused a negative impact on the other partner's pocket.

Punching him mildly, Manab said, "Rahul, please concentrate on the game. Otherwise you'll drain me out today."

Sekhar pitched in, "What's happening to you? You look terribly distracted."

Pradeep intervened lightheartedly, "Let him play. Don't make him so self-conscious."

Rahul felt his game mates were observing him closely. An alarm rang inside him. He knew he had to look normal or else one thing might lead to another.

He replied, "It's nothing really. I didn't get proper sleep last night. And with this drink I'm feeling a bit sleepy. Don't worry, comrades, I'll pull myself up." As he slowly regained control over his mind and actions, he began to get bad cards and continued losing. He whispered, complaining, "You can't fight your destiny after all, can you?"

Pradeep overheard his whisper. He said, "Coming to think of destiny, my man, won't you marry ever? How do you carry on in this lonely manner?"

Before Rahul could reply, Sekhar butted in, "I think Rahul is enjoying his life. He is his own master. What is in a married life after all? Conformance and adherence of the most primitive kind. You keep on doing your duties like a bloody slave. What's the difference between office and home? If you think rationally, you'll find: you get higher degrees of freedom in the office! At least, there you're monitored against tangible parameters; at home, there is an ever-changing, opportunistic set of incomprehensible parameters to suit to the occasion."

Pradeep chided him, "That's because you have an over-possessive, hyper wife. You've pampered her and created a demon for yourself."

Manab suggested, "You can still escape if you want to."

Pradeep asked, shock in his voice, "You mean divorce?"

"That's too drastic. There's something which will require you to brush against the law. Seeking permanent relief out of marriage, at least from the man's side, based on disillusionment is not considered favourably by the law-keepers. But if you're smart enough, you can manage a parallel life filled with pleasure and fun."

Sekhar was listening carefully. He said, "It's easier said than done. It's very difficult to manage time. How do you account for the lost time to your boss in office and the boss at home?"

Pradeep asked wryly, "But, Manab, have you ever tried doing such a thing and succeeded? I'm not trying to puncture your privacy. But I'm really curious, man! How do you manage and where? We live in a tiny world in this colony. If we ever try such things, I fear we'll be left with no option but to poach each other's homes."

Manab said, "Who told you: that's not happening already?"

Sekhar was not amused. "That's pretty blasphemous and simplistic, man. You mean to say this colony is becoming a den of home invaders?"

Manab defended his viewpoint. "I'm not saying that. I'm only saying a home is as porous or impenetrable as it can be. There can be no permanent safeguards."

Pradeep said, "I agree. This colony houses people segregated from the happenings of the outside world. In fact, we take pride in such a thing. We're bothered about making heaps of money, staying fit and healthy, filling our homes with furniture and gadgets, sculpting our children to be philosophers of greed under the garb of excellence and talk culture and charity now and then. What can you expect out of such phony lives?"

Manab made an impassioned speech to drive home his point. "What is that other kind of life where you think you won't be a sexual predator in your friend's home? That's very simplistic. I think there is no straight-cut formula. There is a highly romantic view that pits a life of renunciation against a life of consumption. But the fact is a man has to live both these seemingly mutually exclusive lives to survive. I'm not talking about pure saints or pure consumers here. I'm talking about a man; more precisely, the kind of men we are.

"I heard a story about a beautiful woman who hated her husband for his ugliness; she wanted to sleep with a real hunk. She found one. But the moment this hunk penetrated her she felt suddenly withdrawn and distanced, wearied down by the image of her bloated husband and his sad eyes. She couldn't go on.

"But the husband was not a saint. The day she was with the hunk, he bribed the servant maid to give him a blowjob first and then sit on his rolls of flesh and fuck him from the top. When his wife caught him red-handed she burst out crying, screaming and abusing him. She accused him of violating and betraying her trust. She was morally scarred and suffered from depression after this. Her view was that she had brought this intense pain upon herself by her own betrayal. What would you say to this?"

Sekhar gave up. "I won't say anything. It's complex to take a stand on such things."

Pradeep seemed to be in a dilemma. "I agree. It's impossible to rationalise our acts of saintliness and devilishness."

Manab said triumphantly, "Correct, that's the key! Accepting that a fundamental ambiguity rules our lives is the starting point of becoming tolerant to our differences. The problem is: the life we lead eats into our souls and makes us incapable of such acceptance and appreciation."

Rahul had downed three drinks by this time. The

discussion, as always, had penetrated his mind in bits and pieces. Such intellectual discussions were not new here. The style was like this: first, everybody disagreed on an issue, which caused a discussion to erupt; then everybody took elaborate conflicting stands and suddenly everybody agreed with each other on an exquisite conclusion. The conclusion, in essence, was a critique of their own lives in general, and the conversations ended happily: masks of thinking know-all persons shrinking on their anxious faces.

Rahul shifted awkwardly in his seat. He was a bit surprised that a discussion which started as a query on his personal life never returned to him. It also hurt him a bit. The game was over by this time. He wondered for a moment whether to give them a jolt.

He said all of a sudden, "Guys, what would you do if you found that your wife was having an affair with someone on this very campus?"

Manab, Pradeep and Sekhar were taken aback for a moment. Then they started laughing loudly as if to slight the chances of such an event ever occurring.

Pradeep had downed six drinks. He said, booming and laughing wildly, "It's high time we got Rahul a bride. Otherwise, I fear he will end up becoming a leopard, a woman eater. Man, if I see my wife doing something nonsensical and making shit of my reputation here, I'll burn her face with acid. And let me tell you this: if I find you doing anything hanky-panky with Nandana, I'll shove a bamboo pole up your backside so hard that your ass will burn like a blooming furnace in hell."

Manab chipped in, "You're overreacting, man. He's drunk. In fact, I believe he'll be relieved to share his pain, I mean – Nandana, with anybody willing to volunteer. I don't know how I would react. There'll be a spell of violence initially. I'll try to reason it out. Who knows, I might even succeed! What about you, Sekhar?"

Sekhar said, "I might ask for a divorce straightaway. I don't know. I will like to run away from rejection as fast as possible. You know, the problem is with the law, our increasing madness with creating a meaningful society, a resplendent future. It wants us to be transparent and live in cohesive glass houses. It would be wonderful if all of us could live the varied chapters of our life in opaque quarters guarded from each other with no burden of creating and making out an integral story of a man's life. But gosh, that's not to be!"

Rahul was touched by the honest strain in the replies of his friends. He walked out of the club, confirming to meet all of them again in Manab's house at night. He felt the excitement within him dying down.

When he returned home he asked Anil to serve lunch. After his meal, he scanned his new cell phone for replies. He had received three messages. Tension built up in his chest. There was no reply from Nandana, Kakali and Shruti.

Bakul had replied, "Don't disturb. I don't write or talk to strangers."

Chaitali had replied, "Who are you?"

Nilanjana had also asked the same question.

Rahul thought for a while whether he should reply to these messages. He decided to go ahead.

Rahul replied to Nilanjana and Chaitali: "I'm a plucked thorn. I dream of growing on a tree twig once again."

To Bakul he wrote, "Would you talk or write to me if you knew I was not a stranger? But you can't disclose my identity to others."

After sending the messages, he surrendered himself to a long, dreamless siesta.

3.

When Rahul awoke, it was evening already, and cold. There was a hint of fog outside. He remembered the messages he had sent to Nilanjana, Chaitali and Bakul during the day. In a short while he would have to get ready to attend the party at Manab and Kakali's house. He asked for tea and sat down with the new cell phone. There were three messages docked in its inbox.

Chaitali had written, "I don't like thorns. I'm not a

twig for god's sake. Do you suffer from astigmatism or what?"

Nilanjana had written, "You're barking up the wrong door."

Bakul had written, "Do I know you? I'm not sure whether I will like to talk or write to you. I might. It depends on who you are."

A fresh message arrived. It was from Nandana. She had written, "I like your style of writing. I hope this is not a carefully crafted prologue to a proposal of sleeping with me. I'm an ugly seventy-year-old granny with six children and four grandchildren."

Rahul felt queerly happy reading these messages and shivered with the excitement of communicating with people anonymously. He marvelled at the addictive grip of technology and its validation of voyeurism in modern times. Was technology helping shy and lonely people like him to communicate or was it simply destroying their will to confront and experience the real world and its involving ambiguity? He didn't know. What he found compelling was that in a day's time he was freely and stylistically exchanging emotions with a few women of his choice, which he would not have dared to do otherwise in regular life.

Anil brought his cup of steaming black tea. As he sipped it, he imagined various drafts in which he could reply to these new messages.

To Chaitali he wrote, "A twig is a connection between the earth and the leaves, flowers, fruits and thorns growing on a tree. A twig is that conduit of life without which a tree would have lost its fun of standing out there. You can view this in the right perspective if you want to."

Rahul wondered whether he should reply to Nilanjana. He decided he should. He wrote, "I was not barking. It was a signal. A call. A signal is sent through the thickness of sky. If it reaches the wrong door I can't help it."

Rahul replied to Bakul, "Yes, you know me. I don't know how to disclose my identity. You might be shocked. You might not expect me at all. I fear you might not like me as well."

Rahul wrote back to Nandana, "You make me laugh. You don't look seventy. You look no more than thirty-five. Where are your children and grandchildren? Have you locked them up in some graveyard?"

Rahul felt tired writing to so many women. He was happy Kakali and Shruti did not respond, otherwise he would have had to write two more replies.

Finished with tea, he suddenly noticed it was very dark inside his apartment. He asked Anil to put on the lights and went to get dressed for the party. He considered for a moment whether to masturbate and then go to the party to fend off any chance of being attacked by a sudden erection in front of everybody. He decided against it.

Rahul entered the party scene late in the evening. The others were already there. The party was arranged on the terrace of Manab and Kakali's apartment building. The buffet in brass and silver containers being heated by bluish jets of flame was laid out on one side. Stewards were serving liquor and snacks to every guest with tutored care and elegant hospitality. The men were either in formal suits or kurta-pyjamas of pure cotton and khaddar with cashmere shawls draped around them. Some men looked like top-notch business executives while others resembled manicured, new-age politicians. Rahul wore denim trousers, a full-sleeved cotton shirt, a turtleneck woollen pullover and a woollen cap on his head; he was prone to sinusitis. He savoured the cuts of women's dresses specially blouses, kameezes, dresses, gowns and tops. He eyed them without drawing attention to himself, a skill he had mastered over the years. The children were playing in the lawn below. A separate arrangement was made for them and their accompanying ayahs to keep the adults free of unnecessary hassles.

The sky was clear, dotted with a constellation of sparkling stars and a slice of moon appeared like a boat sliding down the crest of a tremulous wave. The air carried a thawed freeze of sharp coldness, pinched at times by the slow movement of a northerly wind. There were trails of fog that had settled on the ground in the evening. There was no sign of fresh fog falling. To beat the cold, a wrought iron portable fireplace was organised in which wood was fed at intervals by an attendant. The flames drew large groups of guests towards it, leaving the periphery of the large marble-floored terrace filled with islands of garden chairs, centre tables and umbrella coverings spread generously -for the strong hearted to group together to exchange and transact ideas and opinions in comparative privacy.

Kakali greeted Rahul cheerfully, her face affected by a wide blush, as he entered the terrace. She played the part of an excellent hostess. She darted like a butterfly from one guest to another. Shruti sat warming up near the fireplace, eyeing Sandip and, more specifically, the number of drinks he was gulping. Nilanjana was talking to an elderly woman on the southern edge of the terrace and sipping red wine from an ornately carved glass. Bakul stood alone on the northern side looking at the adjoining jungle. It was popularly believed to be infested with hyenas and vultures. She held a tall glass of multi-coloured cocktail in her left hand. Nandana, Chaitali and a few men and women were in animated conversation with each other on the far eastern edge of the terrace.

Rahul imperceptibly moved towards Bakul. Kakali intersected him on the way. She said, "Rahulda, you're looking dashing. The colour of your pullover is damn good. It's as red as the centre of a flame."

Rahul said, "Is the centre of a flame red? I thought it was bluish yellow."

Kakali said mischievously, "Whatever, you look dashing. As I told you on the phone, we're planning to do a play on Poila Boishakh. We'll discuss it in detail tonight. You have to play a role, all right?"

Rahul replied hurriedly, "No way. I've never been on stage earlier. By the way, what kind of a play are you planning to do?"

"Nandana and Chaitali have shortlisted a few plays. They're perhaps discussing it now; you can see. We'll do an open house discussion on this. You can also share your views there if you like. I prefer that the final play is selected by consensus."

"Will you play any role?"

Kakali answered, "Who knows, I might. Did you see my gown, Rahulda? How do I look? You don't look at women at all!"

Rahul looked at her more directly now from top to bottom and said, "The cut and colour are marvellous. You look beautiful. You always look beautiful, irrespective of what you're wearing. That's what beauty is. Who said I don't look at women? I do look at a few of them."

"Then it's high time you marry one."

"Why, what's in a marriage, Kakali?"

"Give me one good reason why you should remain a free bird when all of us on this island are suffering the levies of imprisonment."

"Well, for one, a free bird is a positive change of perspective for so many prisoners, no?"

Kakali asserted, "No. Jokes apart, no. Think about yourself. There's an imbalance in your life."

"Do you think all balance is good?"

Kakali reacted – genuine concern ringing in her voice now, "You're digressing Rahulda; you're talking philosophy. I meant something else. You have nobody other than your servants to look after you. You're involved in your job and career; some day you will feel terribly lonely, Rahulda. You will want to talk at length in the evening. You will want to hold somebody dear. That's not philosophy. It's a primitive instinct to be cared for. Family provides that in a basic and fundamental way. I've seen my elder brother steep into brain-shattering loneliness; he left the family at an early age to live in the forests as an environmentalist. Today he fits nowhere. How I wish the world could have absorbed into its folds people like my brother and you without batting an eyelid, but it doesn't. A person refusing to rear a conventional family is considered a rebel. What they never care to look at is, such a thing could have happened by chance, circumstance, youthful chivalry, some kind of an engaging responsibility or a debilitating disease and not out of choice."

Rahul was intensely touched by the depth of Kakali's

concern. He said, "Kakali, thanks for your kind sentiments. But I feel at home here. I don't feel discriminated against."

"Don't pretend, Rahulda. You're a gentleman. You get embarrassed by others' meanness. Don't you know, the married men here jeer at you, are envious of you, do everything to avoid you: they feel threatened by the thought of their wives enjoying amorous, reckless affairs with you. The women are secretively spinning horrid tales in the backyard about you to distance you from the other, tackling competition in the process. Rahulda, you're just not aware how much of an enigma you are here. It's your personal choice. But I strongly believe marriage could actually be of great use to you."

Rahul wanted to change the mood of the discussion. He said mischievously, "You can go to great lengths to convince me, my dear. But where are those women who can provide company and care the way you can!"

"Oh, my god, you can flirt, too! That's something new. I'll join you later. Manab, it seems, is calling me for something."

Kakali moved on, leaving Rahul wanting more. He looked at Bakul. She was still standing at the edge looking in the distance towards the jungle and sipping her drink. She had turned her back to the crowd. Was it out of some kind of disgust? Amit was talking to another woman at the other end. Rahul moved the distance towards Bakul. When he was at arm's length he said, "Hi, Bakul, what're you doing? Anything the matter?"

Bakul looked at Rahul with a peculiar gaze; she was not looking at him; she was absorbed elsewhere. Her eyes looked swollen. Her face looked pale and pensive. She wore very little make-up. She needed to be brought out of the jungle, Rahul thought.

Rahul repeated, "Bakul, this is Rahulda. What's the matter? You look jaded."

A faint smile formed on Bakul's face, as if embarrassed at being caught in a forbidden act. She said hurriedly, "It's nothing, Rahulda. The jungle out there makes you invariably wistful, doesn't it?"

Rahul said, "Don't look at the jungle, then. I hear there is a plan to do a play on Poila Boishakh. Are you playing any role in the play?"

"Manab has requested me to do the costumes."

"You'll do a fine job."

Bakul informed him, "The gown Kakali is wearing today is done by me. The top Nilanjana is wearing, just look back and see, is also done by me. Are they good?"

"They are very good, Bakul."

Bakul asked, "Do you have an eye for women's dresses?"

"I don't know; I can recognise excellence and craft. Were you crying, Bakul?" Rahul asked unexpectedly.

"No. What made you think I was?"

"You look extremely distracted. Look at your eyes. They're swollen like walnuts."

"This colony makes me mad. I want to run away from here. If it was not for my son I would've done something crazy, you know, by this time."

"What's the matter?"

Bakul looked away for a second and then said quietly, "You know, Amit has not spoken to me in the last three years."

Rahul couldn't believe it. "But why?"

Bakul confided, "I had a fleeting affair with one of my distant cousins when I was in school. He is in France now. Three years back he wrote me a beautiful e-mail wherein he referred to a few events from our past. It was just a few months after his divorce. Maybe he was seeking solace in those wonderful memories of our youth. Amit got a copy of this mail and took the matter beyond limits. I couldn't reason with him. He stopped talking. It kills me, this silence. But day in and day out we have to put up an image of a happy family for the outside world. I can't confess this to anybody else. With you it's different. You're a loner yourself."

Rahul said, a trace of sadness echoing in his tone, "Yes, I know what it means to fight silence."

There was a commotion near the fireplace. Shruti was talking loudly to Sandip. Straining his ears, Rahul could hear Shruti saying, "Don't drink any more, Sandip. You'll get drunk and create a mess at home. Manab, please instruct the stewards not to serve him any more drinks, otherwise I'll have no option but to walk out of here."

Sandip was inebriated. He heaved from repeated hiccups. A steward made him drink some water. He refused. The water spilled onto the floor. Kakali took charge. She made Sandip get up and asked him to come down to their apartment where he could rest. While going down the terrace, holding Sandip firmly in one hand, Kakali said, "I'll make him sleep in our flat. Please carry on. I'll come back in a few seconds. Shruti will you come with me?"

Shruti retorted back sharply, "I don't want to waste my time taking care of this drunken man. Kakali this is your house, do whatever you feel like doing."

Manab intervened, "Kakali, carry on. Shruti, please don't take things to heart. Sandip is not a drunkard, for god's sake. It's his body mechanism, you know. Alcohol overreacts on him, that's all. Don't bloody spoil the party mood here."

Shruti shouted, "I'm not disrupting the party. It's I who gets broken every time. But I'm not going to be broken down that easily. All right, I'm sorry, guys. I got carried away a bit. Do I need a drink myself?"

Rahul was petrified by Shruti's mood. He decided against talking to her. Instead, he moved towards Nilanjana. She stood closer to the fireplace along with Samar, munching snacks; her eyes, full of unknown intent, were on the lashing flames.

Rahul moved towards Samar and said, "How's life, man?"

Samar answered cheerfully, "As good as it can be."

Rahul asked Nilanjana, "How're you, Nilanjana?"

"Fine. How are you?" she replied.

"Okay, I suppose. So going on a holiday this time?"

Samar said, "No, man. I'm planning to move out of this place."

"Changing jobs? Resigning?"

"You could say."

"Where are you joining next?"

Samar explained, "Nilanjana has set up a business of eateries with one of her friends. It's doing good business downtown. She is fed up of this place. We're shifting to a new flat Nilanjana has purchased near one of the eateries she owns."

"What will you do?"

Nilanjana didn't miss this chance to settle scores with Samar. "Why, he can babysit! I've been doing for so many years. Simultaneously, I ran my business and brought it to a stage where I earn no less than him, in fact, I earn more. I want to gift Samar a never-ending pack of time. He always complained; he had no time to do things that he wanted to do."

Samar winked at Rahul and said, "She's sarcastic, my boy. But I think I'll have a ball with my son, beer, books and comics."

"Good for you and me."

Rahul was all in praise of Nilanjana. "I never knew Nilanjana was such an enduring entrepreneur. That's quite a dazzling piece of news."

"Food is my passion. Making people eat is my passion. When I waited for Samar to come back home all these years I thought either I could make my passion heal me or disorient me. I had a choice to make. I made it."

Rahul said, "My god, you already sound like a business magnate, talking autobiographically about the dramatic moments of your life that made you what you are. Great! It sounds nice really. That's a genuine reason for celebration."

"Thank you, Rahulda. I wanted to tell you something. I have a spinster friend. Good looking. Unmarried and uncomplicated. She's looking for a partner. She wants to settle down by the end of this year. She's a lecturer in economics. Would you be interested?"

Samar vouched, "She's good, Rahul. I've seen her. She's very good looking and the intellectual type. An asset to flaunt in parties. She will get along well with you."

Rahul brought the topic to a close, "Don't bother about me. Marriage is not on my priority list. Not tonight at least."

Nandana and Chaitali were getting ready to make an announcement. They requested for everybody's attention, and then Nandana cleared her throat and spoke out loudly, "Ladies and gentlemen, some time back, Kakali had mooted the idea of doing a play on Poila Boishakh. Chaitali and I strongly seconded the idea. We've had some discussions amongst ourselves, a group working on the idea, and have shortlisted a few plays that we could consider doing. I have involved my niece Tanya in this group. She is here, incidentally, on a five-month vacation from her work in Ladakh. She is mad about doing and organising plays. She directed a number of plays during her college days and did plays with a professional group for some time. Later, she had to migrate to a remote corner of the country on work; she abandoned something so dear to her heart.

"We felt it would be a good idea if she could direct our play; she has a good understanding of theatre to make us work as a team and bring out the best in us. If we agree to this we can move forward. Come here, Tanya. This is Tanya, ladies and gentlemen. Tanya, these are our unit members from the colony gang. We do crazy things together to beat boredom and defend ourselves against the hyenas and vultures in the surrounding jungles."

Chaitali added, like a cheerleader, "Ladies and gentlemen, a round of applause for the lovely young lady."

Meanwhile, Kakali had returned. She said, "Can we have the names of the plays from Tanya? And could you introduce yourself briefly for the benefit of all?"

Tanya came forward. Everybody, including Rahul, looked at her with interest. Tanya was tall and dark with deep-set black eyes, sharp features, an athletic body and short-cropped hair. She wore jeans, a white cotton shirt and a brown tight-fitting leather jacket. She looked agile and attractive like a tennis player. She seemed to be in her late twenties.

A fog had formed. At any time a gust of wind could drag the fog and pull it over the colony like a blanket. Tanya greeted everybody with a well-groomed smile. "Hi, I'm Tanya. I'm a trained archaeologist by profession. I have been working in Ladakh on preserving Buddhist monuments for the last three years. In the winters it is impossible to work there because of the snow and cold. So I move out, travel and take a break at this time of the year. This year Nandana Aunty wanted me to spend some time with her, so I'm here.

"Dramatics used to be a passion with me once. I wanted to be an actor at a point in my life, a theatre actor and director. That was a long time ago. With time I got lost in pursuing a career and travelling to remote places. When I heard this idea of doing a play, I was excited to be a part of it. What better way to spend my vacation than to do something I always wanted to do! So, if you accept me as a part of your team, frankly it would be an obligation to me: allowing me to revel in my passion once again."

She took a deep breath expecting the crowd to do something to show their support to her.

Rahul waited for a few seconds before responding, "Of course, we accept you. After all, the motivation behind this is to have fun. Am I wrong, ladies and gentlemen?"

Sagar said, "You're absolutely correct, Rahul. Tanya, you're a very close relative of our very dear friend. That makes you a part of us automatically. I don't think anybody will have any issues learning something from you that you know and understand far better than most of us. I understand you're already well known to the women here. If you're interested in dashing men, which I believe you should be, please be informed that our colony houses quite a few, my dear. Don't be inattentive to them as well."

Samar added, "You say you're an archaeologist by profession, a theatre worker by passion but I find you talk very well, I mean, you talk more like a corporate communications person."

Tanya asked, "Is this some kind of a black compliment that I should treat as sarcasm?"

Samar said, "No, you should treat this as our ignorance of polished archaeologists and passionate theatre workers."

Kakali said, "Come on, Tanya, Samar is just bitching. He does that to beautiful, young girls all the time."

Rahul said, "Have you shortlisted any play, Tanya?"

Tanya answered, "Yes. We have two and a half months to go for Poila Boishakh, so I think we can produce two plays within this time. They will cater to different tastes and temperaments and this will make participation wider. It'll call for hard work surely, but it will make the process more interesting. What do you say?"

Nilanjana said, "You know, all the children have their annual exams during this time. These exams drain us parents more than our children. I think two plays will be an impossible task to achieve under the circumstances."

Chaitali challenged her. "But I think we can plan this out."

Kakali reiterated. "Of course, we can plan this out."

Shruti suggested, "If the same actors are not involved in both the plays and the rehearsals are done in Rahul's house, I think the distraction can be kept to a minimum."

Samar backed her. "That's astute planning. Rahul, will you provide your house for the rehearsals? You're the only lonely Adam here, away from the cruel grindings of family life. We want to keep our children and servants away from as many distractions as possible. We will invade your solitary space with permission, if you don't mind."

Rahul confirmed enthusiastically, "Come on, you don't have to ask for it. It's done. Which are the plays will you be doing, Tanya?"

Inhaling deeply, Tanya said, "I propose Rabindranath Thakur's 'Dakghar' and a situational comedy, 'Detective' by Sharadindu Bandyopadhyay."

Pradeep complimented her. "Wow! Both the plays will be great to produce and watch. What do you say?" He threw the question around generally to everybody without expecting any answer.

Both the plays were approved after a brief round of discussion. The fog was thickening and the participants showed their eagerness to proceed to dinner. The children were tired and wanted to return home. Rahul started eating. Nandana moved towards Rahul with her plate. She said, "Thank you, Rahul, for your cooperation."

Rahul replied, surprised, "Don't be so formal, Nandana. At least now I'll have my house fully lighted up for the next three months up to Poila Boishakh. That's something like a dream to me; I can't explain it to you."

There was a morsel of meat in her mouth. Once it was chewed and swallowed, she said in a low voice, "I won't ask you to marry like the others are doing; there are other things a man can enjoy in his life apart from marriage. Don't you cherish your solitude? I long for it so badly. In fact, this time during the summers we're planning to go on separate vacations."

Rahul was surprised. "Where will Neel go then? Are you going to keep him with one of your relatives?"

Nandana said, "That's been planned out, mister. We have decided to go on two vacations every year. Summers will be for separate vacations; Neel will go with Pradeep and me, alternately. Winters will be for joint vacations: all three of us together. What do you think of it: a good idea or a bad one?"

Rahul shrugged, "Very good! Well, I have never heard of such a thing,but it sounds pretty rational. Four-five days of private space. Good. Do whatever you feel like doing in those days."

"Yes, that's the wish, but I'm not sure whether we are capable of handling pure fun or pleasure."

"True. I think that's a pretty correct reflection of us."

Chaitali joined in. She said playfully, "What's so correct about us, Rahul?"

Rahul fumbled for a moment with rice in his mouth. He said, "I had agreed to a point made by Nandana: we're not capable of handling pure fun or pleasure."

Chaitali looked puzzled. She said, "What kind of fun or pleasure?"

Rahul replied, "Something that makes us feel light but real, disconnected from having to make and live up to tall pronouncements and proclamations."

Chaitali asked, "Something anarchic you mean?"

"That's too loaded. I didn't mean that."

Chaitali became serious. "I had made a study of these things once. I had come across some kind of an argument that said pleasure in its purest form is not possible to achieve within the realms of a nation-state, family or religion. Which means civilisation is a departure from pleasure."

Rahul said, "I don't think I understand these things with such clarity. By the way, what made you study these things?"

Chaitali went into the details. "I did a post-doctoral thesis on ideas of fun and pleasure in aboriginal societies of northeast India. But all that is rubbish. Manipulating practical life is what matters in the long run. Pleasure and fun are all bullshit, Rahul. Who cares? We've compiled so much knowledge today in our universities. Who uses them, tell me? Art is a pastime. It has no impact on our lives. If it did, we wouldn't be leading such unhappy, egocentric lives. The point is we want more of everything. These things have been said a billion times. But we don't pay any heed, not because of our arrogance, but because nature has played a nasty trick by mixing up a revolting cocktail of consciousness in an animal mind. This unique cocktail has given us the nation-state, family and organised religion as we see them today; they pounce on the same individual generation after generation getting modified, revised and more accurate in decimating an individual's soul."

Rahul was dumbfounded by Chaitali's explanation. He said, "You truly have a way of interpretation, Chaitali. I never expected something like this from you."

Chaitali coughed up her angst, "Why? You thought I was some kind of a decorated doll in Sagar's drawing room? You men never take women seriously."

Rahul didn't protest. He was finished with food. He found it convenient to move on. Somehow, he became wary and no longer enjoyed the crowd. He wanted to return to his shell. He bade everyone goodbye and climbed down the staircase, hurriedly shifting his woollen cap on his head.

At the gate, he met Tanya going up after a round of playing hide-and-seek with the children. Rahul greeted her smiling and wished her good night. Tanya replied,

"Hi, Mr. Rahul, going home so early? I wanted to talk to you. I need to tell you in detail about the rehearsals and understand your constraints and inconveniences of space and time, if any."

Rahul said, "If you don't mind, can we do this tomorrow?"

Tanya reacted immediately, "Of course! Good night."

Rahul walked back home; the road was shrouded in a dense cover of mist.

4.

Rahul headed straight for the bathroom. He had a long hot shower and then masturbated with images of Purnasree clogging the millions of subterranean cavities in his head. However hard he attempted to throw away Purnasree's lusty images from the darkness of his mind, he failed. He could not replace that image by any other woman: Nilanjana, Nandana, Chaitali, Bakul, Kakali or Shruti.

Rahul had never spoken to Purnasree. He had only seen her years ago dancing in the mornings. He had felt mysteriously connected to her, surrounded by the engulfing waves of enchanting music. He had conjured up a life of heavenly bliss with her.

Rahul lived in a world of these harmonious images. The ennui he experienced in the lonely landscape of his life was a combat against the real world and after days of suffering from wild, lovesick hallucinations, he would submit to the conjured images of a happy life that was impossible for him to achieve.

Rahul returned to his bedroom. Was a ship drowning in the ocean of his heart? He didn't feel like sleeping. At a subconscious level, he was walking on a thin line separating the real from the unreal. He looked outside at the colony street dimmed by slowly traversing fog. He looked at the treetops, the silent, strangely shadowed box-like buildings and the top hem of the surrounding forest looming on the edge of his vision; he suddenly felt like running like a long distance runner. Languorous echoes of resonant animal groans seemed to originate from the soul of the adjoining forest. Or were these sounds originating from the craters of his mind?

He suddenly longed for his mother. Till she was alive, he had a reason to live. "How difficult it is to live for oneself!" he thought sadly. Whereas people bound within families were longing to escape. Was it not true that people existed in circumstances irrespective of their will? He wondered about his brother: where was he now? What kind of life did he lead with his wife and children? Did they sleep together or in separate rooms? Did they dream separate dreams? Did his brother have an affair on the sly? Was his sister-in-law capable of infidelity? Did his nephews masturbate? Were they happy? Did they quarrel? Who taught the children? Did the children play any outdoor games? Rahul knew nothing. A sudden realisation shocked Rahul: he could not remember his father. In fact, he had no memory of his father. His mother had, with years of propaganda, erased the memories of his father. During childhood, when Rahul looked at his father's frail skeleton-like body, he would become a nervous wreck with exploding tension from a fear: his father might collapse while walking down a street, hit by a sudden gust of wind or get crushed under a vehicle. His father rarely talked. When he talked, it was mostly in whispers. Rahul faintly remembered the power of his never-ending, vacuous gaze, as if he were on a secret mission to discover what existed beyond death and explore the remnants of a life that existed centuries ago. Rahul tried to conjure an image of his father's face. He couldn't. Surprisingly, Apu's father's face in *Pather Panchali* flashed before his eyes. Did his father look like Apu's father? He was a Brahmin; he wore a string across his body; he was not a practising priest or impoverished in that sense. Did Rahul draw comfort imagining the delicate contours of Apu's father's face, eternally soft and graceful in the heat of hardship and loss? Was there a craving for a father lingering inside him? Or did he want to be a father himself?

He absent-mindedly took out his new cell phone from

his bedside drawer and was surprised to find six new messages. When he read the messages, he shrivelled with consternation and terror. The six messages were:

Nilanjana: "Did you like the pilaf tonight?"

Kakali: "Did you like the meatballs tonight?"

Nandana: "Did you like the fish fry tonight?"

Chaitali: "Did you like the cheese kofta tonight?"

Shruti: "Did you like the vegetable au gratin tonight?"

Bakul: "Did you like the chocolate soufflé tonight?"

He was brought back to the real world by the prosaic nature of these messages. He felt overturned by fate. He knew he would soon be caught but he wondered what had given away his identity so soon. Was somebody monitoring his actions closely, like a television journalist? Had he been declared a dangerous entity for society and the world at large? In what manner would he be punished for the offence he had committed? Would he be caught and paraded while cameras and flash bulbs clicked and triggered on his face? Would he be declared a criminal?

Gradually, as his fear subsided and was replaced by a melancholic spell of being caught, a bell rang inside him randomly. Could this be a trick to force him to declare his identity?

The uniformity of the messages suggested that either one person had written them all or all the six women had conspired to achieve a pre-destined end. Why did they disclose to each other the contents of the message written separately to each? Did they work as a team or were they all members of an occult organisation with a hideous agenda? He cooled down as he pondered these questions one by one.

He looked at the multiple layers of mist slowly moving along the street below. He saw a figure emerge out of the corner of the street like a ghost; the figure walked briskly. The person, although barely visible, seemed to be a woman. Her movements, however fast, were under her control; her strides, at times leaps or jumps, bore the sign of a stable mind. Rahul, for a second, suspected her to be a somnambulist. If she was, she could be in danger. He decided to do something. By the time he came out of the building, the woman had moved forward a few yards. He moved slowly behind her making up the distance with time and as he drew closer he realised he was tracking Tanya.

He whispered her name to check if she was sleepwalking. She turned around immediately; she was panting. At first there was an expression of shock on her face, then it transformed into a wide grin. She said, "Oh my god! Mr. Rahul, you've not slept yet? The way you dashed out of the party, I thought you were feeling very sleepy."

Rahul replied, "What are you doing here at this time of the night?"

Tanya replied, "Are you my guardian? I walk regularly after midnight. That's a part of my fitness regimen. Any problem? By the way what are you doing here?"

Rahul was apologetic, "I did not feel like sleeping after I returned home. I was standing at my bedroom window when I saw you. I thought you were a somnambulist. I feared you might need help in that case."

Tanya at once made up for her rudeness. "Sorry, I didn't mean to be rude. No, I'm not a somnambulist."

"It may not be safe to be out at this hour."

"My experience tells me that the daytime is more unsafe than nights. It's only our perception, Mr. Rahul."

"Maybe."

They started strolling at a gentler pace. For some time they did not talk. Rahul was not sure whether Tanya liked his presence or not. He considered returning when Tanya said, "I've begun to like this place. A company township normally has a suffocating air and its claustrophobia brings out the worst in its occupants. It's different here. A few strange incidents in the last few hours, for instance, have given me a good perspective to understand people."

Rahul asked, "Did anything special happen today inside the colony?"

Tanya explained, "Somebody sent a sms this morning to six women in the colony. Ironically, all six were at Kakali Aunty's house at the time for a meeting on the Poila Boishakh celebrations. Since all the six cell phones beeped almost simultaneously, we were naturally a bit curious to find out what it was about. Notes were exchanged and we found it to be a crank sms sent by a potential stalker. There was a lot of speculation, of course, like, whether this could be the work of an insider. However, soon everybody lost interest in it except me. An archaeologist is essentially an investigator by instinct. This kind of a situation makes my blood race. What do you think about this?"

Rahul had a tough time hiding his heaving chest. He said, partly gasping, feigning this to be breathlessness due to the humid cold weather conditions, "Pretty interesting. I'm listening. Tell me what happened next."

Tanya continued, "Since none of the six women were interested in replying or even knowing who the sender was, I took up the matter in my own hands. I started replying on their behalf using their cell phones to lay a trap. My intuition tells me the sender must have attended today's party in Manab Uncle's house. I sent out a few post-party messages to issue a warning: you're under a scanner."

Rahul said, laughing, "I've attended the party tonight. That makes me a suspect, too."

Tanya said, "But you don't fit into the profile of my suspect. You have a thorough knowledge of the colony. Why don't you help me with the investigations instead?"

Rahul asked, "Do you want to punish him, Tanya?"

Tanya sprang back, "You said 'him' which means you perceive this person to be a man. Why?"

"As far as I know, stalkers or crank callers on most of the occasions turn out to be men. Nothing more."

"No, I don't want to punish him. I do want to find him; I believe he is standing on a wall and the wall runs by the side of a bottomless gorge," Tanya answered. There was a chill in her voice; she looked piercingly into his eyes.

For a moment Rahul wanted to shout and scream into the night. He held himself back. He looked at Tanya's crystal like face for a long time, wanting to see through it and weigh his chances of survival with this girl. Then he suddenly started running back towards his house; he stopped abruptly to turn around and see whether Tanya was still standing and looking at him.

Nightmare

1.

Rahul yawned widely. Sleep lingered heavy on his eyes. If he took to bed he would fall into an endless tunnel of deep slumber. Instead, he fought sleep.

He was pacing like a restless, agitated beast within the shadows of his house. He was alone, the servants having gone to sleep in their quarters. He moved about the ground-floor rooms first. Then he went up to the first floor rooms where he spent most of his time these days.

He spent some time on the terrace. The night was clear. Winter had departed a week earlier. Spring had brought bacteria- and pollen-infested air; it healed souls with an unseen treachery. The house was dark except for the lamps in his study. But he traversed the dark spaces in an organised manner, not interrupted by the furniture, objects and artefacts because he knew his house well. He smoked a cigarette, threw it mid-way and lit another, looking for an effective distraction, which was provided neither by the smoke nor the nicotine.

For a moment he considered listening to music or immersing himself in a book. He knew he would not be able to concentrate on anything. He drank a bottle of water. He was not hungry; otherwise he could have eaten an apple. In any case, he tried one from the refrigerator. As his teeth cut through the chill of its flesh there was a shivering sensation of pain in his dental nerves.

This was a distraction enough! He threw the half-eaten

fruit in the kitchen dustbin and knew he had to go out of the house. He took his car keys, locked the house, went to the garage, opened the locks of its rolling shutter, lifted it up in one shove, got into the driver's seat, ignited the engine and moved out in a whiz. As he hit the road he slowed down, considering for a moment where to go. It was already past midnight. He didn't turn on the air conditioning. The front windows were partially rolled down. The breeze funnelling through the gap in the windows was pleasant with an unknown fragrance. The scent belonged to flowers whose names he didn't know. He couldn't see any flowers or gardens nearby. But the smell was a distraction again. He decided to drive the car at random through the city.

There was little traffic on the road at this hour. He could drive safely without concentrating much on the road since the beaming flash of lights from the oncoming vehicles would alert him in any case. He was not pre-occupied with any intense thought. Instead, he was filled with anxiety about why he was behaving this way – if he was sleepy, why didn't he hit the bed and sleep? This was not the first time this was happening to him. While this was a recent phenomenon, it had happened to him even earlier on a few occasions. Was it someone who was confronting him from the inside against his free will? Tension mounted within him and he felt tremulous, run down by a force mightier than him. He feared losing control of his life, surrendering himself and felt discomfited.

A few days back, he was with Gopa in his house watching a Woody Allen film. Later, when he tried to take her in his arms, caress and fondle her, he froze. Gopa was there on his invitation. It was the first time he did not sleep with her on such an occasion. Such nocturnal invitations would usually end up with making love, shower, dinner and dropping her home. Rahul made sincere efforts to kiss her but failed to manage anything except a few pecks. Gopa was wearing lingerie that Rahul had brought for her from Paris and had wanted him to do something outrageously raunchy that night. She had felt desperately rejected and hurt. She left the house without eating and refused to be dropped by him.

Rahul had crossed the eastern part of the city and was now driving through its central corridor. He looked straight ahead in a relaxed manner and did not concentrate on anything else outside. He was in no mood to observe and understand the interesting night-time details of the city. He turned around suddenly at a square and drove back gradually towards the southern fringes. Soon he was no longer driving through the spinal main roads. He had entered the narrow, cave-like lanes of middle-class colonies. He had trouble navigating the car through the snaking roads dotted with crater-like potholes and bordered with open surface drains. Where was he going? Why did he have to enter these arteries of darkness? He thought for a moment. Was he trapping himself in a womb of despair?

Suddenly, the narrow road led to a wider, brick-lined pavement without the decaying ghost-like buildings on its sides. Instead, it was lined with tall, closely-spaced, stooping trees that made the darkness thicker. There was a huge paved pond at the end of the street. Rahul reluctantly brought his car to a halt. He had reached a dead end. He would have to turn around to return. Something attracted his attention at the point where the pavement touched the pond. He saw it clearly in the scorching headlights of his car.

He was filled with terror, rocked by waves of a deathly fear rising through his body. Rahul sweated profusely. There was so much of an upheaval inside his belly that he felt like passing tonnes of excreta and gas.

How could this be happening? Am I hallucinating? But the swollen body smeared with blood and soil lying in front of him looked more than real. The face was crisscrossed with deep gashes. Its wide immobile eyes seemed to stare at him.

He waited for some time. He stopped the car. He did not switch off the headlights immediately. He switched them off for a second later. He was suddenly engulfed in an impenetrable blanket of infinite darkness. He feared that demons would erupt from the treetops and strangle him to death. He switched on the headlights once again and made a Herculean effort to escape from this scene of horror.

As he drove back through the street, he felt his respiration returning to normal. He longed to reach home as fast as he could and fall asleep. He thought of the face that had made him restive a few moments back. Was it a face he knew? Was it a face that resembled a woman he knew quite well?

He slept that night with vultures, bats and owls prowling on a burnt red lonely landscape. He dreamt of a purple baby boy. When he woke up the next day, he had miraculously forgotten the expedition and the dreams of the night.

2.

Rahul often felt like crying although no tears would fall from his eyes. He also felt like laughing or smiling lightly at times but his jaws and lips would not move. Rahul felt like contemplating about his future in the mornings. He would feel dull and empty in his head, incapable of retaining a single stream of thought. He felt like running home from office in the evenings. He felt a numbing weakness in his knees and waist; tiredness crawled through his limbs like an incurable illness these days. Gopa, of course, was a very pleasant getaway.

He soon apprehended this crippling sickness would come in between him and Gopa. She was a hard-nosed professional like him, focused on her career. She had to re-build her family consisting of her mother and two brothers, after her free spirited father died suddenly, leaving them with an uncertain, debt-filled future. She had done well in her life by making fleeting chances pay dividends through her determination and hard work. She believed it was her achievement to have a huge house with a garden, a battery of servants, two cars, her brothers settled abroad with their families and a rocking career. For some time she had been considering marriage and, to find a suitable man, she had mingled with marginally older men with solid financial credentials, mostly focusing on bachelors and widowers in office parties and other outings.

Gopa involved herself gradually in such fishing exercises. Initially she felt guilty and found the whole game oafish and cheap. However, as she started rolling the heads of men (who had earlier never made a move towards her on the assumption that she would live up to her underground infamy of wearing undergarments made up of porcupine thorns) she felt a secret pleasure of a successful conquest, which she had never considered herself capable of earlier. She was not conventionally beautiful. She was tall and dark. She had an imposing frame, toned over the years by sticking to a diet rich in fruits and baked vegetables, light exercises and a long stretch of walking that she did religiously, five days a week. She had clear skin and angular features. She had decided not to sleep with anybody (however much she might take to the fancy of a man) until he had demonstrated his commitment beyond a reasonable degree of doubt. Because of this, she faced many complications. The men with whom she socialised by experience had realised the destined death of all angelic dreams associated with romantic transgressions of inexperienced people; they were mostly chasing a vague mirage of exotic animal like release of their carnal instincts.

Surprisingly, it was the married men who were mostly interested in Gopa; this was because they outnumbered the bachelors and widowers in the age group of men she socialised with. So she was saddled with a double whammy of having to run away from married men and scour the group for fortyish bachelors and widowers.

Then she met Rahul at the Christmas party of a common friend and got intoxicated by a feeling unknown to her. She could no longer stay within the defence of her norms. She slept with Rahul the third day after meeting him without even knowing his marital status. She didn't know what made her wildly passionate about him. Maybe it was because he was afflicted with an eerie calmness and sudden invasions of indecisiveness, which made him look unsheathed and raw. Later on, Gopa found in Rahul a companion who listened to her with great attention, made her laugh and made love to her inventively for very long durations.

Although she had no experience with other men, she had heard and read that the pivotal difference between men and women in the act of sex was their difference in time periods of reaching individual orgasms. She felt blessed by the fact that Rahul could delay his orgasm to such lengths of time. After about a year of their first meeting, Gopa had asked Rahul mischievously, "What's the secret behind your durability, darling?"

Rahul had answered, smiling mystically, "Yogic control, my dear."

Flushed with happiness and yet tense with anxiety, she had asked, "Will you marry me, Rahul?"

Without a blink, Rahul had said, "Yes. But only if you agree to give me a baby." Gopa felt as if she was flying on the moon.

She lowered her mouth on his member and said, "Not a baby but a hundred babies, you fool. Now gear up, I'm feeling horny."

For Rahul, Gopa was a deviation from his life of voluntary exile and professional work. He liked Gopa's old-world beliefs in god, family and patriotism; he was devoid of such mushy patronising beliefs. In many ways Gopa complemented him and that made her all the more desirable.

Rahul and Gopa were going steady, basking in love and lust, and planned to get married soon. It was only recently that Gopa had noticed a cloud of reticence and withdrawal in Rahul whenever they were together. This was not his usual self. Was he losing interest in her? Was Rahul unwell? Gopa felt sad seeing the growing wall rising between them. Turmoil brewed in her; she doubted she could take it if Rahul decided to distance from her now. She felt bitter, sour and found her search for a man at this late stage in her life pathetic. But she knew that Rahul would have unsettled her anywhere, any time. She felt like crying. Rather, she felt like howling. She would do anything to get back Rahul's original childlike self and devoted attention. Was Rahul undergoing a secret trauma, which he was unable to tell Gopa? She decided to talk openly with Rahul.

She fixed up an appointment with him on a Sunday afternoon at the Taj. Rahul reached the venue on time, took Gopa holding her arms from the lounge, got seated comfortably in the coffee shop in a secluded corner and ordered a cappuccino for Gopa, a black coffee for him and chicken rolls for both of them. Then he gazed at Gopa for a long time. He said, indulgently, "Tell me, mademoiselle. It seems you've something burning inside you to tell me. Come on, speak."

Gopa was silent for some time, collecting her scattered thoughts. A trace of a scream formed inside her. She resisted it with all her strength. She locked her eyes with Rahul's for a few moments. She focused her vision through the viscous fluids, crust and pipelines of blood inside his skull and see for herself the essence of his self; she believed there were two petals stored inside a human being: one deep inside the skull and the other deep inside the heart, which contained in their capillaries the colours of a person's essence and destiny. She lost her sight momentarily as her eyelids wiped across her irises and in that fractional darkness she realised she had to talk to Rahul. She said, "Rahul, I've told Ma we are marrying sometime next winter. I've also told this to Riju and Indra on phone. All of them are very happy to hear the news." She wanted to say something more but fell silent. Rahul smiled. "Great! I think we've discussed this. But your brothers haven't seen me yet."

"But they have heard from me quite a lot on phone. I have sent one of your photographs by mail to both of them."

"What do they say? Are they comfortable with me? Are they convinced their sister is in stable hands?"

Gopa pretended she did not notice the sarcasm. "Riju says you're ravishingly handsome but you smile very little.

But that's because the snap I had sent him captured you in a grim mood. Indra made a strange comment about you."

"What?"

"That you have deceptive eyes."

Rahul felt trapped. "Is it a kind of a forewarning?"

"I wouldn't know even if it was."

"What do you think?"

"There's something about you that gives me the creeps and goose bumps. Can I talk to you frankly?"

"Please, please, Gopa, tell me. Your voice is making me tense."

"Why is it that you stay absolutely alone? Why is it that you don't allow any of your relatives inside your house? Why is it that they never want to contact you? I find this weird and hard to explain."

"I think I've told you about this. Why do you need to explain this in the first place? Why? And to whom? Who is seeking such explanations?" Rahul turned red in rage.

Gopa, too, lost her cool. "Don't blow up. Nobody is asking anything. I've only told you the way I feel about things. Can't I speak my mind to you?"

Rahul wanted the conversation to end. He said, "You're only raking up my old hurt."

The food and drinks were served. Starched and embroidered cloth napkins were placed and cutlery re-organised on the table silently by the waiters. There were a few moments of controlled silence until this was done.

Gopa regained control over her emotions as she sipped her steaming cappuccino. Warmth and intimacy settling in her voice, she said, "Don't feel hurt, Rahul. I wanted to have a very conventional marriage. With in-laws and stuff like that you know? I wanted the whole parade of your relatives greeting me and welcoming me to your house. I wanted my marriage to be a starry affair."

Rahul reacted in an unaffected manner, "That's a fair enough wish. But I can't provide that, and you know it already. Will you back out of this mess in that case?"

Gopa replied, flecks of ember returning, "How could you even say that to me? In fact it is you who has been behaving oddly recently. I wanted to know if you were losing interest in me."

Rahul asked surprised, "Oddly?"

"Yes, oddly, Rahul, very oddly, as if I no longer matter to you. You don't even look at me nowadays properly. You don't attend to what I want or I don't want. You seem to have completely immersed in yourself. It's not as if I was demanding it, but because you have been doing all that from day one and that you're no longer doing it, does make a difference the way I look at things. I hope you will appreciate that. I don't remember things very clearly. Since the time we discussed our marriage plans possibly, I find you behaving oddly."

Rahul was furious. "Are you demanding an explanation from me?"

"No, no, not really! But I would be happy if I was told the factual position. Are you going through something terrible?" said Gopa, trying to appease him. "I assure you I can take anything. Anything at all. Do you want our relationship to end? Are you not comfortable with marriage or marrying me specifically?"

"It seems I've hurt you. I've hurt you terribly. But it's nothing to do with you. Not you. It seems I'm under some spell. I know that at times I'm behaving oddly. But am I behaving that bad? Do you think I need therapy or help?"

"Something is eating you up from inside," Gopa said softly.

"What?"

"I don't know. But there is something. It could be something from your past. I'm not saying this to bother you unnecessarily I suppose."

"You're my sheet anchor, Gopa. Don't make me say this a million times."

"But I want to hear it a million times!"

Rahul gave in. "All right. But that makes me feel as if you don't believe me, trust me enough."

"It's nothing to do with trust, honey. Let's cut this crap. Now that I've talked to you, I feel fine. Take me home and make love to me," Gopa said lovingly drawing the conversation to a close.

3.

In the evening Rahul and Gopa made love on the bedroom floor, gently savouring every moment. Gopa didn't hurry to the bathroom after they were done. Rahul went in for a shower. Gopa got up from the floor clumsily; she went towards the carved wooden cupboards on the opposite wall and brought out a few photograph albums from a stack that she had not seen earlier. She felt deeply curious and interested.

She saw photographs of various people from Rahul's past life, some of them caught in interesting frames. She knew most of the faces as she had seen them earlier in a few portrait photographs, displayed on the walls of the study in gilded frames. She looked at three photographs closely: a photograph of Nilanjana, Rahul's first wife, standing relaxed on a mountaintop. She was in a flowing pink dress with a loose fitting green sweater. Her hair was cut short. She looked infectiously jovial, smiling like a queen at the photographer. She looked beautiful and shone like a pearl against the backdrop of a clear blue sky. The second photograph was of Nilanjana and Rahul riding a horse. Rahul was seated behind Nilanjana, holding her in an embrace. His hands were clasped around her waist. Nilanjana's face was turned back to look at Rahul. Ironically both were looking in different directions, their lines of vision intersecting each other just in front of their eyes. Rahul looked like a Greek god in the photograph. The third one was a photograph of Nilanjana and Rahul along with her parents, boisterously enjoying a fabulously laid out dinner on a grand marble dining table, eating, talking and laughing in the vacuous cocoon of a stately hall.

Looking at these photographs she was hit by a sudden pang of jealousy. From the sounds inside the bathroom, Gopa concluded that Rahul would come out any minute. She returned to her position, having kept back all the albums.

When Rahul came out, there was a sudden rush of a

sweet (yet distinctly saline and sour) fragrance in the room – scents of soap, aftershave and perfume mixed together, forming a heady sleep-inducing sensation in the brain. Gopa continued to remain alert.

Rahul said, "Won't you have a wash, honey?"

Gopa said, "Yes, I will."

Then she said, "You know, I was thinking of Nilanjana."

There was a fleeting shadow across Rahul's beaming face. He looked a trifle anxious.

She could understand he was trying not to show his feelings, which arose at the mention of Nilanjana's name. He was making veiled attempts to look normal.

Rahul spoke gently. "Why Nilanjana?"

Gopa said, "God has been unkind to her. She died so early. You said she died of a heart malfunction, no?"

Rahul became restless. "She had a congenital heart ailment. This was diagnosed a few months before our marriage. It was a fatal disorder. But we lived happily for five years before she died. You know this already, don't you?"

"Yes, I do", Gopa said. "You told me she was extremely possessive about you. She was so possessive that she even denied you a child in fear of your divided attention."

"I understood her agonies in the backdrop of her impending death. At a young age we feel we are immortal. But she could never enjoy such pleasant aberrations of youth. She knew she would die any moment. In a way, she felt I was her true companion in life. She held on to me like a baby would hold on to her mother."

Gopa didn't want to ask but couldn't restrain herself finally, "But why did you insist on having a child?"

"It was an act of selfishness, of course, seen in retrospect. I agree. I wanted to be a father. I wanted to secure my future with a companion when Nilanjana would no longer be there in this world by my side. I always believed our child would be a daughter; she would look as regal and frail as her mother. Am I hurting you, Gopa?"

Gopa took Rahul in her arms and whispered in his ears, "You're a very nice man, Rahul. You stood by Nilanjana like a rock. I don't believe people can be so good and I feel blessed to have you in my life. Darling, what all you had to withstand – your parents and relatives deserting you forever because of your choice to marry a dying girl, your wife dying a slow, horrible death and finally your in-laws deserting you, accusing you of neglect and medical conspiracy! Oh, my god, I can't believe this classical battle of good and evil could be so well etched out in today's times of absolute consumption and greed. Look at me. Don't be sad. Now that I'm here; till death do us apart."

Rahul held her tight in his arms. "Don't talk of death again to me, Gopa."

They made love once again, desperately, with melancholic ferocity and later surrendered to a slumber filled with happy dreams.

4.

A few months later, the rains had set in. Rahul sat in his study looking vacantly at the evening downpour. His marriage to Gopa was scheduled for December. The phone was ringing. It took some time for Rahul to realise that he had to react to the phone call. He rushed to pick up the phone.

"Hello," Rahul said, in a low voice.

There was silence at the other end. Rahul repeated, "Hello, who is this?"

He thought there could be a technical problem in the line because of the incessant rains. He patted and lightly banged on the body of the telephone. He kept saying, "Hello, hello, who is this?"

There was a twitching sound at the other end; followed by a nasal response from a male voice he recognised instantly, "Rahul, this is Pradeep. I have come to India on vacation a few days back. How are you?"

Rahul felt irritated and somehow devastatingly disturbed by the call. He made an effort to sound normal and unaffected. He replied, "I'm fine. Thank you. How are you?"

"I'm fine, Rahul. Actually, I wanted to meet you. Yesterday, somebody told me that you are marrying this winter. Is that true?" asked Pradeep.

Rahul wanted to end the conversation immediately. He was agitated beyond words. He strained hard to control his emotions. Instead, he spoke calmly, "Yes, you've heard right."

"That's quite a development. I never thought that after what you went through last time, you could ever decide in favour of marriage."

Rahul sounded exasperated. "Pradeep, can we stop this now? I don't want to discuss my past with you."

Pradeep, hell bound on settling scores, said, "I'm not going to leave you or my father for killing my sister, Rahul."

"Your sister was my wife, Pradeep. Who has put all these dirty notions in your mind?"

"Rahul, I have incriminating evidence. My father bribed you into marrying his sick, dying daughter in exchange for hard cash and a robust career. He was a successful businessman and politician." Pradeep sounded menacing.

"Why would he do such a thing? Nilanjana was beautiful, well read, articulate and educated; of course, she was not too well."

Pradeep reacted sharply. "Don't you remember how she had become a liability and a source of utter embarrassment to my father and family because of her espousing radical politics openly and so defiantly? This conflicted with his and his party's interests. Only recently I've come to know; his party's the then president had instructed him to either silence his daughter or face political extinction. He planned a trick to make his daughter fall in love with a dog like you. A hired killer appointed by her own father to use his suave mannerisms and charming ways to woo my sister and then remove her from the way. But Nilanjana was not a fool; she soon realised she had been tricked."

Rahul lost his patience. "Be careful with your words, Pradeep. Nilanjana was madly in love with me. What do you know? You were a kid at that time studying in a faraway boarding school. Don't fantasise a story out of nothing just because you're a crazy nut, constantly in love with conspiracy theories."

"I repeat, I have incriminating evidence, Rahul, to nail you and my father. Nilanjana was not in love with you. She was in love with your image, fabricated by you in cohorts with my father. She understood every passing day what was happening to her after marriage," Pradeep said. He continued, "She was trapped in claustrophobia further surmounted by her disease. Lastly, after years of torture and suffering she was despondent to leave and run away in spite of her poor health, when you both conspired once again; you killed her by throwing her from the terrace of our ancestral home in Malda to the bottom of an adjoining pond and later dressed it up conveniently as a sudden congenital heart failure, manipulating doctors, police, administration and records."

"Pradeep, I hate being threatened by a moron like you. If you believe what you're saying please go to your father and let him know."

"Rahul, you're forgetting something. My father and his party are no longer in power. The present disposition wants evidence against relics like my father to finish them off. I'll do anything to annihilate you and my father," Pradeep said, his voice filled with hatred and disgust.

Rahul wanted to say, "You ignorant fucker, what you don't know and understand is, your father is an invisible Goliath with his shadows eclipsing every nook and space of this universe. Pure evil and saintliness can't be segregated in between partisan politics. They cut across borders created by human understanding. The present disposition that you think will finish him off, also runs its writ in his area by co-opting his menacing control over the local people built over years of manipulation and power play."

He didn't say all this. He only said in the coolest manner possible under the circumstances, "Pradeep, do whatever you feel like doing. You don't have to tell me and then act, my boy." Rahul banged the phone down like the final swing of a ferocious fencer.

He looked at the falling rain and the grey, wet landscape outside. He was mentally detached from his immediate surroundings. He had digressed into a vortex of plunging thoughts. There were hardening movements of muscles on his face reflecting his thoughts. There was a shade of terror mixed with dark aggression looming large on his eyes.

Rahul made a phone call and talked in a low, hushed voice for a long time. He looked rested after that.

Apart from the impact of the ongoing monsoons, the lash of rains became harsher on the city due to a prolonged depression in the Bay of Bengal. The rains continued for a couple of days without a break. The city and the suburbs were flooded. The government and administration were profusely and relentlessly criticised in the print and electronic media for their slow response and lack of preparation to such a crisis. People were dying in scattered incidents at various locations.

Pradeep met with an untimely death in a city manhole. As he hailed from a well-known family, the news of his death became a popular item on TV and was used effectively to embarrass the administration. However, two people in the city were enormously happy with this sudden death. The news item died a gradual death, just as everything that is born has to die one day.

5.

Rahul married Gopa. She was sad because there was no one to greet her when she entered his house in her bridal attire. She was not too happy to know that she could be the queen of her husband's palatial house without any battle. Her friends and cousins felt otherwise and were slightly envious of her good fortune. When she had asked Rahul if she could ask her mother to join them, he had been condescending, so Gopa did not go ahead with that idea.

Rahul asked Gopa to organise the house the way she felt comfortable and aesthetically satisfied. Gradually,

Gopa made the changes and felt the intoxicating satisfaction of being the only decision maker in a big house with an efficient staff and an agreeable husband.

Gopa wondered if God was ultimately blessing her in exchange of her earlier struggles. In her moments of heart-warming rumination of such marital bliss, she even considered leaving her career and become a devoted homemaker. Rahul would oppose such moves, saying, "You shouldn't do such things. You'll get bored in the house alone."

Gopa would say, "Why should I be alone, darling? Give me babies, honey." Rahul would caress Gopa, locking her within his arms tightly but would not reply.

Gopa got restless for babies. One day, she said, "I've crossed thirty-five, Rahul. I think I should get pregnant now. Otherwise, delivery at a later age could be problematic. And you wanted babies, didn't you?"

Rahul did not respond.

Of late, he was plagued by a dream. He stood transfixed in a morgue illuminated by a streak of moonlight pouring in through a tiny hole in the ceiling. The room was filled with empty, open, fungus-eaten timber vaults. The floor was scarred by dead bodies of babies of all kinds, their terror-filled blue, green and black eyes gazing vacantly in the moonlight.

He would wake up sweating and panting every time, careful not to alarm Gopa who would invariably be gently snoring in her sleep. He would gulp glasses of chilled water one after the other and wander inside the dark house like a ghost.

Then, one moonless night, when he was thrown out of his sleep by the same dream, he saw in the wavering darkness the outlines of Nilanjana's body running desperately with a pregnant abdomen. She took a sudden turn, like it had happened before, elsewhere, rushing upwards screaming through a spiralling stairwell as if she was on fire and seeking help. She ran in absolute panic, not slowing down even after reaching the terrace. She struck the short parapet wall and, with her weight and momentum, fell to her death like a bag of stones and hit the pebbly bottom of an adjoining pond. Rahul saw two men standing in the darkest corner of the terrace like brothers in arms with dead remorseless faces. One of them was Nilanjana's father, and the other resembled him.

Rahul woke up screaming. Gopa sat up, alarmed. After she calmed down, she took Rahul in her arms and consoled him. "Did you see a nightmare, my baby? It was only a dream, honey. You must be suffering from indigestion. Come on, take some antacid and a glass of cold water."

Rahul said, gasping for air, "Just let me be alone. I don't need anything for the moment. I'll go to the study and sit on the easy chair."

Upset by Rahul's response, Gopa asked, "Are you hiding something from me, Rahul? You don't look normal."

Rahul snapped, "Shut up, Gopa. It's nothing. I'll be okay by morning."

Rahul slept on the easy chair in the study and in the morning, made love to Gopa on it twice.

After forty-five days Gopa found out she was pregnant. She was ecstatic. Gopa phoned Rahul and asked him to come back home immediately and take her to her mother so that they could break the happy news together.

Rahul was bewildered but he followed his wife's advice and planned to return home early.

On the road, Rahul's car was smashed by a speeding trailer; it was instantly turned into a ball of pulp. Rahul never returned to Gopa.

Instantaneous Death

1.

Rahul had written six notes on the night of January 2. The notes were addressed separately to his mother, father, wife, daughter, lover and a concubine he had been frequenting in the last year.

The paper and pen he used to write these notes were procured from an up-market shop on the evening of January 1. These, he believed, were his New Year gifts; it did not matter if he had given them to himself. He had dreamt of writing letters in long hand on such neat, thick paper for a long time. In fact, he had been eyeing this shop for the last two years (since its inauguration by the Minister of Commerce and Industry). He felt shy entering the flashy shop littered with multifarious glittering stationery products, sold by nymphets conducting themselves like steel robots behind sterile metallic counters.

The notes had all shot from the reserves of his memory one after the other, without a break, in remarkable spontaneity. They were crystal clear and very well rehearsed. He felt enormously thirsty after completing the task of writing. He downed three glasses of chilled mineral water in quick succession. He used a separate sheet for each note. After writing the notes, he read each one a couple of times and reflected on the imperfection of each with a strange glimmer on his dark, ugly face. Then he folded the letters neatly in rectangles and engraved the name of each recipient in a calligraphic style on the corresponding envelopes. Thereafter, he went to the living room window to take a final view of the world as it existed at that moment and contemplate his next line of action.

2.

The note to his mother read:

"You are a leftist, feminist, sex maniacal, opportunist, selfish, big-mouthed bitch. I was sick of your helpless, well-oiled, sycophantic cavalcade of earnest, ill-treated personal slaves who propped up your sagging boobs, bottomless ego and perennially hypocritical, ambitious lifestyle. They were there to carry out your daily, mundane chores. When I kill myself, I will kill a part of you. I don't know whether I am happy killing me, but killing the part of you that is holed up inside me will be a big time thrill. Bye, you inflated bitch of a woman!"

3.

The note to his father read:

"You have been suffering from a dysfunctional penis for billions of years. At one point in time, I truly doubted if I was your son or somebody else's. There is a similarity in our (yours and mine) breathing patterns, that is, the gravity of our respiratory function; based on this I concluded on an autumn afternoon (some thirty years back) that I was your son after all. Are breathing patterns congenital in nature? I believe they are. But I can't explain how. I've always hated being your son. You know this hatred is fundamental in nature. I never liked to be associated with a weak-willed man who could never stand up to face his unfaithful wife who ranted and ranted, every second at you and me for no rhyme or reason. You, to gain her favour, you bloody son of a swine, switched sides and dared to doubly rant at me. I dreamt of killing you day and night (every moment, with the music of your fuming voice playing in the background), hurling ten gallons of petrol on your body, wiring you to the bed stand and lighting your bent body with an Olympic torch. What a pleasure it would have been to see you burning all the way to hell! Because I could never manage to do this (I was afraid of petrol, wires, bed stands and matchsticks, the way these have been used on me), I finally decided to kill myself to end this pathetic experience of being the son of a spineless bastard like you."

4.

The note to his wife read:

"Jealousy is the epitome of love. I was never jealous of you. Which, conversely stated, would mean I never loved you. It's true. I've never felt anything for anybody that could be described as love, the way they do in books, say it in films or in the shadowy corners of public parks. You used to say that you loved me and fell in love with me twice over the day I didn't react when I found you in bed with that cowboy cousin of yours who was a hunk in body and punk in mind and could ram you non-stop (which you described to me quite graphically later). Then you both went on doing this everywhere inside the house (following some dirty manual you had ordered on the Net from Sweden) in front of my eyes, I don't know how many times, a million times may be! You loved me to watch you both surreptitiously, catch you in the act from some corner. The knowledge of my presence invigorated you so much; you beasts brimmed with the all-conquering ego of well-paid, legalised porno stars. Was that it? I was amazed by the compatibility of your acrobatic movements (which I always believed could only be special effects in porno films), especially your brother, whose fucking skills were beyond my imagination; I ended up every time gratifying my needs myself. One day I was overpowered by a sudden desire to suck your brother's cock. I told him about my desire the next day on phone. You remember how you both giggled at me in contempt and would keep giggling in front of others every time I was there. You stopped this torture only after we were separated, two or three years later. Your brother had told you I was a homo, which I was not. My overpowering desire, I suppose, originated from my genuine respect for such an astounding monument of flesh and my craving for the insides of your body, which this monument had the opportunity of piercing a billion times. When you are denied even the slightest opportunity to shower respect on something that amazes and awes you, the natural consequence that looms on your destiny is death. The memory of you and your brother in bed is so well etched on my soul that I will carry these images into the life after my death. I would not leave my quest to conquer them and have them as my own in my next life."

5.

The note to his daughter read:
"You are not my daughter. I hope you know that. Somehow you like me in a special way. That is sweet of you. You keep on suffering from ailments: flu, diarrhoea, and endless sneezing. You are weak, pale and fragile. That makes you beautiful in my eyes. Last year you crossed 14 years of age and I crossed 42. Remember the glass of wine we shared on each other's birthdays? I have no fatherly feelings for you, like the desire to protect you from villains or bad omen or demons. But I do want you to be happy. You must know I hate your muscular, idiotic father (I mean the real one) and your peppy, white, manicured, pedicured, bleached skin, hair waxed, hair dyed, blistery, brittle mother (I mean my wife). The other day I read in a book that children born out of incestuous relationships are always in danger. They suffer from various diseases repeatedly because of congenital defects and a weak constitution. Which means you could have been born weak because you were born to a pair of first cousins. I felt terribly burdened by the tragedy of your destiny. I was outraged by the possibility of sharing this limitless weight

of being made to care for you for a lifetime (although you are not my biological child in the first place) while your real parents, whom you hate from the core of your heart, make hay. If I lived, you would never agree to be with them. This soured my attitude towards your special liking for me. I chose death to escape from this sticky situation of doting and caring for a child not mine."

6.

The note to his lover read:
"I don't love you. I don't love you. I don't love you. But then I don't know why everybody refers to us as lovers and sometimes, as eternal lovers. Could it be because we shared the stage once and enacted the roles of melancholic lovers in an ancient play on a stormy night? Remember how you refused to act with me the next time because when I was supposed to hold your hand, I ended up drawing you so close to my chest that you nearly died out of asphyxia? You complained to the director: you would never act in future with a sex maniac. Baby, this happened fourteen years back and this (your guttural complaining against me to the director and the slow whispering among the intelligentsia of this city that cost me my career) played on my mind so many times that instead of getting angry, I felt like crying for you, for your deep sense of violation. I actually wanted to apologise to you a number of times. It was not possible because you had left the country by the time I had made up mind to express my unconditional apology to you. And then, it struck me all of a sudden; one could always express a sincere apology to anybody by choosing one's own death. What do you think?"

7.

The note to the concubine read:
"I've not seen your face properly. At times, I feel, I've

not seen you at all. What really draws me towards you? I remember touching you. I do remember sharing a drag of hash with you. I remember the jungle and the cheap lavender odour of your bulbous body. I remember your efforts to give me pleasure. I remember the green sherbet you used to offer me after we had been in bed. Surprisingly, I insisted on condoms and you insisted on having my cock raw. I was afraid of germs and diseases that you may be carrying secretly to transmit into your clients' blood stream in an act of revenge. You explained to me: you and your pimp were so happy with the amount of money I was giving you that you relished being confined to one client. You said you had got yourself tested only a month back, that the test was negative and that I should concentrate only on enjoying the pleasures of your body. A few days later, my office colleagues had organised a party in a five-star hotel over heaps of cocaine and I was aghast to find that the party was planned to end with an orgy where your highness was invited to entertain five men in a single feat. When I caught you red handed in this act, you invited me to join in as well. I was shocked by the extent of your lying and ended up thinking, 'Sluts will be sluts, after all'. I could not sleep that whole night, horrified by your betrayal, the rising terror of a deathly disease, stigmatised existence and a painful death. This continued for a month. I didn't even have the courage to face a blood test, fearing the worst. Since I couldn't kill my attraction for you, which I realized with further agony, after the initial rush of hypochondria had subsided; I decided to kill myself instead, to avoid future bouts of hypochondria that could cause fatal damage to my endocrine system."

8.

Rahul had gathered a revolver and a few bullets, a long nylon rope and a hundred sleeping tablets as various tools to kill him. The process of collecting these items had taken him over forty-five days. He had obtained the revolver with its matching bullets from an old uncle who had been, at one point, minister in a royal family notorious for hunting animals and birds inside their private jungles. Rahul had pleaded with his uncle saying that he wanted to flaunt the gun among his colleagues in a party as proof of his royal connections. The nylon rope was available in a departmental store. He procured the sleeping tablets from two different medical shops against a fake, photocopied prescription, in batches of ten tablets each time, with a gap of seven days.

9.

Rahul re-read the six letters. It was a cold and quiet night outside. People in the neighbourhood were mostly tired and sleeping after the elaborate New Year parties. He was thinking seriously whether his letters would have any impact on his target audience.

He summarised their reactions methodically on another piece of paper, which read:

I. Mother – She will burn the letter, plead for my body to be donated to a medical institution for on-going research in the study of human anatomy and organise a condolence meeting in my flat, fret on children born with neurosis who require special societal care and how civil institutions need to react to such issues.

II. Father – He will shred the letter into pieces and throw them into a public dustbin in a neighbouring *mohalla*. He will be relieved to be rid of a lunatic who had the potential to kill him any day.

III. Wife – She will throw the letter into an open sewer. She will not waste any time thinkingof me.

IV. Daughter – She will keep the letter with her for some time. Then she will lose it the way she keeps losing her things. She might cry but she would focus within a few days on finding a long-term caretaker for her.

V. Lover – She will frown, feel disgusted and violated by my letter and will make it suffer the tyranny of a paper shredder. She will call me and my parents names (quite rightly so) and spit at least one hundred and one times to ritualise the ceremony of forgetting me.

VI. Concubine – She won't read the letter but will give it to her pimp for further action, if any.

Rahul read the list of reactions in front of him and suddenly realised he did not want to die at all. On the contrary, he yearned to switch over to an invisible life, declare himself dead, deliver his letters to the six and observe their reactions from up close without their being able to see him. After an hour of contemplation, he concluded that this was not possible and abandoned the whole idea. He burned the letters on a candle flame, drank a glass of wine and was suddenly confronted with a massive hard on, thinking of the seventh floor maid, Maya.

10.

Rahul had been eyeing Maya for the last six months or so. He lived in a twelve-storey apartment building with two penthouses on each floor. He lived on the ninth floor.

A retired High Court senior advocate, after slaving for the tax- and law-evading corporations his entire professional career, had settled three years back in his posh penthouse apartment on the seventh floor to enjoy his retired life. Meanwhile, he had got separated from his wife (for whom, it was believed, he had bought a similar penthouse in another part of the city), de-listed his son (who was an astrophysicist in the US, married to a German; he hated scientists and Germans) and daughter (a financial consultant who mingled (God knows why) with red-headed aboriginals in the outskirts of Sydney; he hated aboriginals because of venereal diseases) from the list of beneficiaries of his property.

He employed a twenty-four-hour maid named Maya who was around fifty years old and had a wiry frame, a deep wheatish coloured, cunning face, and a charged pair of eyes possibly emitting sex signals, which resonated with Rahul's sex signal receptors. It was rumoured that Maya had very efficient hands, legs and mouth for all kinds of work. There was gossip that Maya, who was an illegal immigrant from a neighbouring country, had a husband and a son. They were well provided for by the advocate with regular income and a house in an unknown location in the city in lieu of the dedicated, slave-like services of Maya. It was said that Maya was permitted to meet her husband and son once a month under the watchful gaze of the old man.

Everything went on fine until rumours of male residents sleeping with Maya started floating all around the place. There were processions by local women's organisations and NGOs demanding the immediate intervention of the police and administration to stop brothel-like activities inside a retired advocate's residence in such a posh colony. Nothing came of all this except that the advocate had to take care of the local police and administration, the women's organisations and NGOs in the best possible manner, which was done without losing any time.

To begin with, Maya was not a whore. She had had an insatiable urge for sex since the days she was involved in harvest work in paddy fields in humid, muddy conditions. There, she would invariably end up sleeping with two or three men in a day. Gradually, as she developed her carnal skills, men started showering her with cash and gifts of all kinds.

In this apartment building, she would insist on precious ornaments from her clients. Services differed for people according to the offering: silver, gold or diamonds. The retired advocate did the cataloguing including preservation of the bounty. He treated Maya with daughterly love. He ensured her nourishment and mental relaxation by making her listen to pre-recorded talks of spiritual and motivational gurus from time to time. She did yoga and followed a hygiene regimen that allowed her to take care of her maid-like duties of cleaning, washing and cooking along with entertaining one guest every alternate night efficiently.

Maya took summer and winter vacations every year.

This was to re-charge her vigour and take care of the effects of her advancing years.

Rahul had seen Maya a couple of times from a distance but face-to-face only once in the elevator, alone, when he was floored by a thumping desire to stop the lift, tear off her clothes and rape her by lifting her on top of his cock till he went faint with pleasure. But this was not to be since Maya did not look at Rahul even once. After the initial bout of excitement, Rahul felt overwhelmingly rejected.

Rahul's first reaction to this rejection was to forget Maya. However, he failed. On the contrary, he got so obsessed with her that he started masturbating two or three times a day using his fantasy about Maya. Rahul could no longer bear the onslaught of fantastical images. He decided to seek Maya's favour and services without any further delay.

However, one night, in the end of autumn, when his mother slapped him in front of his wife and her hunk lover-cousin in connection with a property dispute, he was invaded by a sudden urge to kill himself. That night his entire life of shame, paralysis and horridly different ways of functioning of his brain and body came back at him like cannons, erasing the images of Maya and firing his mind with ideas of death to escape from this hostile world forever.

Early on the morning of January 3, when Rahul was confronted yet again with erotic images of Maya, he felt he was returning to a primitive period of his life.

Rahul decided to rape Maya that very morning. He vaguely remembered that the advocate was away from the city on some work, which meant Maya was alone in the seventh floor penthouse now. Rahul proceeded accordingly.

11.

Rahul knocked on the seventh floor penthouse boisterously and continuously as if the world was on fire. Somebody opened the door cautiously.

"Who is it?" she said, disgust in her voice. It was Maya. When her eyes had adjusted from sleep to sudden waking and could finally locate Rahul, she said, "What's up to you kicking us up from our well meaning sleep, you moron? If your house is on fire call the fire brigade, if you are burgled call the police or the security, if you had a heart attack call the emergency of any hospital. You've no business of waking us out of our sleep. We're private people with private lives of our own."

Rahul was panting with excitement. He had never seen Maya in such an aggressive mood earlier, with a strange scent of sleep and ancient caves coming out of her flesh. He was within a feet of her and yet so far. "Maya, this is Rahul from the ninth floor. I want to sleep with you Maya. Let me in," Rahul said this almost imploring.

"Your selection of date and time is wrong, mister. I've heard stories about you. You are a suicidal vegetable, a rich, ugly kid with too terrible a mental deformation to be useful to anybody or to yourself, abandoned by your parents, wife, lover and slut. They say you have a peanut instead of a penis. You wear a rubber phallus to show a bulge on your crotch. Was that your ma who made you learn this?"

Rahul pushed Maya inside. She was taken aback for a moment. Rahul grasped Maya and felt a volcano erupting inside him. He hissed in her ears, "All that you are saying is true, Maya. There are other things as well about me. I can pay you anything to fuck you once under the shower. Once! I've been dreaming about this for months, Maya. I was going to kill myself tonight. I returned to life thinking about you."

"You are going to get killed anyway, man." This was a man's voice from the hazy darkness of the living room behind Maya. Rahul saw a stout man in boxer shorts, a wooden club in his right hand lifted midair, aimed at Rahul's head.

The club hit Rahul's head with a ferocious force. His skull split into two pieces. He fell down like a log of wood, clinging to Maya with blood gushing from his head and nose. Rahul died instantly without any sign of pain or struggle.

12.

As Rahul entered his afterlife, he saw a moonlit valley with snow-peaked mountains all around. The valley was lit with a bluish expanse of darkness. He saw his mother running, naked, with a club in her hand, long hair flowing down her back, chasing an ugly little boy resembling Rahul thirty-nine years back. He saw his father selling cannon balls under a Krishnachura tree.

As Rahul looked up at the moon, it resembled Maya. She was looking at Rahul with a lusty smile on her face.

Love

The girl with pearls in her eyes
Dived into the crater of a fuming mountain
In search of luminous stones and
An isle that was edged with trees of fire

The girl and the mountain leapt on to each other with
insatiable hunger

I have seen this mountain weathering wind and snow
Waiting like a pyramid
Millions of years for this girl to slip inside the crevice of
its soul
It was shaken with unending desire, at long last

I saw this scene while I was running through a desert
like a
forsaken phantom

Then I saw my brothers and sisters with ashen faces
Marching past with burnt out torches
Humming a lyric of love
Worshipping the shaking mountain and the girl with
pearls in
her eyes.

Face and the Bookcase

I saw my face in a bookcase, the skin parched from
burning and even
melting at places
Queries leapt inside my mind like flowers of spring.
Where are the books in the bookcase?
What is the point at which human skin melts?
Then I saw ants, red and green, eating into my face in
the bookcase and
thick chunks of wood

In the morning, I saw my face in the mirror
The face was the same like it always was

I went to the bookcase
The books were gone
Those were books collected day by day
Those were books of suffering and pain
Those were books shared with lovers of various races
and times

I sat down feeling empty and drained out

I looked at the bookcase with intent and frown
It resembled a cave abandoned and gone like a
mother's womb

Will I fit inside the bookcase and become another book
in time like a

child at play
Happy and gay
While the world ends in the fury of winds and waves
and
My delinquent mother searches her road in ancient
caves.

Clouds of Life

It is strange that in the thick of every summer a gang of
clouds invades the city.
Well for one, travelling through clouds can be
uncomfortable – humid,
blinding and not so spongy as they look, almost airless
to the core.
But I remained adamant.
I carried on with my daily business as if nothing had
changed.
As if the endless announcements on the radio, TV and
the public address
systems were all wrong.

It was difficult to separate night from day.
When I was awake, I felt despairingly blinded.
I could not see the usual faces that I saw while on way
to work, the stooping
trees that were planted opposite my house, the sky
burning with stars and
planets, the dying contours and milestones in the city
that I used to navigate
and find locations within its serpentine alleys.
For that matter, I could not see myself most of the
times.
Mirrors were no longer of any use to the city dwellers.

The government expected accidents and collisions to
happen under the

circumstances.
Surprisingly no accidents or collisions were reported
any more.
Neither did anybody hit me nor did I hit any one
during my work in the
day.
I was like an automaton conducting his business to a
well memorised
script.
Had every one become automatons like me?

It was sad to think of us city dwellers – independent
thinkers, rebels,
writers, artists, professionals and government officials –
as automatons.

One day I thought of walking down the lake to
Debolina's house.
Not to meet her really, but to see her from a distance.
She was a fiercely independent woman in college, now
a docile homemaker
to a well-known bureaucrat.
She had wonderful skin, smiling eyes and a small
frame.
I was madly in love with her in college. When I knew I
would not be
successful in love, the flame of love had turned itself
into a throbbing ache
on the nerves.
The pain came back in the summers. In the winters it
was reasonably less.

I had not seen Debolina for years. The last time I saw
her she looked at me with a
mocking smile a few days before her wedding.
I must confess; I had wanted her to fail in marriage and
even gone to the
extent of cursing her in my mind.
I would enquire about Debolina from common friends
and acquaintances.

When I gathered, she was happy in marriage, had a
loving husband, two
healthy sons, a fabulous house by the lakeside and a
side career of a cuisine
writer; I stopped fishing for news about her.
I knew my curses had failed as much as I had failed
with her.

While on the way to Debolina's house, I realised
something special: a
blanket of clouds covered our sorrows and invisibility
so well that
we were no longer sad to make a new beginning.

Should I tell Debolina for once how much I loved her in
college, the fall of
her hair that reminded me always of a wild mountain
stream?

That afternoon I saw Debolina standing on the
verandah sipping coffee
looking vacuously at the lake.
Strangely there did not exist a single ball of cloud
between her and me then.
I tried to look at her hair and eyes as closely as I could
from that distance.
She had become older gracefully. She looked ripe and
desirable now.
My body was filled with a pain whose origins I knew.

I stood there a long time.
She went inside. She cooked a Spanish omelette first
and ate it with a loaf
of brown bread. I looked at the motions of her lips and
cheeks as she was
eating. She instructed her housekeeper to do this and
that.

Her voice had changed. It sounded fuller and
contented. Then she went

into her study, a room lined with wood panels
containing millions
of books and manuscripts and at the centre a writing
table and a finely
polished upright wooden chair.
She sat on the chair, looked outside the window with
her smiling look as if
she was smiling in slow motion and soon started
writing with a black Mont
Blanc on handmade paper.

I touched her shoulder lightly with my right hand.
She looked back and focused her sight on me. She did
not recognise
me at first. When she did she jumped and embraced me
like a friend, planting a fleeting kiss on the right cheek.
I felt happy and gay.

Then I saw a rush of clouds rising up from the lake,
crossing the
streets and entering the room where we were.

Debolina said, "Sandy dear what do you do?"
I said, "I collect taxes."

She looked surprised and said, "Taxes, oh dear! What a
waste of a life! Do
you love me still?"

I was shocked by her question. How did she know that
I loved her?
I had not told this to anybody.
I kept quiet.
I think the silence miffed her.
She said gleefully, "Remember you were such a foodie
in college? I'm a great
cook now. Can I cook something for you, Sandy?"

The clouds engulfed us.
I found Debolina sublimating in my hands.

She had become a cloud.

As I walked back home still warm from Debolina's
embrace, I saw
the city had become normal.
The clouds were gone.

There was a crowd in front of me.
A huge car had rammed into a wall.
A beautiful, middle aged woman was at the wheel.
She was dead, in a pool of blood and flesh.
Her face was smashed on shreds of glass. Her hair ...

Debolina had told me something queer.
"Sandy I was always curious about you. I wanted to
know about you.
Although, I never showed it.
Frankly I know quite a bit about you by now. Check
with me if you don't
believe me.
I have grown a deep regard and affection for you. The
way you have carried
yourself sanely through misfortunes with money and
women.
Somehow I envied this mysterious sanity of yours.
Would I've been happy
being married to you?
I can't say this today."

This was the last she spoke before becoming a cloud.
My eyes were filled
with tears.

On a Hilltop

In the evenings Rupa rode up the hill.
She went up the rocky incline holding the hand of her
fragile son.
Rupam, barely on the edges of an awkward
adolescence, often played on
the way fondling the wild growth of violet mountain
flowers.
The flowers grew between damp crevices of rocky
boulders breathing a
magical scent in the air.
Looking at the moist petals from close incited a melody
of a popular
tune of her college years in Rupa's heart.
The tune, its melody, playing in her mind lightened the
toil of climbing
heights.

On the hilltop they – mother and son – sat on moss
lined rocks.
Night dripped from the sky like oozing fluid.
The darkness gradually was filled with a halo of bluish
light from
heavenly bodies.
Tiny lamps in the distant town radiated a haze of pale
yellow ochre light
in ether.
Rupa and Rupam sat stoically by each other like a silent
ritual not

talking,
only seeing through the darkness all around with wide
gaping eyes,
rarely blinking.

Were they searching for someone dear and far?

Rahul had left them eight years back.
While leaving home, he had told Rupa, he planned to
travel the world;
marriage had frustrated his soul.
Rupa had turned into a rock not able to understand the
impact of
Rahul's words.

It took years for Rupa to come to terms with her loss.
Every time she remembered the whiplike lashes of
those words, she
shuddered with horror.
At first she remained blurred in mind, unaware of her
existence and
uncaring towards Rupam.
She avoided looking directly at Rupam's eyes.
One night while making him sleep she saw his eyes,
every curve, lash and
colour in detail.
An arrow of fresh pain shot through her longing body.
She buried her son's face in her bosom, let out a sharp
wail and then fell
silent all of a sudden.
Rupam wiped her tears with his soft swollen hands
falling on his face, their
– mother's and son's – eyes locked within the glow of
each other's gaze like eternal lovers.
Rupa knew she was a devoted wife.

She wished Rahul well, wanted him to be a happy poet
writing
beautiful tales of successful love.
She treasured his manuscripts the way she kept as a

child, almost with
fervent love, old leaves of guava and mango inside her
encyclopaedia.

Where did her love go wrong?
Were Rupam's eyes not sad enough to hold his father's
soul from
abandoning them so recklessly?

Two years back Rupa had read Rahul's last novel,
About a hilltop, from where he would, once upon a
time, see
night falling on his native town every evening, sitting
alone on a treetop among
bats and owls.

Was this the same hilltop?
Or, was it another piece of Rahul's fertile imagination?

Mother and son would look at each other at times in
the darkness haltingly,
thinking about similar things about the other.

"Will my unloved ma ever be happy?"
Rupam knew he would never be able to share his ma
with anyone.
"Will my fatherless darling son ever be happy?"
Rupa trembled at the thought of Rupam falling in love
and her having to live
alone, without her son.

Araku

I saw another night falling on the green mountains and
valleys of our youth
A silent crucible of unknown trees, grasslands and
tribes
Pouring a rhythm in my soul

For a second I thought: where was I, where would I go
When I saw you running through the diffusing beam of
smoke breaking on
the southern mountains
Like a deer

The stars twinkled like never before
Showering your path with ancient light
The green mountains and valleys of our youth suddenly
shone with another
light fired from within the tired earthly layers

You came so near panting and gasping looking into my
eyes
I opened my arms

Was it real?
Was it a dream?

I knew it was happening in another world
Where you and I lived.

Café Kali

Café Kali is a wasting hole at the end of town
It is a den of kings and queens without a crown
It is a place of pale blue lights, smoke, rummy and lust
Here kings and queens go on till they go bust

This is a place I visited on a rainy damp night
With a red kite flying in my head and willing to fight
A slogan on the kite in black said: Life is a perpetual
loss

Something happened as I entered this hole, I really
don't know what
I gulped glass after glass of cheap sour wine
As I sensed my intestines burning, grating on charcoal
fire
I was overwhelmed by the sight of this creamy woman
Dancing on her toes lonely in a swarthy part
Tumour-infested goons with bloodshot eyes cheering
her up
But, hell, she was looking at me really with an
indecipherable signal in her
eyes

Later when I was gulping gallons of that uncouth wine
Almost on the verge of crying
She came to me, still dancing, looked now inside my
tired eyes and
whispered in my ears, "Do you remember me, darling?

I am Zeenat. We
made love on a rocking boat by an endless coast."
For once, I thought I might puke and ruin all my
chances of winning a hand,
But then Zeenat, holding my trembling hands, declared
in a raunchy voice to
the boss of the table, "This boy is mine. His losses are
mine. Get going, you
dirty fellas while we catch up with time."

Café Kali is a wasting hole with a large terrace
blooming on its head,
opening up to a vast cauldron of heavenly bodies and
dreams.

Zeenat and I spent some time on this terrace
remembering and forgetting
our days from an earlier life
When we were man and wife

Somewhere in the distance
The music was playing
The wine was flowing
The cards kept falling

Zeenat and I by then were sailing on a lighted boat in
the sky that sheltered
this eternal wasting hole named Café Kali

Wishes

If wishes were horses
You wouldn't find horses leaping on the tracks
If wishes were rockets
You wouldn't find rockets shooting through the stars

Wishes are wishes

They are ripples in your heart
They are ripples of desultory signals flying from other
distant hearts

But wishes get mauled and end on stones of time

Momentarily when you see the shadowed hooded
figure of fate crossing
your path while you were crossing a valley full of
tombs
You look back at your passing life like a child trapped
in a hall
How you wish then if you had other wishes to carry
back home

Cocoa Brain

I've seen on some special nights something happens in
the air and a
few things catch fire almost instantaneously
Like, the other night the circus tent of the Great Russian
Circus laid
out opposite Lady Brabourne College went up in
sudden flames
Hordes of skeletal animals and half starved gymnasts
invaded the
city like diseased rats, horribly swollen and bleeding
The dwellers of Park Circus area were once again
eyewitnesses to a
terrible night of mayhem
Then the 14th floor office premises of an insurance
company, went
berserk in lusty mysterious lashes of fire, cocooned in a
tall empire
on Chowringhee, the coldest night last year
Surprisingly, people laughed the next morning reading
the
news in the papers
A few weeks later on the first Sunday of spring Subimal
told me, the
Howrah Bridge was on fire and melting

I was thinking about these fires in an oblique manner
while
sauntering along Red Road

It was the night of winter solstice this very year
While the city was sleeping barring a few out-of-
business whores
on the streets, a pair of feminine dogs, a dishevelled
tramp and a
few banished lovers roaming around here and there, I
was wholly
concentrated in my thoughts, shivering from the chill in
the air
As I crossed the racecourse; like always it was trapped
in a halo of
darkness
I thought of a valley of flying saucers on a deserted
moon

Just then something erupted in front of my eyes
But I don't know what
The racecourse was suddenly lit from nowhere by
thousand glaring
torches of fire

The air boomed with the resonating voices of horses,
jockeys, trainers,
owners, stewards and boisterous gamblers and glasses
and porcelain
The styling of caps, hats, headgears and headscarves
were all there to be
seen on the heads of gyrating men and women

I saw a pitch-black limousine slowly travelling down
the Victoria
Memorial road like a leopard on a reconnaissance
prowl.
Was this awesome limo crawling towards me in rabid
hunger?
As this giant of a car came very near almost dredging
me off my stance, it
halted panting for momentary breath
I looked with a full-eyed gaze at its full-bodied shining
metallic splendour

I kept on looking like a star-struck boy

Just when one among the many black-lined glasses in
row rolled down
slowly in rhyme
I found a woman behind the glass rolling, sitting on a
red leather-bound
seat full of poise, grace and calm in black, as if she was
wearing
the night on her skin
Once upon a time I knew her well;, her name was
Kokila,
but I loved calling her Cocoa Brain, a brat to the core, I
thought at that time
she was a petite selfish woman, a girl really then, a
serpent who was good to
spend some time with but not forever
Well I thought she was a pigeon brain, not in
understanding of finer
nuances of life and death
Last year I met her under dramatic circumstances in a
traffic jam at
Ballygunj Square
After some hurried small talk she said she was writing
a novel now and if I
had the time she could meet me at the Oxford tea bar
and read out to me
some chapters of her novel
I agreed. Almost immediately and instinctively out of
primitive
curiosity.

We did meet soon, she read to me in her deep wooden
voice over cups of
the finest leaf tea
First I heard with fractured attention but later in
shaking raptures of awe
She had sliced and disarmed the lies of our youth as if
in a joke
I had no words to praise her, so I ended up saying –

Darling I'm in love

She questioned me with her smiling eyes – In love, but
with whom
I blurted – It has to be you
She raced out of the bookshop and before hitting the
road she just about
made a hissing remark – Men who fall in love so fast
are dangerous men

Cocoa Brain did not come out of the car but looked at
me with brilliant
luminescence dancing on her hazel eyes
All of a sudden she said softly almost caressing me with
every syllable she
uttered – Cocoa Brain leads a very complex life now.
Love is hardly on her
agenda. Love can hardly save her now. You are twenty
years too late my
dear. Now she often sighs, thinking in a dreamy
manner, rewinding to
that peaceful night when you washed her hair in your
garden and gave her a
small homemade bouquet of lilies and roses and later
made horrendous fun
of her

Cocoa Brain broke my heart finally
When she was speaking those words the racecourse
behind us caught fire
She for once held my hands within her beautiful palms,
brushed them past
her cheeks and lips

All of a sudden she seemed very alarmed
She instructed her chauffeur in a shrill voice to move
fast and be on the run
Cocoa Brain vanished inside the impending air and
smoke and at last
became a poem in my heart

Spectacle

What does one do with a pair of blue wings on one's
back?

Fly.

This is what the man had said whom I chased since he
came out of the
crumbling hospital building block smelling of death.
I never lost track of him chasing through the intricate
network of roads,
hordes of cars, miles of window shoppers and wailing
beggars and tired
men till he entered a shadowy park where the river
took a minor bend.

There were swarthy boats parked inside the waters
with exasperated lovers.
A few tiny cargo ships sauntered hooting along the
river to the sea.
Their chimneys coughed up a sad pattern of white puffy
smoke in the air.

The man sat on a broken worm-eaten wooden bench,
smoking cheap
cigarettes one after the other.
I kept watching him from the darkness behind a banyan
tree.
The man looked furtively around, all around as if he

was in great danger.

After some time all of a sudden a pair of blue feathery
wings grew on his
back, flapping and fluttering creating a silent wind.

I looked at them in childish awe.
The whole thing reminded me of a childhood game – a
spectacle.
Was the river shaking in the wind?
The question almost hurled off my mouth in a whisper.

He looked around once again with burning phosphorus
in his eyes.
The light showed the melting scales on his oval face.

But he said calmly now looking at me with poise and
candour, "Fly! Fly! Fly!"

As he went up the air high above our city and looked
like an atom with
passage of time, I, by the stroke of an electric spark,
remembered the
madness in Gurung's eyes.
He, a sturdy nomadic mountain boy, once drove my car
like a jet.
Years back in frozen nights we often rushed through
the lonely winding
roads, as in racing sport, between dangerous jagged
mountain cliffs and the
wild waters of Tawang Chu making fun of life and
death.

As I kept looking at the sky with nostalgia, I found the
stars falling from the sky like dead birds on imagined
fields of acacia!

Ladder to the Moon

Come what may, time will pass!
The days will fall into nights; the nights will slip down
the abyss of forgotten
weeks and the weeks into tedious months. The months
will then seamlessly
form prickly years and the years will flow into
ceremonial columns of
decades in ravaged layers.
Each decade in the annals of history will be
remembered for a cause.
The truth is whatever we might do; notwithstanding
the technologies we
have invented, we will never be able to halt the passage
of time, the
decay of our bones and flesh.

Did I wake up after many, years of deep slumber?
Where had all the chimneys gone erupting with
voluptuous layers of
productive smoke,
the rush of colourful vehicles, big and small, that huffed
and puffed and
clogged the arteries of our city so badly that we
preferred to walk,
the submarines and the warplanes that were to protect
us all,
the pungent acidic air that we almost loved to breathe,
the concrete paths and dams and the balloon like shops

with glaring lights
where everything was sold and bought?

Was everything gone?
Was everything gone?
Did we surrender it all?

Where was I?
As I set out to think, I knew, Samiran and I had gone to
sleep arguing over
the ethics of war,
battling to defeat our lust for Seemanti Kar.
We had gone to sleep long back in time singing a war
rhyme in a mansion
on the riverfront that was gifted to my grandfather's
fourth wife by a
reputed writer of his time.
But we had woken up in the ambience of a bombed
citadel full of bodies,
debris and stones, the river gone, the city gone and all
landscape that we
remembered gone.
I looked at the barren world glowing with an unknown
rage it seemed.
Was it the way the first man felt on earth?

All around there were gaping craters and blisters of
rock and soil.
It was difficult to walk. It was impossible to go out in
search of people that I
knew.
I surrendered myself to the breeze of time.
My skin was burnt.
There were sores with pus in my mouth and gut.

The strangest thing, you know, I never felt like sleeping
anymore.
Although felt like weeping so many times but could not
weep as the bombs
dried up my glands.

So I walked and crawled as much as I could and
remembered my life before
I went to sleep.

How much time could have passed in this way? I had
no guess of time.

One night as hot ash was falling from the sky I saw
Samiran and Seemanti
playing tennis with an iron ball on the surface of the
moon, giggling and
giggling, it sounded like water falling from a stream.
Seemanti after winning the match waved her beautiful
hand at me.
She said in her husky voice,
"The war is over. Well it was over long back. But you
just didn't agree to go
up the ladder to the moon because you loved your
sleep like it was your
lover. Most of the guys are dead and the rest of us are
here. We are at work,
Sandy, a new kind of work. Re-doing all the defects in
the ways we lived on
earth. We are working at a new civilisation. How I wish
you were here."
Seemanti turned back slowly having talked to me
planting a longing kiss on
Samiran's lovely lips that looked swollen with a flash of
mauve on them.

The image of the illuminated nylon ladder to the moon
exploded in my
mind, all varieties of men and animals clinging on it to
escape a war.
I don't know how I felt but I felt like screaming, "When
will the autumn
come blooming?"

Sujata Sinha

Last night I had a dream.

A storm raged across the universe.
The oceans invaded the grasslands.
There was a spray of foam and blue on the landscape.
A group of rickety boys played tirelessly with bats and
balls.
Unaware of what was happening elsewhere, they hit
sixes and fours.
Men and a few women in embroidered clothes,
Leisurely seated on the deck of ancient ships like relics,
were clapping and
cheering.
A deathly silence hung loosely on their faces.
In the sky a sand-coloured furry deer was flying, a few
hungry leopards too.
A green snake played on my palms and one on my
shoulders.
I walked for a few miles through water and submerged
grasslands.
After a few hours walking, I reached the confines of a
huge conference hall,
done in brown wood and thick upholstered chairs.
A group of adolescent girls with fine eyes, clear skin
and lovely lips,
were talking animatedly inside the hall.
They spoke a language I did not know.
For a trifle second they were distracted by my arrival,

And then they returned to their noisy relentless
chirping.

In the distance one girl in a pink headscarf was looking
at me.
There was a strange light in her eyes.
Her gaze was fixed on me. I felt an intense and yet
invisible helix of smoke
rising from beneath her irises.
Almost instinctively I looked away, not coming in the
path of her gaze,
embarrassed.
It suddenly struck me she was Sujata.

In my young days in school I played marbles and loafed
around with her,
Until that night she died in a cornfield struck by a beam
of lightning on her
head.

When the dream was gone,
I walked inside the darkness of my room with a faint
trail of smoke
lingering in my head.

Sujata Sinha always blazed with an unblemished
vivacity paling all of us.
She loved marmalade like no other food.
Her ma warned her against eating too much
marmalade, lest she should
grow fat.

One day, she suddenly sat on my lap in her study, once
we were back
from school. She asked me looking inside my eyes
holding my chin, "Tell
me Sandy am I growing fat? Tell me, am I fat?"
I did not replied. I fell silent knowing the storm rising
through my body.
She erupted almost suddenly and started giggling

unrestrained falling from
my lap to the ground.
She said in the end, "Bloody idiot, give up your body!"
Sixteen days later, she died.

I did not understand what Sujata meant.

I raked my mind for a long time after the dream to
think over once again to
comprehend the meaning of that sentence.

I had no clue. That was Sujata Sinha.

Sand Dune Man

This man who normally lived inside sand dunes
entered my soul on days
when I was down and out
He helped me laugh and talk when I hated doing these
but
could not avoid people otherwise.

A few days back I needed him so badly that I saw
myself thrown inside a
floodlit fully packed stadium
Millions of faceless orange skinned men were screaming
at me,
"Sandy, what's happened to you my dear; we're asking
you about the
weather here and you're bloody silent as the sky; we're
telling you Santa-
Banta jokes and look at your morbid face, what are
you, a dumb paraplegic
moron dear,
What's happened, *yaar*?"
I must have been sweating like hell in anticipation
hoping to be hit with the magical entry of the sand
dune man soon into
my soul

But nothing happened really
Late in the night I was caught by the city police and
thrown into a smoky

cell below a jungle.
I was charged with causing discontent among men and
women with normal
faculties of laughter and talking.

After the interrogation started
I was catalogued, bathed, dressed and fed
The guys with bulging biceps, rods and revolvers were
asking so many
questions
I replied to none of them
The muscles on my face were taut with anxiety, they
never tweaked even by
default

But I knew all the replies by rote
I found the whole procedure so funny; I truly wanted
to burst out laughing

Well I did what I did missing the sand dune man

Later I read a piece of news in my cell

There was a storm
It had washed the sand dunes from the face of earth
and gone was the sand
dune man.

Peling

The rumbling sound of fallen leaves under our feet felt
like music

Baba and I walked through the somnolent spaces in the
woods, slowly
step-by-step following an ancient rhyme
Rays of light and clouds of shadows played
intermittently through the
canopy and leaf strewn branches of tall alpine trees
We reached a strange lake
Locals believed mermaids and fairies rose from its
depths on full-moon nights
The lake was endlessly calm and silvery clean like the
third mystical eye
of our gods and goddesses
There were scavenger birds all around us hiding in
nests to clean the lake,
with their tireless beaks, of any falling dried out map of
leaf or speck of
dirt

Baba and I sat on an emerald stone slab by the side of
the lake
The mountains surrounding the lake looked like waves
of frozen grey and
green
Hyenas from their narrow caves came out in the nights,
a few people said

We were safe now, I thought, in the light of day
But for the sight of broken idols of divine angels on the
stone-lined
pathway awoke a slight tremor in our hearts

I looked at baba's face
It struck me I was looking at this face after ages, after a
very long time
The face looked shrunk and dry, crossed by tunnels of
infinite darkness
There was an occasional flicker in the eye
He was looking at the still serene waters for some time
before looking at
me into my eyes

Suddenly he wrapped his frail hands around me, kept
his head on my
shoulders and started weeping without a start
Later when he had finished crying in silence, he
mopped his eyes, without hindrance, against my tweed
coat collar and kissed my cheeks

He said slowly in his breathless wheezing voice, "So
many people are living
peaceful loveless lives; you had to undergo the ordeal
of loving a woman and
yet live away from her. You are madly in love; that
speaks on your face.
Why does she not fly into your life the way butterflies
are supposed to fly?"

Can you tell me what happens between fathers and
sons in the depths of
woods when hyenas are resting in the mountain caves?

I held my baba's face shrivelled and reddened from
anguish now, between my
palms and thought of his love
In his younger days he dreamt of becoming a mahout
for he was in love with

elephants of all kinds and ages
He was brought up in a northeastern forest now
ravaged by timber trade

He had told me once, "Have you seen an elephant's
eyes? What peace and
calm they hold in them! My son, if you look at them for
long you will lose
yourself in their innocent pools of charm. But ask all,
elephants are only
famous for their silly size, ivory teeth or trunk!"

Baba knew if he cried once again looking at my eyes, it
will make me cry and
so, he smiled his trademark playboy smile, which made
his face twinkle with
illuminated kites – kites of love and kites of loss

I said with hope and fervour, holding him close to my
soul, "Don't you worry
old man, she has come and won my heart! When you
fall in love with the
ferocity of a beast, having failed in the past and past
your prime, with a
woman embedded in cavernous layers of memories and
dying, it takes some
time to come. But since she has come, so, I believe she
will come, don't you
bother my old man, but yes, if you can, enjoy the sun!"

*Peling is a place in Sikkim

Killer and a Cop Story

A prisoner told me once,
In a dark cell you lose count of time, days and nights
You are constantly falling and rising
You feel the ambiguous world of zero gravity

These words reverberated in my mind
As I looked at the sleeping city
From the glass panelled walls of my suite on the
twentyfirst floor
The world seemed soundless
An ocean ushering into a muddy bay, a peripheral
concrete topped
road wet with sudden gush of midnight rain, blinking
signs of neon,
apartment buildings looking like dark UFOs and a few
jet like cars
waiting like tense shadows on the street-sides filled up
the landscape
All waiting for the break of dawn
There was nothing strange about the landscape except
that its familiarity
made it look like an eternal blind wall directing my
eyes inwards to a tunnel
of memories and dreams.

It was one such moment when I remembered the
prisoner talking to me

It was in this city I had captured this serial killer after
years of chasing
and plotting
But when we finally met – guns and chains in hand – I
felt the journey of
catching this nut was more intoxicating than catching
him in person

The first lines he screeched at me were:
I am the suffering of god
I am the fly that bites and thrives on others blood
Even the blood that pumps the chest of god

After an arduous judicial battle fought acrimoniously
between lawyers on
both sides,
He was jailed for life
To be cast inside the darkest quarters in the capital
prison for ending the
lives of nine coquettish women during consensual coitus

I had asked him,
Why was it that you had to kill them?
He had replied in his whining voice with eyes burning,

I did not kill them, they had asked for it themselves,
they had screamed for
death in my hands for I granted them with unbearable
pleasure

We met in the prison meadows from time to time for
idle chat

The last time I met him he had asked me two questions:
Tell me who finds lovers for us?
Tell me who takes away our lovers from us while we
are still making
sunshine love?

I did not speak much and I had no clue to these
questions

The morning was breaking on the city
My memories fading with light
I was back in this city with another mission, running
behind another killer
of young men with coloured streaks in their hair.

Jelly-ness, Fears
and Masks

There are moments
When I feel like a mass of jelly
Jelly stuffed inside me
As if I am floating inside an ocean of jelly
The jelly inside and the jelly outside are different and
they are very different
from the jelly that I am myself, you know

Purple beams of light that travel from far away
asteroids through this chaos
of jellies slowly with time get completely jellified

In this utter jelly-ness of life
One realises one's fears in the most intimate manner

Like
I fear mothers waiting for their dying children
I fear chubby kids staring in awe, behind coated glasses
of their longish
cars, at glue sniffing rickety urchins loitering on filthy
street-sides, while on
their way to fancy schools
I fear bearded men puffing and puffing, jutting their
bodies out, stooping
menacingly from the parapet walls of their lonely and

time ravaged
terraces, looking at the smog falling over the city in
melancholic gaze,
waiting for nobody, mummified in air by an agenda-
less life
I fear skinny dried out women with pus-filled pimples
exploding on their
cheeks, spending most of their time looking at
themselves in all sorts of
mirrors and reflecting objects everywhere wherever

I fear waiting for sleep
Actually, I fear sleep might rob me off my sight

These moments are best spent walking through narrow
crowded lanes
Negotiating with the jelly-ness of living
Sometimes drinking sweetened milk tea in clay cups
from underground
teashops
Smoking one cigarette after another
Tackling fear with smoke
When suddenly, but invariably, in a street corner I
would find my face being
sold off as a beautiful mask

As I would tread back home
I would ponder
How many masks can you make out of one ageing face?

Faces and Pipal

Chasing the music on her feet I entered a cave
A cave by the shore of a wild green sea full of foam and
rocks
Its walls, dark from outside, now lighted with a soft
glow
Showed faces, unique and lost

Face of Purnendu*kaku*, who loved my ma like a slave
failing to win her
support in the end, died wretched, like a dog.
Face of Robby my brother, horribly shy, a genius in
solving mathematical
riddles, breathed his last falling from a coconut tree
Face of Pipal, who had shown me sparkling ways of
making love in bamboo
jungles, drowning her black agile body on a full moon
night
She had burnt like forests burn turning into mountains
of ash.
Face of Naren*dadu*, my ancestor, a boatman and
charmer of errant tigers
He had hopelessly lost his soul to a girl who made fried
sweetmeats for
lovesick sailors.

All these faces looked at me in awe
I looked at these faces as one looks up in the sky at
stars

They were mystically connected to my life
I was connected to them
By the intervening plasma of aromas and years between
us
One night I heard the music on the feet of a woman
whom I had called
My wife, my soulmate, my lover, my concubine, my ma
and my daughter
many, many times over
As I followed her sound deeper inside the cave
I saw all of them sitting around a brown conference
table waiting for me in
silence,
Expectant and gazing
This woman showed me the way and my seat with a
musical movement of
her hands

I saw her veiled face
She was Pipal.

Threesome

Rahul, Gargi and I sat down by the sea.
The stars sparkled in the night sky like fine cut
diamonds.
The moon slowly travelled upwards, as if rising from
within the sea,
shading the sea near the horizon with crimson.
The sea rose and fell in melancholic motions of a
defeated lover.
The air was laden with familiar seaside scents – saline
and fishy.
We drank from white plastic cups originally meant for
tea or coffee.
Were we counting stars in the sky? We were, I suppose.

I knew similar movies were running in the theatre of
our minds.
Reflections of togetherness seventeen years back before
we had left for
separate lives.
Moments of explosion with pot and rock.
Moments of reading aloud Camus on the riverfront.
Moments of writing laboured poetry.
Moments of illusions of waging a war against
commercial lords.
Moments of entrapments of immortality.
Moments of longing and loss.
Moments of nothingness and simmering void in the
cacophony of ideas

and a greater life.
Moments of not knowing the bliss of love and the
blanket of
companionship.
Moments of an aching strain of growing up restless and
blazing.
Moments of finding meanings where none existed.

As everybody abandoned the ship of circus one by one
to get embedded
in the tried ways of life, we too left one day without
any alarm or
declaration of a farewell.
We got lost to each other suddenly with an unsaid vow
never to meet
again in life.

Gargi said in her musical voice, "Boys I could count
fifty six stars in the sky,
then got bored and concentrated on following the
moonrise."
Rahul looked at her with a sad yet glowing smile in his
eyes unable to speak
confronting her lovelorn beauty. Gargi looked more
beautiful than she was
in college.
I looked at Gargi for some moments and then at Rahul
wanting to say
something not knowing what to say.
Rahul said, "We had to get back, I knew. I had thought
this, the night we
were parting."
Gargi put her hands around our shoulders and ignited
a speck of magical
fire somewhere deep inside our souls and said softly
almost crooning
against the wind, "This is a family story, boys, a ma
with her two sons finally
lost inside a seaside jungle. Remember this is where it
had ended, to start

now after so many years. There are fires, boys, that will
never die down how
much you beat them down!"
I knew we felt like colossal losers; getting vanquished
year after year
doggedly building blocks of happy, buoyant and
successful families.
Did we end up as pathetic caricatures of conquerors of
men, ideas and
wealth in everything that we did?
We had guarded ourselves every moment from an
unfettered longing.
The purity of this longing was drowned in the noisy
proclamations of our
youth.
We had believed we were strangers brought together
by fate to become
friends for a span of time and fate would eventually
scatter us into other
orbits.

We lied down on the sandy shore, now looking straight
into the sky.

Rahul was bored to death chasing politicians and
returning to a
sterilised home.
I was bored to death listening to ad jingles and
returning to a messy
home.
Gargi had lost hope writing screenplays that went
berserk and losing her
twins in a boat accident in the tsunami.

Rahul asked, "Gargi, Sandy should we start a family?"
Gargi said, "Yes, of course my baby. Ha! People will
gossip around us."
I said, "Yes, at last" smiling at a green star, shivering
like a blade of grass.
Then there was a beam of light travelling above all of

us exploring the
darkness on the sea.
It came out of a crumbling lighthouse standing in the
background.
The beam of light as it panned from side to side located
three ships standing
lonely and listlessly in the deep waters, gradually
joining them by the streak
of its incandescent glow.

Wayfarer

What music rang inside your soul
When you almost by chance discovered a new patch of
land in the city where
you had lived for so long
A city you thought you knew so well like the weeds
growing in your backyard
A patch of land with untrammelled avenues, minarets
and teashops rising as
would happen in a movie set contradicting what existed
in the chapters of
history texts
A park laced with trees, grasses and flowers never
grown in the climate of
your city
Unknown birds and butterflies flying in the air
Children and women with strange patterns of smiling,
faces and shoulders
walking along its boulevards
Most of all an engulfing silence that you craved for so
badly but was always
denied
In the night as you crossed this new land, you looked at
the moon, a pale disc
of light, looking so different from here and so near that
you saw its potholes
of darkness with a terrifying clarity

This happened to me last Sunday

As I walked I thought I must not have belonged here
ever and I shivered with
this thought
Would I have to make a new start, a new beginning
after all these years?
Should I embark on the last journey of my life in search
of a place on the
edge of my homeland with my sad son on my back?
Hours later I had crossed other streets
Filled with noises and fumes of cars, buses and auto-
rickshaws
Laughter spiralling out of cheap gambling joints
Laboured roars rumbling out of vegetable and fish
vendors - their emaciated mouths
When I came back home I looked at the face of my son,
the most beautiful
face I have seen in my life.
I saw a faint moustache on his face and soft follicles of
hair on his hands and legs
I shivered once again for a while thinking,
"My son may not remain my son forever
He will soon become a man of the world."

Last Sermon

We sat among ruins
A metropolis lay beneath our feet, crushed by money,
time and bombs
Waiting for each other to speak,
Listen to our words and the sounds of tombs

There were fiery splinters and missiles flying in an
ashen sky
A strange scent of gunpowder and decaying flesh
choked our voices, god
knows why,

But our silence apart from the war must have had other
reasons
Like, the end of seasons
The pall of grief before we die
The rising crooning of a faint cry

That is one moment when you long to hold your
beloved in your arms
Freeze the shadow of your advancing annulment
forever
And dive in the unending layers of her delicious
bosoms
To listen to the songs of her heart another time

But we sat in silence avoiding each other's eyes
A history of forbidden love, agony

And relentless conflicts of passion, duty and meanings
In the end moving away stoically from each other like
rivers do.

Do rivers meet before vanishing inside the turbulence
of oceans?

Suddenly, she was trapped within a vortex of flames
lashing from the sky
Like always, she had moved ahead of me and ahead of
time

She talked to me at last from a spiralling cage of smoke,
"You would make a better writer Sandy
If you made loneliness your only strength."

Unfulfilled Dream

The image of a happy death lingered in his mind for
sometime as he breathed
his last
Dying, looking at the lovelorn face of his beloved
As if, falling endlessly from the dearest mountain cliff
Wind rushing past his ears, stars growing dim
The smile on his tired face grew softer and magical
with time as he fell deeper
into the dimensionless abyss layered by light and
darkness
Entering a new life slowly and irreversibly
Diffusing within the cells of an unknown womb
Losing memories of a life spent in torment and angst

His beloved sat alone like a stone with her hands
outstretched looking at this
miraculous fall
Looking at the spell of death crushing a beautiful face
For her everything had become a memory in an instant
She sat there year after year decomposing in thin sandy
air

The valleys replete with flowers were gone
The farms of food-grains were gone
The woods of thick, tall and shady trees were gone
The rivers flowing with silvery waters were gone
The sky marked with stars was gone

Yet his beloved sat there looking at this nothingness,
breathing dust and soot
Remembering her days of glorious love
Their stolen moments away from multitudes of crowds
Their quarrels about whether to eat a burger or not
Their travels in jungles and mountain deserts
Their dances in a sudden rain
Their heat when they melted in pleasure and pain

She knew; they had fallen in love in a dangerous time
When people preferred a popular war rhyme

One night after making love on the terrace they had
vowed to each other to
make love once on a treetop in the moonlight among
birds, bats and owls and
jinns
She had said, 'But darling, the branches would hurt my
skin'
To which he had kissed her deeply and replied, 'Never
mind dear I will hold
you in a manner that no branch or rough patch would
touch you ever'
She smiled remembering the silly fervour in his voice
then

But it had remained an unfulfilled dream, making love
on a treetop

Mainak and I, a Night in the Ocean

I caught Mainak by his collar and pulled him inside the
deck-side lawn on
the ship.
Seeing Mainak almost on the verge of plunging inside
the moonlit ocean, I
stood frozen for a moment.
I gathered myself instinctively in a hurry and rushed
towards him.

Mainak cried inconsolably as I held him close to my
chest.
He resisted my firm embrace at first but later
succumbed to its intimate
warmth.

He said, "What's the use of living a life without Rupa?"
I argued, "What's the point in dying in the name of
Rupa?"

Well Rupa had fled Mainak irreversibly for sure. She
like all the normal
men and women preferred success and power to the
happiness of love.
Rupa had turned out to be a celebrity actor. She
worked hard to reach
where she is today.

It was rumoured she was in a new relationship with another
successful actor.
He was a much married man with children. There were other
complications.
But Rupa was experienced in such matters.
The news of this torrid springtime affair was mercilessly splashed across all
national dailies during the last fortnight, including the local news channels on
TV.
This affected Mainak more than anything else.

I explained to him, "Forget her. She was not your type."
Mainak remained silent. His chest was heaving, the excitement cooling
down with every passing second now.
His black eyes in their deep sockets were transfixed at the moonlight-tinged
darkness. The darkness had engulfed us wholly in its magical trance.
Mainak did not talk for a very long time.
I remained silent thinking about the defeats of my own life.

He said at last indicating by the tone and tenor of his voice that he might talk
at length.
"Sandy, to begin with, I was not much in love with Rupa, you know.
I was in fact more in love with Debolina. I was head over heels for her.
But she never liked me, my attitude more specifically. She stopped even
meeting me after some time.
Then I tried my luck with Kaushiki. She was the intellectual type.
With time she found me utterly ignorant and was

embarrassed of
me before her friends and family.
Well I failed once again. Then came Rupa. She was
available in a way.
Even when I met her for the first time, in spite of her
dazzling beauty, I knew
I would be successful with her. But somehow I did not
feel for her the way I
had felt for Debolina or even Kaushiki.
She allowed me to sleep with her the third time I had
met her.
I went mad with happiness.
I forgot everything because of her indulgence.
I committed my life to her.
And then this ... Bloodyshit!"

I kept quiet. Mainak did not speak any more.
The ship sailed slowly cutting through the cold placid
waters in the ocean.
The moon was playing a silent spectacle with its rays.
The universe looked magical in glowing silver.
Terror rose in my heart as I digressed in my thoughts.
Is loneliness like smoke with unseen claws that will eat
up freshly abandoned
souls?

Is loneliness as deadly as the vampire trapped inside a
castle of fog waiting?
We felt for a moment so tiny compared to the universe
that was laid out in
front of us. This was not a fleeting feeling.
It took control of us.
We felt goose bumps. There was a quivering anxiety
pumping against my gut.

Suddenly, Mainak and I locked hands as if to be sure of
each other's
presence there.
We felt terrified by the vault of the sky, its arch, the
boundless ocean, the

imperceptible movements of the ship and the
moonshine piercing through
the universe.

We dreamt of the hill of happiness and the sea of
sadness where Mainak
and I had played in our childhood.
Within our dreams we prayed for the night to pass as
fast as it could.

In the morning over a cup of coffee I said, bracing
myself against the railing of the deck,
"Mainak, we don't fall in love with the person we love
desperately.
We fall in love with the person who is available to us
most conveniently.
That is the story my boy.
Falling in love is mostly building a castle in air."

Author's Note

Frosted Glass contains 14 stories and 21 poems written between 2007 and 2009. They are about melancholy, lyric and politics of love and loss. I hope readers find this collection enjoyable, and at times, thought provoking.